LIVERPOOL LIBRARIES AND ARTS

WILSON
Voyage to a beginning

John O'Grady
Amazon
Jan 11

Voyage to a Beginning

by courtesy of Oswald Jones

The author in 1956, at the time of publication of *The Outsider*

Voyage to a Beginning

A PRELIMINARY AUTOBIOGRAPHY

by Colin Wilson

CECIL WOOLF·LONDON

First published in 1968
Reprinted 1987
Copyright © 1968 Colin Wilson
Introduction copyright © 1968 Brocard Sewell

Cecil Woolf Publishers. 1 Mornington Place, London NW1 7RP
Tel: 01-387 2394

British Library Cataloguing in Publication Data
Wilson, Colin
Voyage to a Beginning: a preliminary autobiography
1. Wilson, Colin, 1931 — Biography
2. Authors, English — 20th century — Biography
I. Title
823'.914   PR6073.I44Z/

ISBN 0-900821-02-7

FOR J. W. SIDFORD
FOR THE REASONS SPECIFIED
ON PAGE 48

CONTENTS

	INTRODUCTION BY FATHER BROCARD SEWELL	ix
1	AIMS AND MOTIVES	1
2	THE TUB OF DIOGENES	9
3	STIMULI	24
4	NIHILISM	39
5	THE AIR FORCE AND AFTER	57
6	PARIS, STRASBOURG, AND LONDON	76
7	LONDON AND 'THE OUTSIDER'	108
8	THE SUCCESS PROBLEM	126
9	AFTER THE DELUGE	137
10	STARTING AGAIN	149
	INDEX	179

INTRODUCTION

Colin Wilson has given this book, *Voyage to a Beginning,* the subtitle 'A Preliminary Autobiography'. It is, therefore, a sketch for the earlier part of the full autobiography which may be expected from him in, say, another forty years' time, and should be judged as such. Some people may feel that thirty-six is too early an age at which to write an autobiography. But at thirty-six Mr Wilson is no longer a 'young' writer. Plenty can happen in thirty-six years; and after all, there is the precedent of Mr Beverley Nichols's autobiography *Twenty-five.* Colin Wilson's life so far has been full of outward incident and inner development, so that he has an interesting story to tell.

Mr Wilson himself, however, rather discounts the narrative interest of his book and says that for him its chief interest is as a record of the development of his thought. *Voyage to a Beginning* is, in fact, as much autopsychography, to use a word coined by Eric Gill, as autobiography.

It ought to be realised by now, when the noise of earlier sensations and controversies has died away, that Colin Wilson is a serious writer whose main concern is with ideas. But if this is beginning to be understood, the public has not yet accepted Mr Wilson's claim that himself and Mr Bill Hopkins are the only two geniuses alive today. But in all probability there is still plenty of time for this assertion to be made good. I certainly know of no one more likely than Mr Wilson to end his days as a revered and patriarchal centenarian to whom the term 'genius' is almost fated to be applied.

When his first book, *The Outsider,* appeared Colin Wilson had the misfortune to be taken up by certain highbrow upper class critics who thought it was wonderful that a working class boy should so educate himself, read so many books, and grasp their contents so firmly. And, of course, it *was* wonderful. But, as Henry Williamson has pointed out, it was not unique. The critics forgot, among a good many others, Robert Burns, Thomas Hardy, and D. H. Lawrence.

The Outsider and *The Age of Defeat* were remarkable books for so young a writer to have written. But it is a fair and indeed obvious criticism of *The Outsider* and its sequel *Religion and the Rebel* that they are so clogged with ideas and quotations illustrative of the ideas that it is difficult to grasp just what thesis the writer is propounding. From this point of view *The Age of Defeat,* a book which attracted much less attention, was a great advance. But for a clear view of Colin Wilson's main positions as a thinker *Voyage to a Beginning* is perhaps even better, since it covers a wider range of problems, and reaches a more definite conclusion.

What Mr Wilson is trying to do is to create a new kind of Existentialism; he sees it as his mission to work for the discovery or creation of existential values – which he says come curiously close to what are called religious values. And this New Existentialism, he believes, involves an attempt to 'deepen the foundations of literature'.

Mr Wilson conceives of his thought as going 'a long step beyond Heidegger and Sartre'; and here I at one time felt a certain apprehensiveness. If this 'long way' was to be in the same direction as that taken by Heidegger and Sartre, then the only result that could be expected was philosophic bankruptcy. For what else can come from a philosophy whose key words, at least for Sartre, are *le néant, la nausée,* and *l'absurde*? And with Heidegger 'la finitude de l'être humain devient absolue et essentielle. Il n'y a pas d'achèvement, il n'y a pas de totalité de la vie. Il est donc absolument exclu que l'homme puisse jamais être ou devenir avec l'histoire le maître de son existence.' (Emmanuel Mounier, *Introduction aux existentialismes,* Paris 1947; p. 51.)

But the essence of existentialism is precisely man's affirmation of himself as an existent. This may involve at one stage an attitude constituting almost a *challenge to God,* a wrestling as of Jacob with the Angel; and after centuries of a Christianity preached in the context of a faulty cosmology and a static view of the universe, such an attitude is natural. But a philosophy that is atheist in the sense of holding that man is *all,* and, at the same time, that his existence has *no meaning,* ought rather to be named Inexistentialism. 'If one believes or tries to believe literally in nothing, if nothing makes sense, if we can assert no values whatever, then everything is permissible and nothing is important. There is no pro or con; the murderer, for instance, is neither right nor wrong. One is free to stoke the crematory fires or to give one's life to the care of lepers. Wickedness and virtue are just accident or whim.' (Camus, *The Rebel*, Peregrine Books edition, 1962, p. 13.)

To insist on this is not to deny that Sartre and Heidegger are important writers and thinkers at the present time; but in the last chapter of this book Colin Wilson makes it clear that his 'step beyond' these thinkers will be in the 'personalist' and meaningful direction explored by Blondel, Bergson, Berdyaev, Karl Jaspers, and Gabriel Marcel, all of whom are in some sense existentialist.

To me it seems that the trouble with Mr Wilson's own new existentialism is that it is still dangerously man-centred, in the sense that it lacks an apprehension of the *contingency* of all the existence and existences that we directly know. But here and there he gives hints of a certain awareness of the Uncontingent: 'Immediate problems and miseries are unimportant; but there *must* be a tomorrow; there must be an emergency exit, a final assurance of safety.'

One of the most attractive features of *Voyage to a Beginning* as an autobiography seems to me the moderation of its judgements on persons and events concerning which a good deal of acerbity might have been expected from the author. This is especially noticeable in Mr Wilson's comments on those critics who first over-praised him and then, resentful of the too great success which they had helped to create, reversed their judgements and tore his work and his reputation, as much as they could, into pieces.

Here and there, it is true, when writing of others, Mr Wilson shows himself a good deal tougher than he is in real life; but even so, *Voyage to a Beginning* seems to me a very generous-minded book. It is also a very truthful book. The author has not sought to disguise some of the more indelicate aspects of an experienced human life, but neither has he written anything for sensation sake. Nor does he seek to commend what is not commendable.

It would have been difficult for him to avoid mentioning what is, from a moralist's point of view, the most debatable action of his life, since although a strictly private matter it became at one time a public topic because of newspaper publicity. He has set down the facts with candour, and those who have been spared the necessity of making a similar crucial decision would do well to abstain from comment.

Colin Wilson is entirely right when he says that 'mankind shares a common sin: the devaluation of life'. Somewhere in this book he quotes Chesterton's remark about the extraordinary contrast between the number of enchanting children in the world and the equally vast number of dud grown-ups. What happens to the children in the years between? Whatever the answer to that question may be, Mr Wilson has successfully escaped the too common fate of becoming a mediocre grown-up.

Chesterton would have understood perfectly what Colin Wilson means when he says: 'The homing instinct is strong in me. I am happiest when I have long empty days ahead of me, and I can sit in my own home, surrounded by books and gramophone records, with a typewriter conveniently near.' I like to think of him with his family in his house above the cliffs at Gorran Haven, doing his daily stint of six or more hours' writing – he is a hard worker – and then relaxing with his music, his books, and his friends. His home is a real *foyer;* the newspaper, which is left in a hole in the hedge at the bottom of the lane, is simply inscribed 'Colin' on the outer page; and the postman, plumber, and electrician, when they call, address the master of the house in the same direct and familiar fashion. Acceptance by Cornishmen of people who come from other parts as one of themselves is not easily won.

In his home Colin Wilson has created or is creating – for creation is eternally continuous as the theologians tell us in their paradoxical and analogical language – what Eric Gill calls 'a cell of good living'. This he has achieved by energy and determination. If genius lies in the prosecution of great designs through unremitting hard work and refusal to admit defeat, then Colin Wilson has the basic qualities of genius. Perhaps also the genius is the man who never accepts boredom and unfulfilment.

BROCARD SEWELL, *O. Carm.*

VOYAGE TO A BEGINNING

I

AIMS AND MOTIVES

MY INTENTION in these pages is to lay bare, as honestly as I can, the basic aims and motives of my work and to relate them, where it is relevant, to events in my own life. It is not intended to be a formal autobiography; the events of my life do not interest me enough to make me attempt such a thing, except where they can be used to illustrate an idea. Besides, the proper place for autobiography is fiction. A friend of mine once asked Ernest Hemingway how he felt about a certain volume on his early life as a reporter in Kansas City. 'Disgusted', said Hemingway; 'I intended to use all that stuff in my books, and now it's wasted'. This expresses my own attitude to autobiography.

There is a certain problem that nags me all the time, and has always done so, in one form or another. It is this: on the one hand there is the world, an immense and complex and beautiful place, with enough interests in it to occupy a man for a million years. And on the other hand there is the curious narrowness, the limitedness, of human consciousness. We are like blinkered horses; we are aware of almost nothing except the minute we are living in, the room we happen to be sitting in. Why? Why has nature blinkered the human will? Why do so many of us die, bored and discouraged, at the age of seventy, complaining that we have exhausted the world?

One of the first stories I ever learnt at school was called 'The Old Woman in the Vinegar Bottle'. A good fairy is flying over a ditch one day, when she hears a voice complaining, 'Oh dear, oh dear'. She investigates, and finds an old woman living in a large vinegar-bottle and complaining about its narrowness. With a wave of her wand the fairy changes the vinegar-bottle into a lovely little cottage; the old woman thanks her, and she flies off. A few months later, she passes the cottage and drops in to see how the old woman likes her new home. The first thing she hears is the same complaint: 'Oh dear, oh dear.' The sanitation is inconvenient, the well is too far from the house, the thatched roof lets in the rain, and so on. So the fairy waves her wand and transports the old woman into a splendid house with water closets and h. and c. in the bathroom. A few months later she drops in again, and still finds the old woman moaning: 'Oh dear, oh dear.' The servants are dishonest, the noise of traffic keeps her awake at night, the tradesmen are disrespectful ... So the fairy again waves her wand, and the house becomes a magnificent palace. A few months go by; the fairy drops in once more. But still the old woman is wailing. The place is too big and cold; the rooms are difficult to heat and keep free from draughts, the kitchen staff are always stealing, the view isn't all it might be. So with a final snort of exasperation the fairy waves her wand and transports the old woman back to the vinegar-bottle.

For me this story is symbolic of human nature – as symbolic as the story of the Fall of Man. Every day I realise that an ironic Nature has given us everything we could desire – and has omitted to give us the ability to enjoy it. I have seen it recently in the case of my own father. All his life he has worked hard in factories, with no more holiday than an occasional day at the seaside. He loves the countryside, and spends his weekends fishing, or searching for mushrooms and blackberries. When I first began to make money by writing I rented a cottage in Cornwall, and the family came down regularly for their holidays. My father revelled in it; he was up at dawn every day and out with a fishing rod, or trapping rabbits, or looking for mushrooms. He made a habit of saying that if he could live in a cottage in the country, with a decent back-garden, he would need very little money to support himself. Finally the lease on the cottage expired; I decided to look for a larger place to house my books and records. We found a large bungalow, with two acres of land and an enormous greenhouse. It seemed to be the ideal opportunity for my father, perfect in every way, so I invited the family to move in. My mother and father and my ten year old sister Susan came down from Leicester; we moved into the new house during a perfect summer.

Confronted with an endless holiday my father seemed to get bewildered. Instead of vanishing every morning to look for rabbits or mushrooms he would do a few hours' weeding in the garden, and then wander up to the local pub. This was not out of any real need for a pint of beer, but to kill time. The fishing expeditions stopped. Plainly, he was bored and at a loose end. After six months of this my mother decided it was time for the family to return to Leicester. My father went reluctantly; although he had found living in the country less of a pleasure than he had expected he felt no enthusiasm about returning to work in a factory. But they went, and my father found it as hard to readjust to factory and city life as it had been to settle in the country. He developed an ulcer, and had to spend months in hospital.

It is true that my father is at a certain disadvantage when it comes to the problem of freedom; he is completely the practical man, who likes to have something to make with his hands. He reads newspapers, but never a book; if there is time to kill he prefers to do it in a pub, talking with a friend over a leisurely pint of bitter or a game of dominoes. But how far can any of us claim to be at an advantage when it comes to the problem of leisure? Fifteen years ago I wanted nothing so much as a quiet home crowded with books and records. Now I live a mile from the nearest village and ten miles from the nearest town. If I began playing steadily through my record collection tonight it would take two months of non-stop listening to reach the end; if I were to read every book in the house at the rate of one a day, it would take me ten years. In spite of this, I find myself occasionally becalmed in a period of mental sterility; my consciousness is as narrow as a keyhole, and there is not a book or record in the house that can rouse me out of total lethargy. I cannot write, I cannot read, I have no desire to see friends, or to eat, or even drink. How can I claim to be any less of an 'old woman in a vinegar-bottle' than my father?

These are the problems that never seem to be mentioned in autobiographies. Neither do any of the other problems that occupy my attention unceasingly. This is a perpetual challenge to me. *Why are they not stated?* Have we some reason for preferring to avoid them? Or do we not see them? Or do we see them and attach no importance to them? If the latter explanation is the answer, then we are fools; for these problems are killers. To ignore them is like ignoring the regulations about boiling malarious water or pasteurising tuberculous milk.

In most technical matters our civilisation demands accuracy and definition. Every scientist knows the importance of pigeon-holing each piece of data; every business man knows the importance of keeping his books in order. Even our philosophy and our literary criticism are becoming scientific, loaded with jargon and definitions, impatient of vagueness. But living and its psychological processes are still a matter of *laissez faire*. We ask for no definitions of aims and purposes and of basic rules. And although living is like nothing so much as an obstacle race where the obstacles are invisible and highly dangerous, we still approach each new day in the same vague and empirical spirit.

Let me try to give an example of what I mean. The other day I read a novel by Artzibashef called *The Millionaire*. Unlike his earlier novel *Sanine*, this was very bad indeed. It is about a young and handsome millionaire, who is unable to rid himself of a feeling of uselessness and purposelessness. He feels that no one is ever sincere with him, because he is a millionaire. He is also bored because he can do anything he likes with his money, and has no desire to do anything in particular. Nothing much happens, except that he quarrels with his mistress and best friend, tries unsuccessfully to mediate at a strike in his own factory, and ends by committing suicide.

I finished this book in a state of deep dissatisfaction. What was Artzibashef trying to say? That life is gloomy, even for millionaires? This is unlikely, for *Sanine* is a singularly cheerful and heartening book. That you had better be poor than be a millionaire? I doubt whether the author would be so naïve. No, the real trouble with the book is that the author is too much identified with his bored millionaire. He also can see no reason why, if one has enough money to turn life into a continuous holiday, life should not be a complete bore.

If Artzibashef had been a fear greater writer – and more honest – he might have begun by saying: 'Now gentlemen, let us draw up a balance-sheet on life. Unless we are suffering from some disease, or starving, or being actively tormented, there is no physical reason why we should not go on living. The body's capacity for pleasure is considerable. For the civilised man who possesses an intellect the possibilities of the world are immense. And yet here we have a millionaire, healthy and good-looking, who finds life exceedingly dull. Why? Is life really as dull as all that? What are these invisible forces that finally drive him to suicide?'

Instead of trying to define these forces, in the way that a biologist stains an invisible germ so that he can see it under a microscope, Artzibashef continues to describe the trivialities of his millionaire's pointless sex life, and remains completely involved in the confusion.

Another example: Somerset Maugham once edited an anthology of modern writing, and he wrote an introductory note to each passage that he included. His comments on certain famous writers had a somewhat astringent tone; Henry James, T. S. Eliot, James Joyce and W. B. Yeats were all dismissed as boring or prolix or pompous. But, as a well known critic pointed out, you would never guess from Maugham's notes that Joyce and Yeats were on a completely different level from Michael Arlen and Katherine Brush, whose work is also included. And you would certainly suppose that Mr Maugham himself was on a very much higher plane than bores like Yeats and Eliot. Again, the important things are left unstated; and an open-minded reader who came to Mr Maugham to learn about modern literature would go away with some weird and topsy-turvy notions.

It seems to me, then, that the task of the writer is to give a shape and definition to ideas by stating them clearly.

I can remember when this idea first came to me. I was twelve at the time. We had in our class a boy named Simpson, who was not especially clever or remarkable. One day he asked me if he could borrow my fountain-pen, and I refused, claiming that the nib had worn itself to the slope of my hand. Simpson immediately said: 'That's not the reason. If So-and-so asked you, you'd lend it to him without worrying about the nib.' 'So-and-so' was a boy of strong personality and generally admired. Simpson was right, of course. But what struck me was his psychological penetration in ignoring my excuse about the nib, and going straight to the heart of the problem – that it would be of no special advantage to me to lend him my fountain-pen, but that I would be happy to lend it to someone I respected and liked. It may seem that this is not a particularly profound observation. But schoolboys are curiously unperceptive creatures, and self-analysis is not their strong point. Simpson surprised me several times by remarks that showed him to be aware of motives that would be invisible to most schoolboys. I began trying to be the same. I can still remember how pleased I felt when one day it struck me that the personality is a strangely fluid thing, which depends completely upon the personalities around it. You speak to one person and feel weak, to another and feel strong. A certain person makes you feel positive and masculine, another yielding and feminine. These are the simplest shades of the matter, the degrees that can be expressed. But each person also produces in you an individual reaction which defies definition as completely as the odour of a rose. You may find someone curiously irritating, and yet be unable to understand why; you may not see that person for five years, and completely forget your reaction. Then you meet him again, and instantly the old irritation returns, as unmistakable as ever.

Shaw once said about Wilde: 'He came and spoke to me, with an evident intention of being specially kind to me. We put each other out frightfully, and this odd difficulty persisted between us to the very last, even when we were no longer mere boyish novices, and had become men of the world with plenty of skill in social intercourse.' Shaw makes no attempt to define the nature of the difficulty, and the probability is that it was quite indefinable. The contact of these two chemical compounds produced strange effects; some of these effects can be explained by taking into account Shaw's intellectual seriousness and Wilde's lack of it; but such an explanation is as crude as the chemistry of Cornelius Agrippa.

We have no language, no science to deal with these problems. And I became aware of this at the age of thirteen, when I tried to write an essay on the way people affect one another's personalities and self-assessments. I suppose I have been attempting to create a terminology for these problems ever since.

This is perhaps the place to mention one of my 'private terms', a convenient piece of shorthand that I use frequently in journals and notes for books. About ten years ago, on a hot Saturday afternoon, I happened to be hitch-hiking north from London along the A.1. It was dusty and windless, and I was depressed. There was very little traffic, and lifts were short and infrequent. A point came when I was waving my thumb at lorries with no real expectation that they would stop, and with almost no interest in whether they stopped or not. I was on my way to interview my girlfriend's parents, and I did not expect to be welcome. One lorry I had been in had broken down, but I was too bored to care. So when finally I sat in another noisy diesel lorry, rattling towards Peterborough at thirty miles an hour, I realised that I felt absolutely nothing: no relief at having found a lift, no anticipated pleasure in my destination, no particular desire to be there or elsewhere. Then I wondered how I would feel if this lorry also broke down; I realised that I would still be indifferent. I began to run through various catastrophes in my mind, until I thought of one that aroused some response in me. Then it came to me that human beings can lapse into a mood of indifference where pleasure has no power to stimulate, and where only active discomfort or pain can penetrate the boredom. We happened to be passing through the town of St Neots at the time, and to keep the conception in my head until I could write about it I scrawled on a piece of paper 'St Neot margin'. It would probably have been as effective if I had simply called my conception the indifference margin (except that, since the concept needs defining anyway, it might be preferable to have a term that does not look deceptively self-explanatory). In the past ten years I have found myself returning again and again to the conception of the St Neot margin. Why is human consciousness so narrow? Is this not another name for the concept of original sin? Why are human beings not grateful for the lives they possess? And most of all, how can we achieve control over the mechanism of the St Neot margin, and banish the sense of boredom and lack of purpose from human life?

One more comment, and I have finished with preliminaries. When my mind is at its clearest, and I am working well, I become vaguely aware of some piece of knowledge that would solve the whole problem. It hovers on the edge of my consciousness; but I have no doubt of its reality. The painter Richard Seddon expressed it when he wrote: 'It is certain that the artist intuits something that is just beyond the grasp of human intellectual comprehension.' It is perhaps wrong to call this 'something' knowledge, because it seems to be real and solid, and is no more abstract than a tin of sardines. But if I try to concentrate on it – that is, to *see* it, to define it intellectually – I immediately cease to be aware of the thing itself, and grope around in the concepts that would define it, rather as a shadow is defined by light. I become aware of the strange vacuum of purpose in which we all live, and trying to define it is like trying to write a novel in a language that does not yet exist.

2
THE TUB OF DIOGENES

I WANT to keep to essentials: and the most essential fact about my childhood is that I was spoiled. Although my mother was not the youngest of her family, she was the first of seven brothers and sisters to offer her parents a grandchild. Eighteen months later my brother Barry arrived, and by that time there were several grandchildren, my uncles and aunts having been busy in the meantime. But as the first-comer I was spoiled by everyone, with the exception of Aunt Maude, who later quarrelled with the family on my account and severed all relations with them. As the eldest I was used to being the strongest, and to exerting a certain authority over my brother and cousins; my grandparents were inclined, for some reason, to regard me as altogether remarkable, and their conviction communicated itself to me. I was told that I was pretty and clever, and came in for a great deal of kissing and caressing; but I hated being 'fussed' (which in Leicester means coddled) and can remember wrestling strenuously to escape kisses.

It was not until about three years ago that I first realised the importance of so much attention in my early years. A composer friend was speaking to me about his lack of self-belief and his shyness. I was writing at the time a book called *The Age of Defeat*, an attack on the 'fallacy of insignificance', the sense of failure, the shrinking modesty, that pervades so much literature of the past century. Obviously, the difference of our views was a difference of temperament, not of ideas. I tried to define this. Although there is in me a fundamental 'anxiety' about the universe, the possibility that life will turn out to be a horrible joke, I seem to myself to have a certain basic conviction that life and fortune mean well by me. (I had quoted with sympathy a story Eckermann tells of Goethe. When they were discussing the question of destiny and of optimism, someone pointed out to Goethe that fate had been on his side; but supposing he had been born unlucky, what then? 'Don't be silly', said Goethe. 'Do you suppose I'd have been such a fool as to be born unlucky?')

'But *why*?' asked my friend, and in attempting to answer him the solution came to me. Because I was the first-born of the family and was mollycoddled by my grandparents, envied by my cousins, and frequently told by my mother that I was 'born lucky'. One of the strange paradoxes of this world is that the quality of living experience has nothing whatever in common with the quality of a story told in retrospect. Other people's lives may be a 'story', may have an epic or romantic quality; but sitting here, now, looking out of a window or reading a book, every human being knows that the present is not a moment in a story; it just *is*. We never really grasp the idea that all lives of all men have been like this: a hard nut of the present, an uncrackable nut, refusing to reveal its secrets, jammed between the teeth. And the usual method of overcoming this problem is to drop the nut and retreat from reality, to live in a dream. So the world is made up, for the most part, of two kinds of people: the strong ones, who stick to reality and are rendered purposeless and moronic by it, and the cranks, the self-deceivers, the weaklings, whose sense of meaning is derived from rejection, deliberate retreat. The third class, those who have managed to retain a sense of purpose without too many self-deceptions, is so small as to be almost non-existent.

But to be meaningful, life has *got* to be a story. That is to say, each moment, being a link in the chain of consciousness, has to be connected to the links that went before. So living is always like trying to write a letter with the radio blaring, the children screaming, and the house on fire. Reality beats on us like a factory with a thousand steam-hammers, destroying the effort to concentrate, to retain some thread of motive in the confusion. Sometimes there is a lull; meaning dawns in us, a curious happiness arises, we can look at the world and say, 'I love you, I accept you'. Then the whistle goes, and the racket starts again.

I suppose I must have possessed some obscure need for withdrawal even in early childhood, for I can remember telling my brother long stories in which a boy retreats into a cave deep under the ground, or crawls into a chest and closes the lid. My chest

– with a light inside and a supply of food – was my symbol of subjectivity.

I think I was an abnormally affectionate child, in spite of my distaste for being 'fussed'. The affection was divided about equally between my mother and my brother Barry. Everybody said that Barry was completely unlike me. Where I was forward, he was shy; where I was aggressive, he was yielding. We were always quarrelling, and I was always beating him. But beating him only made me love him more than ever – I suppose it was the opposition of temperaments. I lived in a perpetual agony of affection and anxiety for him. One day he went picnicking by the River Soar with my cousin Roy; all day I was certain he was drowned; when he came home very late in the evening I had spent hours standing by the window, hating my parents for letting him go. On another occasion he was late coming home from school; I walked for miles searching for him, and finally discovered him in a wheelbarrow, being pushed along by an old man. Admittedly, he was coming in the direction of our house; but I was nevertheless certain that I had saved him from being abducted by a sex maniac. (There had been several child murders – this was about 1938 – and we had been warned about going off with strange men.) Barry protested that he had been tired, and the old man had offered him a lift; but we made him promise to refuse all future offers of lifts.

Apart from Barry, my life was completely bound up with my mother. She was nineteen when I was born, and was finding married life during the slump-years exhausting and unrewarding. She and my father were of opposite temperaments. My father had been in charge of his mother's family ever since his father was killed in 1914; my grandmother supported the family by taking in washing. They lived in a tough district, and my father grew up tough and strong willed, given to violent outbursts of temper or of affection. As I grew older, the temper outweighed the affection. My mother also had a will of her own, but she was fond of reading, and had inherited a quiet and gentle disposition from her own mother. My father never read a book, and he liked to spend his evenings in the pub. After drinking half-a-dozen pints at Sunday lunch-time, he was likely to go off to bed without his lunch, and fall asleep with his boots on. He worked hard, but pay was bad (he worked for

£3 10s. a week throughout the thirties), and he felt that he deserved his evening in the pub. So money was always short, and my mother often cried. When she was miserable she confided in me; and I came to regard beer as the tragedy of our lives. One of the first sentences I ever learned to spell (at the age of six) was 'Dad drinks beer'. My father rightly regarded this as a criticism of his habits, and ordered me to tear it up.

But it seems to me now that my mother was frequently miserable during my childhood, and that she manufactured a morbid sensitivity in me by making me the confidant of her disappointments. My father also had his worries, but I knew nothing about these. When I was very young, he often bought me sweets and petted me and played with me; then, quite suddenly – or so it appeared to me – he seemed to push me to arm's length, to become irritable and despotic. He no doubt felt that life had treated him badly in making him a father before he was out of his teens, and forcing him to work in a stuffy shoe-factory for starvation wages. So there were violent quarrels at home; and at least one of them ended with my mother and father hitting one another in the middle of the room. On another occasion my mother slapped my father's face in a pub. My father said that my mother was heartless because she was detached and unemotional by temperament, and my mother called my father a sentimental fool because his emotions were easily touched and his sense of pity could bring him to tears.

Naturally, I was on my mother's side. Apparently I would even tell the teacher at school about the quarrels at home and the shortage of money. (My mother reminded me of this the other day; I retain no memory of it.) One day I asked my mother what I could take to school for my 'lunch' (mid-morning break), and she said: 'There's no food in the house.' I remember being oppressed all the morning by a horrible sense of tragedy: we were starving. I wanted to rush home and comfort my mother. But at lunch time she was cheerful and indifferent, and when I reminded her of what she had said, she replied that she meant only that she hadn't yet been out to do the shopping, not that we were penniless. That morning must have been unusually miserable for me; I can still remember it with clarity, after twenty-five years, and my sense of the irony of life, since everyone at school was cheerful while I was so utterly depressed.

I think I must have inherited a broad streak of my father's sentimentality. I can remember taking a tearful farewell of an old overcoat in the school cloakroom, the day my mother told me she was going to buy me a new one.

When I was eight my mother went out to work at a local hosiery factory, and this eased the family's finances. She disliked the work; it left her perpetually tired. My father wanted her to continue; he was naturally glad to be able to buy his friends a pint of beer without having to borrow from the rent. Two years later she solved the problem by having another baby – my brother Rodney. But in the meantime, she worked and cooked meals and did the housework, and nursed a resentment about the beer that placed a double burden on her.

I find it difficult to say whether my childhood was happy. I suspect that most childhoods are more alike than we suppose. Children have very little capacity for sustained happiness. Dr Johnson suggested that happiness and misery are always pretty much alike for every human being, and the happiness of a great general who has saved his country is exactly the same as the happiness of a girl attending her first dance. This is certainly true of children. They can be made miserable and cheerful, but really miserable or really happy childhoods must be rare exceptions. Most of them alternate between the two, with the same pleasures, the same embarrassments and guilts, the same pride, the same enthusiasm. I certainly had no reason to be unhappy. No one ever treated me badly. I was beaten occasionally – often with my father's leather strap – but I usually deserved it. My grandparents spoiled me. I had various collection-manias – for india-rubbers, for pencils, for geometrical instruments, for comics, for penknives. I did a certain amount of thieving – usually food from the pantry, or apples from local orchards. I was regarded as a good 'scrapper', and usually won my fights. I can offer no sexual revelations of childhood, because although I had the average childhood interest in my own genitals, sex as such held no interest for me. In writing about it I find it difficult not to make it sound as though I was a little prig; but it was not any desire to be a 'good boy' that prevented me having any early sexual experiences at all. I listened with a certain interest if older boys boasted about the things they claimed to have done to girls; but I could never escape a faint feeling of disgust, as if they were defiling themselves. I can only record the fact that during my childhood, I was apparently 'undersexed'. When a schoolfriend explained to me one day how babies came into the world, I refused to believe him. I suppose this kind of puritanism is a matter of temperament, probably commoner in girls than boys.

There were, admittedly, a few traces of things that now appear to have been sexual perverseness. I loved to dress up in my mother's clothes, including her underwear. I gather from Havelock Ellis that this frequently indicates a tendency to homosexuality – like my passionate attachment to my mother and dislike of my father. In fact, I have never observed any trace of homosexuality in my make-up at any time, although I have occasionally been assured by homosexual friends that everyone has a homosexual phase in adolescence. If I had, then I failed to notice it. I also showed very distinct tendencies to sadism, which manifested themselves as a violent intolerance towards anything that seemed to me weak or silly. A little girl at the top of the street used to arouse a sadistic impulse in me because she seemed somehow feeble and too 'girlish', too lacking in vitality, for which she substituted a bleating, sugary charm. I used to pinch her when her parents weren't looking, and then claim that I had no idea why she was crying.

This sadism eventually led to the worst beating I ever had in my life. It was a Fifth of November; I was probably about six or seven. Barry and I had stopped to talk to two small children, and I felt they were 'silly'. We played with them for a while; then I whispered to Barry that at a signal from myself we would both hit them. I gave the signal; Barry and I both punched the children, and then ran like the wind. Their parents came out and saw our red jerseys disappearing round the corner. Ten minutes later they found us watching a bonfire on a piece of waste ground, and went to our parents. We were hauled off to bed, and my father laid into us with his leather belt. In spite of the pain, I yelled that Barry had nothing to do with it, so he was allowed to go after a few whacks; then my father beat me until his arm was tired. The next morning we were summoned before the headmistress at school, and had to say that we were sorry and would never do it again.

I started fighting when I was fairly young. As a child my father had been a champion scrapper, and he often told me how he had defended his sister Lil against a much older boy, and had beaten him. In his teens he had been a good amateur boxer, and had had his nose dented and his ear flattened. There was even some talk about his becoming a professional; luckily, he lost the fight that would have decided his career. But he talked a great deal about his childhood fights, and gave me rudimentary boxing lessons, from which I never profited, since no child bothers about boxing when he is face to face with an opponent. For most of his enthusiasms I had no sympathy or capacity. He had been a star footballer, a champion swimmer, and had taken a pride in polishing his shoes and parting his hair. One of his favourite stories was of how he had been called in front of the whole school so that the headmaster could show them his ideal of cleanliness and tidiness. I was lazy and untidy. I disliked football, as I could never get close enough to the ball to kick it. I like the water, but was never a fast swimmer; my capacity is still limited to a slow breast-stroke. But I could fight. I used to hurl myself on opponents, my fists flailing; and usually they seemed to give way. But I had no love of fighting, and sometimes allowed myself to be bullied, out of cowardice. Occasionally, I surprised myself by losing my temper and beating someone I had been afraid of, as once when I lashed out at a small boy named 'Tich', the school bully. But many years later I allowed the same Tich to slap my face over some absurd misunderstanding, and although I wished him dead I was afraid to hit him back.

The thieving was fairly harmless until I was about ten, when someone showed me how to 'knock off' from Woolworth's and other big stores. I think this was probably my cousin John, who was a fairly constant influence in my childhood. A year younger than myself (which to a child is like five years), he was reckless and self-willed, and was therefore excellent company. He liked climbing trees, while I was afraid of heights and hated trees. He was an expert at scrumping (stealing apples), knocking off, and inventing forms of mischief to while away the holidays. John had one serious fault; he would quite suddenly develop a 'mardy' streak, and go off in a huff, or refuse to do something he had promised to do. But he was such good company when he was in high spirits that we forgave him these fits. Like myself, John was also regarded as 'clever' by the family, so there was a kind of mild but constant rivalry between his parents and mine; this was increased by the fact that my mother and her sister, Aunt Dora, had always been jealous of one another as children.

John and I used to walk 'up town', if we hadn't the bus fares, and do the rounds of the big stores, stealing penknives, Christmas novelties, and anything else that was not too difficult. Children, of course, have no conscience; they are as innocent as savages. Like savages, they love toys and trinkets and gadgets. I never felt any conscience about stealing – and neither do I in retrospect. I was convinced that all the children in Leicester would descend on the big stores like locusts if they were certain of not being caught. As a child, my father had once joined a group of boys who entered a big store, probably Woolworth's, through the roof; I believe some of them were caught. I often daydreamed about my father's story, and spent hours imagining in detail exactly what I would take if I could get into Woolworth's by night. Chocolate, fountain-pens, magnifying glasses, penknives, devices for looking behind you without turning round (called 'Seebackroscopes') and sheets of metal that made a noise like smashing glass when you dropped them. I was also particularly proud of some small red books I stole called 'Inquire Within for Everything' or some such title, giving all kinds of statistics and all kinds of information : 'Do you know the seven highest buildings in the world?' 'Do you know the longest tunnel in the world?', etc.

Luckily, I was never caught – except once, many years later; but then I was allowed to go after promising not to do it again. The reason was perhaps that although I wanted penknives and toys so much, I had also the strongest desire not to be caught, and I exercised every caution.

Looking back, it seems to me that thieving dominated my childhood; it was never far from my thoughts. A few years later I discovered that gangster novelettes sold at a high price; I knew a second-hand shop that would give one and sixpence for a two-shilling paperback of 'Ben Sarto' or 'Darcy Glinto'. (Mickey Spillane was not widely known in those days.) I also knew of a bookshop whose proprietor sometimes took several minutes to emerge from the back premises when a customer went into the shop. So I got into the habit of taking books from one bookshop and immediately selling them to the other. But I never put the books in my pocket or in my school satchel; that would have been too dangerous; I always thrust them under my armpit, next to my shirt. This precaution proved to be a wise one; the woman who kept the shop suspected me of stealing the paperbacks, and one day demanded to see what was in my satchel. She looked bewildered and disappointed when she found only school books. But I took this as a hint that 'the heat' was on, and dropped the re-sale of Ben Sarto as a means of making an income.

No doubt such experiences are not uncommon among children; I mention them because I think they must be relevant to my development as a writer. Lying and deceit are the usual experiences of childhood, but a child lies only to those in immediate authority over him – parents, schoolteachers. But habitual thieving is a different matter; it is directed against the authority of society, and risks greater penalties. The development of a Genêt may be commoner than we think – from thief to rebel and 'outsider'. It would be interesting to have a record of all the criminal activities of all the artists and writers of the past hundred years. The Victorians held that George Washington, George Fox and Gladstone were prototypes of the future leader of men. 'Father, I cannot tell a lie.' I have always been inclined to feel that perhaps Charlie Peace and Jim the Penman are more accurate symbols of the spirit that makes for progress.

I am trying hard to throw my mind back to the essential quality of my childhood. A basic factor was a contempt for adults. They seemed to understand so little; their relations with children were so incredibly miscalculated. So few of them seemed to be natural. I became aware of that question asked by G. K. Chesterton : why the world is so full of brilliant children and dud grown-ups? I never met a grown-up whom I could wholly admire – of whom I could think : I'd like to grow up like him. This may have been because all the adults I was likely to meet had as little money as my own family had. In comparison to most of the relatives of my father and mother we seemed lucky. When I was four we moved out to the Coleman Road estate, into a council house with a tolerably large garden at the back as well as at the front. The roads were wide, and lined with trees and grass verges; the rooms of the house seemed big and light. Most of my father's relatives lived in the neighbourhood in which he had been born, in tiny, stuffy houses with narrow strips of back gardens. In all my childhood, I never went into a house that made me wish *we* lived in it. It might have been different if I had ever met the 'rich'; luckily I never did. So I remained free of any social ambitions, and remained completely unaware of myself as a member of a 'social class'. The only ambition I felt in connection with growing-up was never to become a grown-up like the ones I knew.

In a curious way I was religious. When my mother first explained to me that Jesus had made the world, I took this to be a piece of factual information that explained a great deal. When she said that Jesus would hear me if I swore, I took care not to swear, and prayed for forgiveness if I forgot myself. I was curious about the world, and was always coming across important pieces of information that the adults had inexplicably forgotten to mention. For example, I was seven when we had our first history lesson, and I heard for the first time about the ages before men lived on earth, about dinosaurs and sabre-toothed tigers. It seemed amazing to me that no one had ever told me all this before. In some encyclopedia (I think it was Arthur Mee's *Children's Encyclopedia*) I saw an illustration of Jules Verne's *Twenty Thousand Leagues Under the Sea* showing Captain Nemo discovering Atlantic. I asked questions about Atlantis, and was again amazed that no one had bothered to tell me about such a fascinating subject.

My grandmother was a spiritualist, and attended a séance every Sunday night. It was probably she who answered my question about what happened after death by offering me a brief outline of the ideas of Swedenborg, Conan Doyle and Sir Oliver Lodge. This information I added to the bits of natural history, imaginative fantasy and religious instruction that constituted my picture of the universe. The picture was forming; it was beginning to be filled out. The craving for a 'system', an explanation of the world, seems to date back as far as I can remember. I even explained it at length to friends at school. But I was sure that all adults were possessed of the sum of all human knowledge; and since I disliked being a child and wanted to grow up, I set about acquiring it in gulps. One day, at the beginning of the war, I heard my father and one of my uncles talking about it; my father explained lucidly how we were going to win the war. We would beat Hitler in North Africa because the Germans were not used to desert fighting, while the British had conquered India and most of Africa. Hitler would be forced to withdraw his forces from France, and we would invade Europe again. His theory also depended on the invincibleness of British sea power and, in some way I have forgotten, on France's Maginot Line. I listened with great attention, and for weeks afterwards explained to anyone who would listen how England would win the war. It was one more piece of information, as reliable as the stories about Jesus and dinosaurs and Atlantis; when speaking of it I solemnly cautioned my friends not to repeat it, in case a German spy should overhear and warn Hitler.

I dwell on this at length because it was my attitude up to the age of ten or so. Information was information, and when you had accumulated enough you would know everything. I still remember how horrified I felt when I learned from my mother that cousin John's father was an atheist. I challenged him on it at the first opportunity, and he admitted it. 'But if Jesus didn't make the world', I objected, 'who did?' 'I don't know. Perhaps nobody.' I am not sure whether this was my first realisation that information might *not* be information – might be only opinion; that the problem was to distinguish between information and opinion. I felt like a man who has built a house and then been told that half his bricks are hollow and will blow away in a high wind.

But I am moving ahead of my story. I have been trying to indicate that the impulse behind my religious convictions was the same impulse that led me to steal from Woolworth's. Both sprang from what I can only describe as power-mania. Knowledge was one form of power, material possessions were another. I once read an article in a boy's magazine describing the things that all boys should carry in their pockets. They included a penknife, ball of string, india rubber, pencil, safety-pin, etc. A boy who carried these articles, the writer concluded, would be equipped to meet every possible emergency in life. Immediately, I collected the various items, and carried them around with me for years, until I discovered that I never used most of them. Life seemed too dangerous and incomprehensible, and every measure had to be taken against it.

And yet I must admit that I had few experiences likely to produce a distrust of the world. There were a few, but they seemed unimportant. For example, my father won a red jack-knife in a raffle, and allowed me to take it out with me when I went to play. I was then about four. A butcher's boy saw it and asked me if he could borrow it. I refused, but he used all his persuasion, and said he only wanted to ride around the block with it. Finally, I lent it to him; he rode off, and I waited on the corner for hours, and finally went home in tears. We never recovered it, although my father inquired in every butcher's shop in the neighbourhood. I had the same kind of experience a few years later, when a friend and I went out to Bradgate Park, ten miles from Leicester. A van-driver asked us to help him load some tins, and offered to give us a lift back to Leicester later in the evening, when he had to return. We loaded busily for an hour; then he drove off; but although we waited until the last bus came in, he never returned. On both occasions, when I realised I had been cheated I felt a hopeless rage, and dreamed of sadistic torments; but the feeling was brief.

My contacts with more sinister types of betrayal – with sexual perversion – worried me less. When I was very tiny a youth approached me and asked me to play with him. I discovered that his idea of 'play' was entirely sexual, and went on for hours. When he finally let me go, I went home and told my parents, and my father immediately took me out on the crossbar of his bicycle looking for the youth; but he had vanished. The episode struck me as curious, but not frightening; I had been bored by it all.

A later episode might have had more serious consequences. When I was seven or eight, I was on my way to the public library with Barry and a friend when we were approached by a man with a bicycle, who asked us if we wanted cigarette cards. We had all been warned not to speak to strange men, but I was greedy; I insisted on leaving the other two (who refused to come) and went off with the man. He took me on to some allotments, and into a little wood. As we went into the wood, he saw a man standing by a gate, watching us. So when we got into the wood, he leaned his bicycle against a tree, asked me to wait for him, and went off. By this time I was worried, for he had told me that the cigarette cards were buried. I crept after him, and saw him on all fours near the edge of the wood, peering out at the man who had been watching him. Thoroughly scared, I slipped out of the other side of the wood, and ran like a jack rabbit. A few minutes later I met Barry and my friend, who had come to look for me, convinced that I had been murdered. Perhaps I would have been, or perhaps the man's intention was only sexual assault. But if the danger had come close, I was not aware of it. I never expected anything awful to happen to me, and nothing ever did.

All the same, I was aware that the world could be a treacherous place. I had frequently been bullied and beaten-up by boys from slums, who may have been encouraged by my obvious fear of them. So in bed at night I used to tell Barry long stories about a super-boy named Tom Perry, who lived in a castle in the wild west, led a band of cowboys that included Buck Jones and Ken Maynard, and frequently defeated gangs of ragged-arsed slum-boys single-handed.

Throughout my childhood I was always aware of the two opposing impulses: distrust of the world, and the sense of immunity, complete confidence. This latter seems to me to be important, since it is closely related to the confidence that came of being spoilt. I can recall many occasions on which I have wanted to do something, and have done it with an ease that has astonished me – an ease that is somehow foreign to the subjective and introspective part of me. As a child of five I was taught various poems and songs by my father and grandfather, and a recitation that purported to be a speech by You Ri Reep from Dickens. (I always assumed him to be a Chinaman until I finally read *David Copperfield* and discovered that Dickens spells it Uriah Heep.) These I was persuaded to sing or recite standing on a table whenever we had company. My brother Barry and various cousins could never be induced to do the same, but I was always happy to be placed on a table and receive all the attention. There I would wring my hands, declare I was 'an 'umble man', and end by threatening to squeeze somebody dry like a blood orange. Alternatively, I sang comic songs, particularly one called 'Standing Outside a Lunatic Asylum'. In my teens, when I looked back on these extraverted activities, I found it incomprehensible that I should have felt no shyness.

Certain episodes of tree-climbing and fighting seem to belong to the same psychological category. I remember a boy of whom everybody was afraid; one day at school he annoyed me, and I knocked him all over the playground with an absurd ease. The act of fighting belonged somehow to a different order of events from the ones that engaged my normal personality; it seemed as inevitable and as free from danger as sleepwalking.

And yet I knew this sense of confidence could be deceptive. Near our home was a bridge that crossed a brook, and carried tram-lines. When the trams were scrapped this bridge was partly dismantled, leaving only iron girders across the brook. One day I steeled myself to walk across one of these girders, edging cautiously, step by step. Having crossed without mishap or danger of overbalancing, I did it again, faster. Finally, I was able to run across the girders almost as fast as I could run on solid ground. One day I was strolling casually across the girders, and talking to some friends who were standing to my left; since my head was turned sideways I could not see where I was walking, and I took a false step. I managed to right my balance; but it taught me the danger of over-confidence. A few days after this had happened one of my friends fell off the girders and hurt himself badly on the jagged chunks of concrete in the brook, which redoubled my sense of its danger. I stopped walking across the bridge.

These episodes are trivial; but I am trying to place my finger on what lay behind them. Do men of action – men like Napoleon and Hitler – go through their whole lives in that sleepwalking trance which I have experienced only occasionally? If so, what is the meaning of the trance? Are such men – as Yeats would contend – instruments in the hands of the force of the spirit of history? Inevitably, we live the greater part of our lives in calculation, in the spirit of caution and anxiety, the preparation for defeat or at least for heavy setbacks. The world of neurosis and 'nausea' is reflected in all our art and literature; it would seem to be the essence of consciousness in the twentieth century. Even for the total sceptic, the historian who regards Spengler and Toynbee as 'readers of tea-leaves', there can at least be no doubt that our billions of observing minds are reflecting the spirit of Hamlet, even if there is no real meaning behind the phrase 'spirit of the age'. Neurosis is the disease of being too much awake. Men who have lost the power to sleep may feel an almost superstitious envy of the sleepwalkers. Is this the reason we live in an age of demagogues and 'popular idols', of Hitler and Marilyn Monroe? Are the wars of the twentieth century a reflection of the need for gods? The man of action, moving with the precision of a racing driver, can never cease to be aware that he avoids death by the grace of the gods. (I occasionally achieve the same feeling when night-driving for long distances.) Hence danger becomes a way of re-establishing the sense of the gods and soothing the exhausted ego into the sleepwalker's trance. Hence such curious anomalies as T. E. Lawrence, St Exupéry, Ernest Hemingway – even the late James Dean. The violent death becomes also somehow inevitable.

However, the symbol of my childhood was never the racing-goggles of Lawrence or St Exupéry, but the tub of Diogenes. To establish complete independence, like a youth called Huckleberry Hodge featured in *The Rover* or some other of my favourite boys' papers, who lived in a barrel and fished with the line tied to his big toe while he slept. When I think back on my childhood, and try to focus that impulse again, it seems to me that my life has been dominated by a desire to contract into a point.

3
STIMULI

SPEAKING through the mouth of Jack Tanner, Shaw declares that the greatest revolution of his childhood was 'the birth of the moral passion'; up till that time, he had lied and stolen 'with no more conscience than a fox in a poultry farm'. I seem to remember that Shaw somewhere sets the birth of that passion at the age of fourteen or so. In my own case, it happened earlier. I would be inclined to call it the birth of disinterestedness; for all the lies of my childhood (and I lied extensively and gratuitously) were attempts to interest or impress the grown-ups.

When I was ten I went to stay out at the village of Middleton, near Corby, with Aunt Connie (my mother's sister) and Uncle Frank Carlyle. Before I left, two weeks later, Uncle Frank presented me with a volume called *The Marvels and Mysteries of Science*, which cost five shillings, and was full of photographs of stars, waterfalls and other interesting objects. One morning, lying in bed, I read the chapter on the planets, and learned Professor Lowell's theory that Mars might be inhabited by a race who dig canals as straight as Roman roads. This seemed to be another one of those remarkable pieces of information that I should have been told at the age of five, and had for some reason been withheld from me. I began to read everything on astronomy I could find in the local library.

Up till this time my imagination had been stimulated largely by death and violence. I was known to all the boys of the neighbourhood as a teller of tales of horror, which I invented, or pieced together from fragments of horror stories I had read; these usually included Frankenstein monsters, zombies and vampires, and frequently all three.

With the sudden growth of my interest in science, I became contemptuous of the horror stories. It must have been about this time that my grandfather gave me an old science-fiction magazine, which I read with a sense of revelation. I became a science-fiction addict;

STIMULI

I thirsted after the magazines like a dipsomaniac for whisky. During the war they were not available; but many bookshops ran an exchange system – you could not buy their science-fiction magazines, but once you had one you could exchange it any number of times on the payment of a few pence. I was not satisfied to exchange my magazine; I wanted a collection; so during the next year or so, I turned my skill as a thief to full acount. On two or three occasions I was almost seen by the shopkeeper as I was about to slip a magazine under my jacket; but the collection grew until I had about sixty magazines – *Amazing Stories, Thrilling Wonder Stories, Fantasy Magazine,* and so on. I cannot remember how long the passion lasted, but it was certainly several years.

At about the same time – for my eleventh birthday or for Christmas – my mother bought me a cheap chemistry set. I worked as a newspaper-deliverer to make money to buy test tubes and chemicals (again a difficult matter during the war); and I turned a spare room in the house into a laboratory. Everyone in the family complained; the house stank perpetually of chlorine and sulphuretted hydrogen. I spent every Saturday afternoon and Sunday in my laboratory, producing smells and bangs. My discovery of the explosive potentialities of potassium chlorate and sulphur, when hit by a hammer, started a craze that seemed to spread all over Leicester. Potassium chlorate could be obtained almost pure in throat-tablets. Throughout the winter of 1942 our district rocked with explosions. A kind of bomb could be made by taking two large bolts and joining them with a nut into which was inserted the chlorate mixture. It was then thrown into the air. When it landed the two bolts would be hurled violently apart; many windows were broken in this way. I suspect that I may also have been responsible for the carbide epidemic. Potassium carbide was sold in tins by most bicycle shops; when dropped into water it produces acetylene gas, which is inflammable. Spectacular explosions can be produced by dropping carbide into half an inch of water in a large tin, and then replacing the lid on the tin. If a small hole is bored in the lid, and a light applied to the hole, the mixture of air and acetylene can be guaranteed to blow the lid ten feet in the air, and perhaps to buckle the tin. A more dangerous practice is to mix carbide and water in a bottle with a screw-top, to stand it on a fence, and throw stones at it. If the pressure is great enough, the bottle may explode before it is hit; in any case, it makes a satisfactory bang. I have broken a window fifty yards away when I used an exceptionally strong bottle for the experiment; the explosion also brought neighbours from the whole street out of doors. The caretaker at our school was kept overworked washing and refilling inkwells in which the ink had been turned to a muddy brown paste with carbide; threats of instant expulsion finally ended the craze.

For completeness, I should also add that Leicester had a brief epidemic of cordite stealing. We discovered that the army dumps in the surrounding countryside housed red silk bags full of cordite strips. One day a friend and I cycled out to a nearby dump, and returned with a dozen or so bags. Cordite was disappointing. It burned merrily enough; but try as we would we could not induce it to explode. In disgust, we began lighting strips of cordite and throwing them into the air. A policeman approached and asked what we were doing; we told him we were throwing lighted matches. Luckily, he showed no curiosity, and never thought to search us, or even to look at the fragments of half-burnt 'matches' on the ground. A few days later there was an unholy row at our school, and about a dozen boys were summarily expelled for stealing cordite. Luckily, we were not mentioned, although I was well-known throughout the school as a trafficker in explosives. I either manufactured them from gunpowder mixture and magnesium, with various salts of strontium, cobalt or zinc to produce different coloured flames, or persuaded my grandfather – who was an ARP warden – to steal me the mixture the ARP used in their imitation incendiary bombs. I made a great deal of money selling my explosives in packages at threepence each, particularly as Bonfire Night approached and it was impossible to buy fireworks.

And yet, even if I implemented my collection of science fiction and my chemistry set by dubiously legal methods, I still believe that it was Shaw's 'moral passion' that was born in me when I discovered science. Something altered in my picture of the world. The darkness and fear disappeared. It seemed that I at last understood human destiny. Man might be, on the whole, a contemptible creature, but this was because most men were too lazy to care about anything beyond their immediate needs. I had never met anyone who was in the least interested in ideas, or in knowledge for its own sake – they are still scarce among working class people – but it was possible to transcend human limitations by an idealistic devotion to knowledge. For me, the scientist was the hero of the drama of human destiny. I read a little book by Russell called *Religion and Science,* and it placed the matter in perspective. Before the coming of science the human race had been at the mercy of tyrants, liars and fanatics; now man would not regress; the great spirit of science could never be killed. The Church had tried hard; now it was being swept away by the flood. (I still had unpleasant memories of a large cold church, and hours of hymn singing, and the peddling of moral platitudes as if they were an elixir of life.)

I cannot remember how far this attitude was influenced by the reading of H. G. Wells, although he was the writer I admired most at this time. I suspect that I was aware only of Wells the story-teller and was indifferent to Wells the prophet. I bought some of the weekly parts of the *Outline of History* for the sake of their coloured plates, and was disappointed to find Wells the scientist dealing with a subject as trivial as history.

This was for me the essence of the attraction of science: it divided the world sharply into two halves: the essential and the trivial. 'Facts' were the only essential in so far as they provided a basis for generalisation. All the facts that could not be generalised – which included 99 per cent of my life as a human being – could safely be dismissed.

This is of immense importance to someone with a working-class background, an importance that can hardly be grasped by members of the middle classes. There is a scene in John Osborne's *The Entertainer* in which a housewife has hysterics because someone has eaten a slice out of a cake she is saving for someone else; when I saw the play it recalled the worst elements of my childhood with a reality that disgusted me. If I think back on the most violent quarrels and scenes of my childhood, the cause was always as trivial as that slice of cake. I recall interminable conversations overheard on buses or in other people's houses, hair-splitting spite and malice; but most of all, an overwhelming, monstrous triviality, a parasitic triviality that ate its way into all values. At the time of my greatest revulsion from it – in my mid-teens – the mere sound of a Leicester accent was enough to give me goose-pimples of disgust.

Science meant freedom from all this; unlike religion, its standard of values was cool and unassailable. The Jehovah's Witnesses who came to our door told us that all other sects were misguided, and that some religious bodies, for instance the Catholic Church, were instruments of Antichrist. Science stood above this kind of squabbling like an adult above children.

This was the reason why I seemed to become a new person, and felt a new kind of happiness in borrowing fat volumes on inorganic chemistry from the library, or reading some popular science article on the cyclotron. (Years later, when the radio announced the dropping of the atomic bomb, I ran around the room shouting with excitement, and felt as a Jehovah's Witness would feel on hearing the trump of the Last Judgement.)

But even now, I have not made clear what it was that happened to me with my discovery of science. Suddenly, all the recurrent motives of my life, all the glimpses and urges and brief enthusiasms – came together and united into a theme that became at last a conscious driving force. I suppose it has been the main obsession of my life ever since.

To begin with, it was discovery of the *impersonal* – that one could gain pleasure from something that had no connection with one's needs and desires. All the pleasures of childhood are connected with the satisfaction of various appetites – food, toys, vanity, the need for adult attention and approval. And here suddenly was a pleasure that arose from none of these. It was like discovering you had a spare limb that you had never noticed.

But there is something even more important than this. We tend to accept life as it is, and it is usually pretty dreary. As children, we have our moments of deep satisfaction – at Christmas time, for example – and find it difficult to face the dullness of another eleven months of school before the next one. And these times convince us that 'life' and 'everyday living' are not synonymous.

Well, a great number of these 'glimpses' came to me in childhood, and I was unwilling to see them fade into the 'light of common day'. When you are a child, you assume that they are associated with certain times – Christmas, Easter, the August holidays, and so on; so it seems that there is little to do but to wait for them. What science taught me was that it is possible to go out and look for them.

Later on, I discovered that other studies can bring these moments of intensity – poetry, music, mathematics, painting, history and archaeology; even, paradoxically, the study of murder, which can produce a response of revulsion that awakens the sense of evolutionary purpose. But since I had started as a lover of science, I conducted my search scientifically, and tried to analyse the psychology of these moments of insight. In saying this, I have explained the driving motive behind all my thinking and writing.

All this is important enough to make it worthwhile to leap ahead of the story. I had discovered that there are states of 'higher consciousness', which make our everyday consciousness seem little better than sleeping. When we wake up from sleep, we imagine that we have passed clearly from one state to another; it is not true. We are still only half-awake, or less than that. We walk around surrounded by dreams, half-drugged. This is why we do not appreciate life. It is as if God said: 'I will give human beings the greatest of all possible gifts – life', and the devil replied: 'And I will add a condition: that they should never appreciate it while they have it'. So we live in dreams; we are like healthy men who have been hypnotised into hypochondria, so we sit shivering and moaning, wrapped in blankets and full of imaginary aches and pains.

We are not awake. If something could awaken us, we would arise like giants. This is the absurdity of human life: we are gods who have been hypnotised into believing themselves insects. It is from this perpetual state of semi-sleep that there arises the problem I have called the St Neot margin – and that the Church fathers called Original Sin.

For this reason, we possess almost no free will. We imagine we do; in reality, we are like drunks who have to lean for support on walls, and who would immediately collapse if made to stand up alone. How can we know the extent of our wills when asleep? Sleep is the time of will-lessness, of hidden fears, when you lie

> '....and watch the night revealing
> The thousand sordid images
> Of which your soul was constituted.'

It is the time when you try to run from some obscure menace, and your legs feel like lead. And yet we *can* make an immense mental effort in a nightmare and wake up. We possess that much willpower in spite of the sleep. And in the same way, as we walk around in our everyday sleep, we possess enough will-power to strive to throw off the dreams and delusions. All religions are fundamentally no more than a recognition of this truth : that we live enmeshed in dreams and delusions, and 'salvation' lies in somehow throwing off the burden, the paralysis of our true will.

Because they possess so little real will, men need purpose to keep them sane : they need the demands of everyday existence. When I was in the hosiery class at school, I used flat-bed machines, and discovered that the fabric has to be heavily weighted as it emerges from under the machine; otherwise, the wool climbs up the needles, and in a few seconds the whole thing is a tangled mess. So it is with human existence; unless freedom is weighted with purpose, it can turn a man into an animal.

Most men are contented with their everyday purposes, and do not look beyond them. A few men have tasted another kind of consciousness, and they cannot rest in ordinary purposes. They are like the crocodile in *Peter Pan* that tasted Captain Hook's leg and followed him round the world to get a bite at the other one.

I later came to call these men 'outsiders'. Carping critics were to object that the term is meaningless, as everybody is more-or-less an outsider. But this is not true. The outsider is a man who has accidentally had an 'awakening', and suddenly realised the sheer absurdity of human existence – the incredibly poor quality of the thing that we accept as everyday human existence. The apparently 'paradoxical' conduct of certain outsiders arises from this insight – T. E. Lawrence's enlistment in the RAF, for example. To the ordinary man, they appear to be behaving against their own best interests, to be 'denying life'. The outsider knows that the kind of existence most people accept is not worth calling 'life'.

It was science that first made me fully conscious of this problem, of which most people seem to be totally unaware. From now on, I could no longer 'live'; my existence became a search for something I had lost.

At school I became a 'teacher's pet' in the science department. During my first year at the secondary school, The Gateway, I had been unhappy, and finished bottom of the class; but as soon as I shot to the top in chemistry all my other subjects improved – including my French and geography. A similar transformation had occurred two years earlier, when a friend of my father's offered me half a crown if I could reach top place in the form, and I changed overnight from a very middling scholar to a kind of prodigy. My abilities seem to work entirely on optimism. (I am sure there must be a moral for educationalists in this somewhere, but I cannot see it at present.)

The name of Einstein kept recurring in science-fiction magazines, so I borrowed books from the library on relativity and wrestled with them. Einstein's own 'popular' account baffled me. But Abbott's *Flatland,* Jeans's *The Mysterious Universe,* and various other simplified accounts gave me a firm grounding in the subject. I enjoyed correcting the physics master on problems involving the speed of light.

Looking back on it all, I can see that I was not half the prodigy I thought I was. The kind of knowledge I picked up could have been acquired by any industrious eleven year old without an atom of real scientific ability. But it was just as well that nothing disillusioned me. I got used to thinking of myself as a prodigy; it became a mental habit that inoculated me against the prevailing 'fallacy of insignificance'. Nietzsche answered the question 'Why am I so clever?' by saying that he had never wasted time or energy on questions of morality and conscience; if I ever had to answer the same question, I would probably reply: Because I have never wasted time on modesty.

I have spoken elsewhere of the curious effect that Einstein produced in me. I can no longer reconstruct the process by which I moved from scientific relativity to moral relativity. No doubt it was based on my contempt for most adults. This contempt had to be rationalised, so I created the concept of 'superiority'. It seemed to me clear that all men are guided by the desire to regard themselves as extraordinary. Since we are all more aware of our own existence than of anybody else's, we have a basis for the sense of uniqueness. But sometimes the subjectivity of the individual becomes the last stronghold of the sense of superiority; he has no other reason for regarding himself as unique. (This reminds me of the joke about the psychiatrist who told his patient: 'I have discovered the reason for your inferiority complex; you *are* inferior.') Then the power of self-delusion comes into effect. In extreme cases, it can make a man believe he is Napoleon; but usually the delusions are milder and not socially harmful. How many times had I heard my father's friends in argument declare: 'Now you listen to me...' with the implication: 'I *know*'.

It was a disturbing picture: a world of men all mildly or totally insane; insane because man has no capacity for honesty. But supposing one were honest – what then? I frequently argued with anyone who would listen, adults preferably. I was told I was immature or conceited. The desire for honesty led me to refuse to allow the mechanisms by which we retain our self-conceit to come into action; so I writhed.

I had been completely absorbed in my world of science for about two years when changes came. Every evening I worked, delivering newspapers. Just before Christmas, 1944, a friend of mine opened the door as I was about to deliver the newspaper, and invited me to come in. There were three girls in the house: Gladys, May, and Betty (whom we called Ginger). They wore the maroon blazers of the 'Art and Tech', the college opposite the Gateway school. My friend Andy was Gladys's boy-friend. They were doing their science homework, and wanted some help. I was delighted. The next evening they were waiting for me, and I went in again. May, who was a plump, pretty and rather shy girl, seemed to like me. Gladys was more vivacious, and I preferred her, but since she was Andy's property I was willing to compromise with May. It was all innocent enough. We travelled to school together on the bus in the mornings; we went to the cinema together on Sunday evenings, and exchanged awkward goodnight kisses afterwards. And just before Christmas we went to the school dance together. There, Gladys and Andy quarrelled, and I became aware that Gladys contemplated a transfer to me. Among adults the situation would have led to hysterics and blows; at thirteen we were more civilised about it. Gladys became officially my girlfriend, but Andy and May still made the party up to four.

Nothing much happened, except that I gained a name at school as a womaniser, which flattered me. We managed to see the girls several times a day, since Gateway boys spent a great deal of their time over at the Art and Tech.

But I became intensely aware for the first time of the power of sex. I was still puritanical; kissing was my idea of the extreme limit of the sexual commerce between man and woman. All the other boys of my age and acquaintance seemed to be more sexually advanced, and I was aware of what went on at the Sunday evening cinema when the lights went out. A thirteen year old girl who lived near Gladys slept with American soldiers and made a great deal of money. Sex was a constant part of our conversation. The inevitable conflict developed; I would have liked to take more liberties with Gladys, but was held back by shyness. A previous boy-friend of hers had been less backward; in fact, she had been forced to throw him over because he had tried to rape her. The idea morbidly obsessed me until finally I made his acquaintance, driven by a compulsion I found incomprehensible. He proved to be pleasant, cheerful, uninhibited and not particularly intelligent.

Quite abruptly, I had a period of bad language, which was undoubtedly an expression of frustration. I was totally self-divided about sex. This was reflected in my relations with Gladys; I began to take a certain pleasure in hurting her, as if she were to blame. I knew she had had some kind of rudimentary sexual experience, and this tormented me. I lay in bed with her once – I was telling her small niece a story, and we were both fully clothed – and later could not stop feeling self-contempt because I had not even kissed her.

One day several of us went out to Mountsorrel, near Leicester. I had some kind of quarrel with Gladys, and made her cry. Andy was indignant and decided that I must be taught a lesson, so three of them challenged me to fight. I fought them one after the other. The first I beat; with the second, I was beginning to feel exhaustion, but managed to hold him off for ten minutes. By the time I fought Andy, I was breathless; he gave me a blow in the solar plexus that doubled me up on the ground and made me think I should never recover my breath. This was the beginning of the end of the affair with Gladys. A few days later she threw me over and returned to Andy. (Years later, they married, and now have several children.)

I had known Gladys for nine months; I could hardly believe it was all over. I felt choked with frustration and regret. The August holidays were approaching. I began to read books faster than ever before. Then I conceived the idea of writing a book – a short work that would summarise all the scientific knowledge of the world in formulas. I bought some small notebooks with hard covers, and worked throughout the August of 1945 producing articles on physics, chemistry, astronomy, geology and aeronautics, to which later I added philosophy and mathematics. I had a small library of reference books that had begun with a six-volume edition of *Practical Knowledge for All,* bought at some church bazaar. The work was originally intended to occupy one small notebook; finally, it extended to six. Before I began it I had no kind of knowledge of philosophy, geology or aeronautics. In writing of these subjects I made a curious discovery: the need to summarise the subject and condense it into a few pages seemed to increase my ability to grasp it. Months of reading philosophy could not have taught me as much as a week's writing about it.

At all events, the exercise had the effect I had intended: it stopped me mooning about Gladys.

By Christmas I had reached volume six, which was devoted entirely to mathematics, and realised that my idea of a summary of all knowledge was hopeless. So I gave it up. But the exercise had taught me a great deal; apart from the amount of useless knowledge I picked up, I also became aware of the intense pleasure of being absorbed in work on a book, the feeling of inner-health that comes at the end of an exhausting day's work, the reverse of the usual neurotic world of daydreams.

I was always inclined to do things strenuously. I was about eleven when I discovered that I could ride a bicycle. On Sundays I used to borrow my grandfather's old Raleigh, and go off for long rides. Sometimes I went with a friend named George Baxter; more often, alone.

But I could never bring myself to do a short and reasonable day's ride – say, twenty miles. Neither could I ride slowly and easily; I had to tear along as fast as I could go. In his *The Wheels of Chance* Wells has a large, hot cyclist who complains to Mr Hoopdriver that he has the misfortune to combine an energetic temperament with a contemplative disposition, so that although he would like to drift along and appreciate the scenery he feels impelled to pedal like a maniac. I immediately recognised myself in this nameless cyclist. Some of my memories of country rides are pleasant – the back of the castle at Warwick, with the noise of the waterfall; the coolness of the caves at Matlock; the lawns of the memorial theatre at Stratford. But my main memory is of cycling along against the wind, cursing every motorist who sailed by at sixty miles an hour, cursing the wind and the human race.

This was the kind of exercise with which I alternated long days of working on my *Manual of General Science*. It did me no harm. I seemed to thrive on strain. My mother told me I lived off my nerves; no doubt she was right. But I had been lucky in never having been ill in childhood (except for measles and mumps, which were welcomed as holidays from school); and while overwork made me feel virtuous, it never made me feel ill. The only effect of all the reading was to make me more short-sighted than ever. I had worn glasses from the age of ten – as a result of going to the cinema too often. (My grandparents displayed cinema posters in their windows and got free tickets; I went sometimes as often as four times a week.)

I cannot conceal the fact that I owe a very considerable debt to the cinema; it seems to me to be a medium of incalculable force in the life of the twentieth century – probably more important than newspapers, free lending libraries and the radio added together. Again, this is not recognised because most of our psychologists and sociologists come from middle or upper class backgrounds, and are unaware of the burden of dullness from which young men and women of the working classes need to escape in their spare time. Famous musicians and theatre critics have written about the revelation of attending the theatre or opera for the first time; but every working class child has the same experience when he first goes to the cinema. (I am unable to generalise about the effect of television on this audience, as I am too old to have experienced its impact.)

The first films I can remember seeing were *Trader Horn* and *The Last of the Mohicans*. As soon as I was about six or seven I was allowed to go to the Saturday afternoon matinée (price twopence). The stimulus of the cinema encouraged endless daydreams. Like all small boys, I preferred cowboy films, and never missed an opportunity to disparage 'sloppy love stories'. Compared to most schoolboys Thurber's Walter Mitty is as unimaginative as Sancho Panza; my daydreams were like four-volume novels that proceeded in instalments over weeks. Later, when I had to travel to school by bus, and therefore had a wider choice of cinemas, I developed a taste for Technicolor musicals (and of course, for their blonde heroines). The daydreams also became technicoloured. To describe the effect of these films I should be forced to resort to clichés such as 'world of enchantment' and 'unbearable nostalgia'. And yet they were the source of the energy that was poured into the study of Eddington and Jeans. If life was ever to evolve from the vegetable mediocrity of Leicester into the realms of romance and technicolour, it would be through the effort to be great. Therefore, an 'ordinary' future was unthinkable; it had to be genius or nothing.

On the whole I enjoyed my years at the Gateway secondary technical school. It proved to be disappointingly unlike the public schools of *The Magnet, The Gem* and *The Hotspur*; but it gave one a great deal of freedom. A lot of time was spent in the College of Art and Technology; I proved to have talent neither for art (sculpture, drawing, clay-modelling) nor technology (hosiery, engineering, boots-and-shoes); so any other secondary school in Leicester would have suited me better. But I was never forced to play football or cricket (the flimsiest excuse would serve if you didn't want to play), and was encouraged to do the things I enjoyed doing : speaking at the school debating society, writing for the school or form magazine, organising theatricals.

And yet I must also admit that I learned a disproportionately small amount from my eleven years' schooling. I have learned more about literature in a month of desultory reading than from hours of 'English Lit.' at school; and I learned ten times more about science from writing the *Manual* in six weeks than I could ever have learned at school.

While on this subject, I should mention an observation that struck me at the age of eleven. We were given *Tom Sawyer* as a 'class book'. On the day we were issued with it I took it home and started to read it; I finished it in the early hours of the morning. It was the first book I had ever read that described children from the inside and did not try to evade the immensely important sexual issue. During the next year I re-read it several times.

And yet, for some reason, we never got around to reading it in class. Perhaps the teacher found Tom's love affair with Becky too embarrassing, and wanted us to read the book at home. No one else read it. I asked everybody in the form. And the strange thing is that if we had been asked to read it in class I know I should have hated it.

I noticed the same paradox with a book called *Stories of Detection* that was issued as a class book. I had already read Father Brown and Sherlock Holmes; and yet I remember being bored when we 'did' 'The Blue Carbuncle' and 'The Queer Feet' in class.

I am unable to offer any generalisations about education – except the obvious one that perhaps its aim should be to persuade children to educate themselves. This would also involve giving everyone more free time, which might not be a blessing. And yet surely our educationalists could devise some method whereby a child's free time was governed by his achievement at school? Admittedly, this would mean that the brilliant children would have something like a perpetual holiday, while the dull ones would be unfairly confined to their classrooms; but would this not be more sensible than imprisoning them all impartially?

When I was nine years old all the adults I knew had a habit of speaking disparagingly of comics and boys' papers; I always declared, on the contrary, that they could teach one more than any school text book. On the whole I am inclined to stand by this opinion. I certainly learned more out of school than in it; and my only reading until I was ten was the weekly comic.

After I had read *Tom Sawyer* I realised for the first time that boys' papers have a serious fault: they make no provision for the schoolboy's sexual romanticism. In *Tono Bungay,* Wells remarks sensibly that schoolchildren have as much right as any adult to call their romantic attachments 'love'. For myself, I cannot remember a time when I was not violently attached to at least one little girl; and occasionally the list grew to as many as ten. These 'affairs' were usually very innocent, most of them never reaching even the stage of kisses. With most of my friends it was the same; 'love' was our main concern. In almost any street in Leicester, you could find chalked such inscriptions as 'John Patrick loves Norma Bingley', which were intended to embarrass the two concerned, but more often produced a shy pleasure. *Galeotto fu il libro, e chi lo scrisse.*

Shaw's 'moral passion', then, may be a late comer to most children; but the other passions are there in abundance. I am inclined to add 'thank God', for I can imagine no real development or progress without the influence of these stimuli that most educationalists would dismiss as 'recreations' or condemn as unhealthy appetites.

4
NIHILISM

I HAVE said that a feeling of 'moral relativity' developed somehow from reading Einstein. No doubt my discovery of Berkeley and Hume (in Joad's *Guide to Philosophy*) also played its part. I can remember distinctly the first occasion when I actually began to feel a kind of fear of the unknown. It was in the clay-modelling class in the Art and Tech. The teacher had gone off and left us to ourselves. I was working on the same board with a boy called Flynn, and various friends were close to us. For some reason, we began to talk about astronomy, and someone raised the question of where the universe ends. I kept trying to fling my mind into the conception of endless space. We talked of immense distances, of light years and the expanding universe. But always we came back to the question: Where *could* it end? We thought in terms of an end in *something*, perhaps a wall, or a 'dimensionless hyperspace' (to use the jargon of science fiction writers). My mind began to reel – and I mean this literally. There was a feeling as if I were losing my balance. When we left the room at the end of the morning I felt strange, as if I had died. The world has a comforting surface of stability that keeps us happy. Nothing is final and irreversible. I suppose I had had an exceptionally comfortable and stable childhood. I had never believed that any harm could come to me; I had been affectionate, and had had all the love I needed. If I had ever been in trouble, it was nothing that a few pleas and apologies could not cure. Nothing seemed irrevocable, and my worst nightmares were followed by a pleasant awakening in a sunlit bedroom. My basic attitude was optimistic and Chestertonian; Chesterton had finished a poem with the lines:

> 'Death was but the Good King's jest,
> It was hid so carefully.'

I was like a man who has always been comfortable behind a thick glass wall, able to observe other people's discomforts, but never really believing in them. It was now as if a crack had appeared in the wall. It was the entrance of death into my universe, and therefore of evil. That feeling of ultimate immunity vanished.

What had happened, I think, was that I had come to grasp the idea of the external universe as 'everything', leaving no alternative. That horror still comes upon me sometimes in the night. I have attempted to describe it in my novel *Ritual in the Dark*. The feeling of limitation is death to the soul. No life can exist without ultimate hope. There is the story of the last year of the life of Theodore Storm, the German poet; when he was seventy a doctor diagnosed in him cancer of the stomach; Storm asked the doctor not to deceive him, but to tell him, man to man, what chance he had. The doctor complied. Storm was shattered; he lost all will to live. Then his brother involved two more physicians in a plot; they re-examined Storm, told him it was all a mistake, and that the cancer was benevolent. Storm immediately continued work on his last novel *Death on the White Horse* and finished it triumphantly; he also spent a happy year eating and drinking before his death.

All human greatness, all human effort, depends on the feeling of ultimate un-limitedness. Immediate problems and miseries are unimportant; but there *must* be a tomorrow; there must be an emergency exit, a final assurance of safety.

This discussion about 'ultimates' seems to me to be the first of a long series that took place over the next ten years, always ending with the same feeling of despair, of exhaustion and futility, of inability to get to grips with the problem. The first effect of this exhaustion was a feeling of amazement that the world could go on, that people should continue to be preoccupied with trivialities. William James records that after his 'vastation' his mother seemed to him to be paradoxical in her cheerful unconsciousness of danger. I also felt this of everyone I saw.

My first expression of my sense of revolt at the universal self-delusion was an essay on 'Superiority', written when I was twelve. I still have this essay. It argues that all men are completely enmeshed in self-delusion, and that the universal motive that underlies all human conduct is the need of the individual to feel himself 'superior', to deny the obvious fact that he is a mere insect among billions of other insects.

The title-page of my exercise-book is labelled: *Essays on the*

Life Aim, under which is written: 'The following notes are based on Adler's system of Individual psychology and on the philosophical aspects of the principle of relativity'. I explained that Adler felt that neuroses were all due to a sense of inferiority and inadequacy in the face of other people, and that a healthy man feels himself to be equal to his fellows. I disagreed with Adler, I declared. In my opinion, the healthy man must be certain of his own superiority, and he would be a neurotic if he merely believed himself to be on the same level as everyone else.

Re-reading these essays, I am aware that they spring out of a defensive attitude to the 'adult world'. I keep asking *why* adults should expect the young to respect them. It seemed to me that all human beings are involved in the same total nescience, so that even a Shavian ancient would have no right to regard himself as anyone's superior.

I suppose that, at bottom, this attitude is a religious one: in the face of death and our ignorance, how can we claim to know anything? But it hardly makes for a cheerful and well-adjusted adolescence. There were moments when the sense of detestation of 'people' rose in me to such a pitch that it was a kind of comfort, a certainty of superiority. But no sooner had this thought struck me than I would be forced to regard my own 'superiority' as a mere mechanism. I was trying to live without the certainty that I had a right to live; or rather, I was trying to live *with* the certainty that I had no right to live.

I went around like a man with no skin, shivering with loathing of everyone I came into contact with. Zola says: 'Each of us has to swallow his toad every morning.' My whole life seemed like an act of swallowing toads.

Admittedly, it had its consolations. I read the articles on English literature in *Practical Knowledge for All,* and discovered Spenser and Ben Jonson and Coleridge and Macaulay; this started a passion for poetry. I enlarged my library with characteristic amorality, taking books from bookshops, or from the school or public library. I was able to retreat into my world of literature and avoid contact with 'people'. It seemed to me that literature was an enchanted lunar landscape, beautiful but quite dead, and that to prefer it to the 'real world' was to prefer death to life.

Curiously enough, my discovery of Shaw only deepened this pessimism. I have spoken of this elsewhere (in my preface to *Religion and the Rebel*) – of how I tuned in one night to *Man and Superman* on the Third Programme, listened to it until midnight, and went to bed with a feeling that my life could never be the same again. Up till that time, I had assumed that I was the only person in the world who was interested in the problem of *why* we are alive; it seemed to me that all other human beings were too deeply enmeshed in the act of living to question it. Now I heard Shaw's Don Juan asking the question: What are we doing here? – and what is more, answering it optimistically. I had been troubled by the problem of futility and repetition, and had repeatedly quoted the preacher's 'All is vanity'. Shaw asks: 'Shall a man give up eating because he destroys his appetite in the act of gratifying it?' This was, in fact, precisely my problem – the problem I later called 'the St Neot margin'. What was the point in being a mere draught horse of destiny, pricked on to the effort of living by discomfort and pain? We go through the futile and repetitive act of eating because hunger is painful; we go to work because we would starve otherwise. In short, we are the galley-slaves of life, sweating and heaving because we are afraid of the lash. To me, Oblomov seemed the most sensible man in the world. If I had had money I would have retreated into a tower and refused to emerge. It seemed to me incredibly unfair that fate had been kind to men such as Gide, Firbank and Delius, enabling them to live like hermits, while I had no prospect of ever being freed from the need to earn a living. I have no doubt whatever that if some good fairy had made me a present of a life annuity I would have found my 'tower' and produced the kind of works suited to a pessimist and a recluse – some kind of combination of Schopenhauer, Firbank, and Lovecraft.

While I was at school and studying I had little time to worry about the futility of life. But in 1947 I took my School Certificate examination and succeeded in getting only four credits, instead of the five needed for matriculation. I had hoped to get a job in a chemical factory, and be allowed time for study, so that I could take a science degree. (For some reason, it never occurred to me to try for a university scholarship.) But the failure to matriculate was a temporary setback. I made arrangements to take the mathematics exam again in September. Then I looked around for a job.

Looking back, I realise that this was the most crucial period of my life since my 'discovery of science'. The 'protected years' were over, and I had to think seriously about a career. I would have preferred to stay at school for another ten years. I can still remember the intensity of my reluctance the morning I went to the labour exchange to ask about a job. They directed me to a factory in Cranbourne Street. The place had to be approached down a narrow entry, between dingy houses with tiny backyards. It was a small, two storey building; on the upper floor, women stood by machines that wound hanks of wool on to spindles. My job was to keep the women supplied with wool, and take the spindles downstairs and pack them in cases. It was not difficult work, but it was monotonous. The women all came from the surrounding streets. They seemed so resigned to their dingy houses and dreary lives that I found it abysmally depressing. It was difficult to understand how people could live like this without wanting to go and dynamite the Houses of Parliament and Buckingham Palace; and yet they seemed to expect nothing else out of life.

Working in this atmosphere made me sharply conscious that most people's lives are a long-drawn-out defeat, and that my own might be no better. I became more clearly aware than ever before that I was faced with a choice – between meaninglessness and dedication. No half-hearted dilettantism would do, no spare-time scribbling. It was psychologically necessary for me to perform a mental act of total commitment, like a monk's vow of dedication. Such an act was frightening, like betting every penny you have on a single throw of a dice; but it was the only alternative to fighting a defensive battle and drifting. It was necessary to somehow create within myself a sense of separateness from the people and the way of life of which I was a part. I wanted to be able to echo the words of Shaw's Caesar: 'You and I, Sphinx, strangers to the race of men, are no strangers to one another'.

Therefore I now began to think of myself as wholly and completely a writer, one whose lifelong task would be to investigate the problem of the meaning of human existence. The 'two worlds' now seemed to stand facing one another, and open war had been declared: on the other hand, the futile world of 'everyday life', on the other, the possibility of a way of life that should be completely *meaningful,* creative and self-conscious.

It would have helped if I could have believed – as I do now – that life never witholds anything you want badly and persistently enough. The successful find it easy to believe that fate always meant well by them; but I had no reason for believing anything of the sort, since fate had landed me in a wool factory. It would certainly have helped a great deal if there had been anyone I could have talked to about these matters; but I knew nobody who would have understood. I tried talking to friendly adults occasionally, but they always made me feel that I was taking myself far too seriously, and ought to relax. I think my state of unhealthy intensity genuinely alarmed some of them, and made them feel that it might lead to a mental breakdown. In fact, one Anglican priest with whom I talked said as much, and advised me to read nothing but newspapers for two years. He was right, to some extent. It could easily have led to a mental breakdown, and very nearly did. I came to understand the phrase in *Ecclesiastes*: 'And desire shall fail....' Life became a desert. There were no 'holidays' from the constant fatigue. I felt like someone who has been forced to keep awake for night after night, until the ability to sleep has vanished, and everything is meaningless. It hardly seemed worth going on – but there was no alternative. It always seemed that life was demanding of me more energy than I possessed. In the evening, I locked myself in my bedroom and plunged into poetry – I came to know most of Palgrave by heart – or into Shaw's plays. Sometimes, a few hours of this would leave me feeling cheerful and optimistic again; but when it was time to get out of bed at seven the next morning, my whole being would grind with an immense resentment. I could easily understand how people became social revolutionaries. But I could see that this would only be half a solution. The main problem was to develop as a writer. One morning, packing spools of wool into a crate, I thought about Shaw's *Man and Superman,* and how I would have written it myself. Suddenly the idea excited me. I would write a sequel, in which Jack Tanner is a man in his fifties, with a son in his teens who feels that socialism is no answer to the basic problem of human existence... That weekend, I bought a great pile of foolscap, and began *Fathers and Sons*. I only abandoned it some weeks later, when the first act was already longer than the whole of *Man and Superman*.

After Shaw, Eliot was the greatest influence on my development at this period. This is not surprising. He seemed to justify my own disgust and world-rejection. One of the fantasies that often came into my head was that the plaques on buses carrying advertisements should be replaced by plaques carrying quotations from Eliot: 'Human kind cannot bear very much reality', 'Think of us not as lost, violent souls/But only as the hollow men, the stuffed men', 'I see crowds of people walking around in a ring'. I could never escape a feeling of the absurdity of the lives of these people who could live unaware of the abyss under their feet, unaware of their own deadly second-rateness. I hated human beings, and I hated myself for belonging to the race. It seemed to me that all saints and men who could profess to love their fellow creatures were morons. Shaw once said that it was untrue that he was a champion of the poor; he only wanted to see the poor abolished and replaced by sensible people. I felt that a real saint would be not a lover of humanity, but a man who wanted to see humanity abolished and replaced by some species less futile and stupid. In this respect, I have not changed.

But it would be untrue to suggest that I experienced no other sensation but this unalloyed nihilism. There were also moments, often at the end of a long day of reading and writing, when I became aware of a curious power that made me glow like an electric bulb. In these moments I would suddenly be certain that 'the gods' were on my side, that the misery was a temporary nuisance, that I and all mankind were destined to become gods. In these moments I felt that I was strong enough to bear any burden, that I need never be afraid of anything. They were moments of triumph without a cause. But these moments would disappear after a few hours of work.

I took my mathematics exam, gained my credit, and was all prepared to continue my interrupted career as a scientist. But in the two months of working in the warehouse I had lost all interest in science. The headmaster of the Gateway School offered me a job as a laboratory assistant, and the offer was too good to refuse. But I accepted it unwillingly, because I was aware that this was not the career I intended. I had already made my act of dedication. The problem was that I could think of no way of promoting my career as a writer except to continue the frustrating business of writing short stories or plays in my spare time. In two years' time I would have to go into the army; in the meantime, I had to stay in Leicester and try not to let my hatred of the place destroy my will to write.

So I took the job at my old school, and spent all my spare time writing stories and plays instead of studying physics. It was a disagreeable year. I soon developed a feud with the physics master, who seemed to search for ways of inflicting annoyances and petty humiliations on me. I drank gallons of free school milk, and spent the year in a state of physical and intellectual constipation. Admittedly, there were consolations. I read Shaw until I knew most of his plays by heart; I wrote quantities of plays and short stories; above all, I decided to keep a journal, and was able to pour my frustrations into it for hours at a time until I felt better. 'A timely utterance gave that thought relief...' In the opening pages I stated that I would be a greater writer than Shaw, and that, since I was probably capable of producing better plays than the ninety-year-old Shaw, I had more right to call myself Bernard Shaw than had the old man at Ayot St Lawrence.

I showed my stories to various friends – to the English master and to a woman at the Juvenile Employment Bureau who took an interest in me. But the comment that they were remarkable 'for my age' would throw me into a fury for days.

At about this time I had my first short story published in a Durham factory magazine. It was a story about a meeting of a burglars' society, and the style was largely influenced by Dickens. (I had been reading *Pickwick Papers*.) I came eventually to hate the Dickens style, after hours of wrestling with words and trying to cast my thoughts into a pompous nineteenth century English. But I read *Ulysses* at the time, and thought its style a betrayal of English language, cheap and journalistic. I also agreed with Forster that it was a determined attempt to cover the universe with mud. It had been bad enough escaping from the continual consciousness of Leicester's mediocrity, without having it brought home to me through so-called literature. (When I read the letters of H. P. Lovecraft, I realise how much I resembled him in my mid-teens: the same pessimism, the same world contempt, the same hatred of everything modern.)

I suppose my 'nihilism' reached a kind of climax in that year I worked in the school laboratory. I often suspected, with Berkeley, that other people do not really exist; this naturally led to a kind of terror. If the whole world is a delusion, then *who am I?* What am I doing here? One day, when I had been reading too much (it was a gloomy book on Russian literature) I went into the kitchen to switch on the stove, and had a blackout; I stood holding on to the stove, and felt my mind swept away completely, and all I knew as my identity. When my sight cleared, I was overwhelmed with horror. Through all the hatred and distrust of the world I had at least been certain of one thing – my own existence. But in the blackout I had felt my existence taken away from me as simply as you might take a sweet away from a baby. Suddenly, I wanted badly to know who I was if *I* could still exist when all I knew as my identity slipped away. I understood what Eliot meant when he spoke about the mind under ether being 'conscious, but conscious of nothing'. What I seemed to have been conscious of in the blackout was a kind of electrical flow of pain in the nothingness. Later, I wrote in my journal that it seemed to me then that life is not a movement towards something, but an escape from something – from some ultimate pain on the other side of existence. For days, after this experience, the world became an absurdity; watching it was like listening to a foreign language. What made it worse was that I could not feel: 'This is frightful', or 'This is a tragedy'. It simply negated every possible human value and therefore every human description. I felt as if I should not be alive.

The other experience of this time was the opposite of my 'vastation'; it ended in a kind of revelation of meaning. After a particularly boring and humiliating day in the lab. I thought of killing myself. I felt that even the galley-slave has an alternative, a way of spiting his overseer – to die. The idea grew on me, and I decided that I would probably drink cyanide that evening in the analytical chemistry class. But when it actually came to taking the bottle off the shelf I knew I would not do it; not because I was afraid, but because no matter how little there is to live for, life is better than death. Some tremendous happiness seemed to explode inside me, and I had a strange sensation of *standing beside myself,* looking at the person I called Colin Wilson with mild amusement. It was as if some higher level of my being had taken over. It seemed to me that if I intended taking such an extreme step as killing myself I might just as well utilise that same will power to make my life less irritating. If the physics master was the cause of my irritation, then surely it would be better and braver to kill *him*? If I meant to take an irrational step and throw away all taboos and repressions, then I had better take some irrational step that would leave me still alive. It would be better to rape the rather dim-looking girl working opposite me, or make a tube of nitro-glycerine and throw it against the wall, than to put an arbitrary end to all my possibilities.

I cannot remember how far I put this resolution into action. Probably I took days off from school more boldly, stole books more blatantly, took more trouble to be insolent to the physics master. Eventually, when the end of term exams revealed how little work I had done, they were forced to sack me, and I again found myself out of a job. It all seemed very boring and irrelevant. I went to be interviewed for a job in a wool-merchant's office, and had to claim to be interested in the wool trade and prepared to make a career of it. I got home sizzling with hatred against a society and a life that forced me to tell absurd lies to earn a miserable few pounds a week. But the wool merchant saw through me (luckily) and I was turned down. After this I went to see the Collector of Taxes, a jolly, fat gentleman named Mr Sidford. He could see at a glance that I did not want any kind of job, and that I was going to be endless trouble to him; nevertheless, he gave me the job, and for the next year showed astounding patience with me. I have never ceased to be grateful to him. I hated the tax office, if possible, even more than the laboratory; but I am certain I would have hated any other job still more.

It seemed stupid that I should be forced to live and work with nothing but a sense of total rejection of my life and job. The other people in the office were pleasant enough. There was Miss Pearson, a stately, white-haired lady who adored the royal family and all its doings; there was Joyce, a highly attractive young married woman, who wore expensive clothes and obviously longed for the Riviera;

there was Desmond, a handsome, smart and highly efficient young man in rimless glasses, who looked like Ian Fleming's James Bond but actually seemed to lead a blameless life; there was Ken, who was about to marry, and who often talked to me at length about the joys of married life; there was Mr Joiner, an easygoing Scot, my immediate superior, who was as patient and decent as Mr Sidford. Most important, there was Millicent, who occupied the centre of my thoughts for the next year. She was an attractive, short-sighted, Jewish girl with a sensual mouth and a contralto voice. Recently she had married, and the marriage was unhappy. Millicent's favourite author was Aldous Huxley, and her chief interest was in theatricals; her husband read nothing but Westerns, and thought in terms of 'birds' and horse racing. They were completely ill-matched.

I began to see a great deal of Millicent. We would cycle home from work together, make tea at her house, and then talk about books until her husband arrived from work. He never seemed to object to me – on the contrary, he was always embarrassingly friendly and 'man to man'. The marriage was one of those Look Back in Anger situations. Henry was charming and full of vitality, but he spoke with a cockney accent, and felt that Millicent looked down on his lack of 'culture'. So he enjoyed showing that he was master in the home, ordering her to cook his meals or make tea, and indulging in Jimmy Porter tirades about the books she read. He spent his weekends in bed reading Hank Janson and drinking endless cups of tea. Millicent and I went for long cycle rides and talked about 'ideas'. Inevitably, I was greatly attracted by her, but too shy to show it. On the other hand, I was seventeen, totally inexperienced sexually (unless lurid daydreams count as experience), and found it physically disturbing to be in constant contact with a young married woman whose eyes often had the dreamy look that comes after violent love-making.

In spite of the frustration, I managed to enjoy it. Millicent was a member of the Vaughan College Drama Group, which I now joined. The various activities were a kind of relief, even though it seemed to me that I spent all my time making a fool of myself, knocking over coffee cups and tripping over my own feet. I attended classes on modern poetry, folk dancing and Bernard Shaw, and acted in Dryden's *All for Love*. I also met a young man – whom I shall call Gerald – whose strange affectations and languid manner impressed me much as Starwick in Wolfe's *Of Time and the River* impressed Eugene Gant. We started a curious and rather stormy friendship – curious because I did not share his sexual tastes, and yet was fascinated by him. Like myself, he came of a working class Leicester background; unlike myself, he had a mother who was determined that he should be shielded from the buffets of the world. In spite of the hostility of the rest of his family, she went out to work to support him. When I first talked to him, he gave me the impression of being the son of a rich family; when I first called on him, I was amazed to find him in a tiny, crowded house, the breakfast table still set at midday. But his bookcase in the front room was filled with expensive books, and he talked casually about continental travel. He was two years my senior, and spoke with a deliberately drawling, aristocratic voice. He had succeeded far better than I in eradicating all traces of a Leicester accent.

He talked about the world of the 'beautiful and rare'. When I showed him one of my longest of most philosophical short stories, he remarked casually: 'Completely worthless'. His great admiration was for Oscar Wilde, and the world of the very rich possessed for him the same glamour it possessed for Wilde and Scott Fitzgerald. He read the Elizabethan dramatists – if possible in limited editions – and was encyclopedic about music and painting.

Our tastes were totally unlike; I was contemptuous of the 'beautiful' and enjoyed quoting Don Juan's gibes about the cloying aestheticism of the damned. He admired D. H. Lawrence, and identified himself with Lawrence in his relations with his mother; I detested Lawrence. On the whole he was not deeply interested in ideas, but had a sharp critical mind.

Like myself, he enjoyed walking. We would set out at ten in the evening and walk out along the Groby Road, with its great orange lights suspended from concrete posts. We would turn across the newly built New Parks estate, and sometimes call in on an aunt of mine who lived there. Arriving back at his home in Woodgate in the early hours of the morning, we would make coffee and talk until dawn. Then I would cycle back across Leicester, get an hour's sleep, and go off to work. But at least I seemed to be living a life that was a gesture of defiance against the civil service and the general mediocrity of Leicester.

Our quarrels always sprang from the same cause: he believed that 'the superior man' should possess a streak of aristocratic cruelty. His dismissive judgement on my story was typical. This idea may have been derived from Wilde, or it may have been natural to him. But it meant that, at any time the humour took him, he might turn his 'aristocratic cruelty' on me. One day, for example, when I called on him, he was sitting in the armchair reading. I tapped on the window; he looked up, scowled, and shouted 'Go away'. I went, burning with rage, and swore I would never speak to him again. But boredom and loneliness drove me back a few days later, when he was again amiable and gracious. It gave him pleasure to feel that he might behave like this and his friends would forgive it. 'After all, a proud, aristocratic spirit must be allowed its foibles and tantrums.'

He was engaged on a long novel about homosexuality and a male 'triangle' that involved a young soldier; one of its main themes was the mother-yearning of the homosexual. The novel progressed erratically; he had written the beginning and the end, and scenes from the middle. When he discovered the novels of Proust, he decided that it should be an immense twelve volume work, but retaining the same beginning and end. In the ten years since I first saw it the novel has undergone many changes of style, idea and approach, but the original pieces have been retained, giving it the air of a country house on to which a dozen different owners have added wings in different styles.

Since we were both writing, we spent a great deal of time reading one another our latest pages. It was he who drew my attention to the *Diary of Nijinsky* and to the life and work of Van Gogh; I in turn introduced him to the work of Eliot and Joyce. (He read *Ulysses* from cover to cover in a day, and then re-read it slowly.) In retrospect, I realise I owe a great deal to Gerald.

Millicent's attitude to my friendship with Gerald was mixed; she regarded him with a certain awe, but not, I think, with much liking. It also meant that I saw a great deal less of her. For my own part, I found both relationships unsatisfactory; but each provided a relief when the other became unsettled. Close contact with Millicent I found frustrating, while I suspect that Gerald found my stolid 'normality' equally frustrating. Quarrels were likely to develop unexpectedly, and I often found myself trying to hurt Gerald by telling him what I considered to be the blunt truth about himself; if this upset him, he never showed it. He made it a point of honour to appear untouchable. He told me once that his elder brother had quarrelled with him as they sat eating; Gerald was calm and infuriating, and his brother snatched up his dinner plate and smashed it over Gerald's head. Gerald went on eating calmly, his hair full of chipped porcelain, the blood and gravy running down his face.

I made one other close friend at the Vaughan College, the writer David Campton. He was fifteen years my senior, as plump and good natured as Mr Micawber, a brilliant character actor and a playwright with his own distinct sense of humour. He worked for the gas board at the time, and lived with his parents. Perhaps he tolerated me out of good nature and politeness; at all events, he didn't seem to mind if I called on him twice a week, and occasionally read him my stories or plays. I developed a great affection for David, which still survives today.

These activities made my seventeenth year more tolerable than my sixteenth. Then, early in 1949, I took the exam in order to become an established civil servant; to my disgust, I passed it, and was immediately posted to Rugby, nineteen miles from Leicester. Here again I found myself bored, irritable, and full of impatience for everyone with whom I came into contact. I found lodgings in the Hillmorton Road, opposite the school, five minutes away from Rupert Brooke's cottage. Gerald had introduced me to Brooke's poetry, and I had come to love it. Rugby was idyllic, the summer was beautiful, and very hot; but I hated the office, and was aware that my landlady disliked me. I had to eat my meals with the family; they had a small, snappy dog that would yap incessantly when I was in the room. I did my best to 'fit in', but since I hated the place this was difficult. I began to write a comic novel, influenced by Chesterton, about a crowd of art students who take lodgings in a small and idyllic town and upset everyone with their unorthodox goings-on. (At this time I knew nothing about students, and tended to idealise life in a college.) I quickly became a member of the public library, which proved to be an exceptionally good one, and spent the summer studying *Finnegan's Wake* with the Campbell and Robinson *Skeleton Key*. I also bought Mann's *Doktor Faustus*, which had just been published, and was disappointed in it. I was fascinated by the Faust subject, and could repeat page after page of Latham's translation of Goethe. I intended to write a *Faust* of my own, for in Goethe's Faust I had discovered a man who seemed to feel the same nihilism that I myself experienced. It seemed to me that Goethe had cheated in making Faust accept Gretchen as a substitute for the knowledge he craves; I wanted to try and create a Faust who has the courage to demand equality with God, who would not cringe and cover his eyes when confronted by the earth spirit.

Mann's *Faustus* struck me as atrociously written, clumsy and amateurish. No doubt Mann intended Zeitblom to be amateurish, but this is hardly an excuse for boring the reader. (I was disappointed with Mann's prose altogether, having been assured that he was a great stylist; his masters, Goethe and Richter, are also appalling prose stylists who often use three words where one would serve. While Mann is indubitably a great writer, his style has been absurdly over-rated, much as Dickens's style was over-rated a century ago.) While I now return to *Faustus* more frequently than to any of Mann's other books, there are still many passages that strike me as wholly unsuccessful – the death of the child, for example, which is rhetorical and sentimental.

At all events, Mann's Faust disappointed me by avoiding every single issue that interested me, and I began to write a Faust of my own in free verse, which hardly progressed beyond the first act, since I had no more idea than Goethe of how to solve Faust's god-dilemma.

I also joined the Rugby equivalent of the Vaughan College, and did some folk dancing; but I made no special friends, and left without regret.

At the office, tempers were becoming frayed. The collector of taxes was less patient of my vagueness than Mr Sidford had been; and my immediate superior in the office finally developed a habit of non-stop nagging, which made me one day threaten to punch him in the eye. This did not increase my popularity. Another day, when I had been finding the office particularly intolerable, I decided to stay at home, and told my landlady I felt ill. Half an hour later, to my disgust, the collector of taxes in person appeared to ask why I was not at work. In a fury, I told him to mind his own business, and he went off in a huff. My landlady overheard the quarrel, and took the opportunity to give me notice. I cycled down to the employment bureau, and enquired at the lodging section; they were able to direct me to a hostel out on the Leamington Road. I went back to my lodgings, collected my luggage, and went to the hostel. For my remaining two months in Rugby I lived there, and was happier than I had been for years. It suited me perfectly; no one cared what I did or when I ate my meals. It was a pity that I had not discovered it when I first arrived in Rugby; it would have saved me some discomfort. I shared a small room with a youth of my own age, an engineer. He was very seldom in. I had been reading Maugham's *The Moon and Sixpence,* and had also taken up the study of painting and sculpture, borrowing huge encyclopedias of art from Gerald. For about a fortnight I lived, ate and drank the atmosphere of painting, and found it my most exciting experience since my discovery of science. Certain landscapes of Corot or Giorgione produced in me a feeling that was like drunkenness.

I also saw my first opera while I was living in Rugby; it was Bizet's *Carmen,* and I travelled to Coventry to see it. I had always loved music, and when I was eleven various films developed in me a taste for 'classical' music. (Does any language in the world have a passably accurate word to distinguish the kind of music written by 'serious' composers from popular songs and jazz? I always shudder when I am forced to use the word 'classical' to distinguish Wagner from Irving Berlin.) The most important of these was *Fantasia;* but although its lasting influence was greater, its immediate impact was certainly smaller than that of such films as *Dangerous Moonlight* (with its Warsaw Concerto), *The Glass Mountain* and *Concerto* (which used Rachmaninov's second piano concerto). Later came Eric Coates and Holst's *Planets.* By the time I saw *Carmen* I had been in the habit of listening to the BBC's Wednesday concerts for years. I even listened occasionally to operas on the radio, but found them a bore.

Nothing, therefore, prepared me for the impact of *Carmen* (although, when I came to think about it, I remembered that Shaw had been to see it again and again when he first came to London as a young man). It seemed amazing to me that a composer could keep up two hours of such music and spectacle. I had to leave ten minutes before the curtain fell, to catch my last bus; but I was dizzy. For days afterwards I hummed 'Over the hills and far away' (Suis-nous à travers la campagne) or the Gypsy song. It plunged me into a Yeatsian melancholy, for I dreamed of Spain and travel instead of the civil service and hostel dinners, and freedom seemed infinitely distant.

When I was posted to Rugby I had applied for a 'transfer grant' on the technical grounds that I had been working as an established civil servant in Leicester for several weeks before I was posted, and could therefore claim that the posting was actually a transfer. One morning, to my surprise, twenty pounds arrived in the office. I immediately decided that I would use the money to try and get 'over the hills and far away' before my National Service. I bought a good bicycle for about £14, and went off to the Lake District on my August holiday. (This was rather selfish of me; my family needed the money far more than I needed a holiday; but this did not occur to me.)

This holiday was the first of my life, if occasional days at Skegness before the war are not counted. I took a tent on the back of the bicycle, and a single blanket. The first night I slept at Matlock, and was frozen to the bone. After that, I hit on the sensible idea of wrapping myself in the heavy canvas tent; this kept me warm and dry, even when in heavy rain.

Unfortunately, my idea of the geography had been vague; until I consulted a map I had always thought that the Lake District was in Surrey. When I discovered that it was more than two hundred miles from Leicester I was taken aback, but was still determined to get there. I had very little time and not much money. On my second day I cycled through Manchester and Bolton; on the third I reached Kendal, where heavy rain forced me to sleep at the Youth Hostel. I arrived at Windermere the next afternoon, spent a night there, and set out for Leicester again the next morning with only about half a crown to feed me. I reached Huddersfield that day, and the following day cycled from Huddersfield to Leicester in about twelve hours, eating bread and margarine, and cocoa mixed with sugar – all I had left. Like most of my cycling trips, this one had hardly been relaxation. And yet I can still remember the tremendous excitement of the first two days, of freewheeling down the long, long hill that stretches from Derbyshire into Stockport, and making a resolution that I would get to know my own country before I went abroad.

I had expected that my call-up papers would have arrived while I was away, but I was disappointed, and returned irritably to Rugby. As I had given up my room at the hostel I had to travel daily by train, or, occasionally, bicycle. Finally the papers arrived; I went to Coventry for my medical examination, and went into the RAF some time in September.

5

THE AIR FORCE AND AFTER

AN HOUR BEFORE I left home to catch a train to Padgate in Lancashire I made an entry in my journal. I wrote that I was now going to 'face life' and find out whether it was really hostile or indifferent. Since I was eleven I had been a bookworm, and consequently had no idea of the real nature of the world. My phrasing of the idea betrayed my usual anthropomorphic tendency; what I really meant was that so far I had not given 'destiny' a chance to show its intentions towards me, since I had always kept close to the shelter of home.

I felt that the RAF might prove to be grimmer than my worst expectations. My father, who had always disliked and mistrusted my bookish tendencies, often said in moments of anger that the army would 'teach me a lesson'. If it was the kind of lesson that my father wanted to teach me, I had no doubt it would be disagreeable enough.

In fact, it proved pleasanter than I expected. There were a few unhurried days at Padgate, during which I read *Faustus* and *Finnegan's Wake,* and finished writing a short story about a middle-aged Jehovah's Witness who allows herself to be seduced by a youth of eighteen. (To gather 'material' for this story, I had attended several meetings of the Jehovah's Witnesses.) I called the story 'Maze of Maya', for I had by then discovered the *Bhagavad Gita.*

We were then transferred to Bridgnorth, in Shropshire, and 'basic training' (square-bashing) began in earnest. But I had always been used to exercise, and found it no hardship. For the first time for many years I felt physically healthy and happy. The *Bhagavad Gita* also contributed to a mood of optimism, and I carried it with me everywhere. It now seemed clear to me that the only power worth anything is mental power. The problem was simply to appreciate being alive. This would seem simple enough; and yet, because they live so shortsightedly, most men never learn to enjoy themselves. Through my years in offices or classrooms I had felt that my intellect was simply a burden that made living twice as difficult. Now my body was healthy it seemed to me that intellect was the power that makes for freedom from the stupidity and triviality in which all men are entangled. The *Gita* gave me detachment from the everyday, made me aware of the possibility of existence over millions of years.

> You and I, Arjuna,
> Have lived many lives
> I remember them all,
> You do not remember.
> I am the birthless, the deathless
> Lord of all that breathes.

I also liked repeating Yeat's poem *Mohini Chatterjee,* and the lines:

> Brahman is the ritual
> Brahman is the offering
> Brahman is he who offers
> To the fire that is Brahman.
> When a man sees Brahman
> In every action
> He shall find Brahman.

I found myself repeating this on the parade ground or in the mess hall. It was the kind of certainty I had always needed. 'No one who seeks Brahman ever comes to an evil end.' I was not worried by the fact that certain parts of the *Gita* contradict the Shavian notion of evolution. (On re-examination, I am not sure that they do.) All that mattered was the guarantee of the power of the will directed towards ultimate freedom.

> 'Though a man be the greatest of sinners,
> This knowledge will carry him like a raft above his sin.'

It was this conception that invigorated me: the idea that one day all men will be selfless and idealistic, concerned only with overcoming the evils of the human condition and learning the purpose of life. I found this same religion in Plato – particularly in the last pages of the *Symposium* – in Shelley and in Shaw. There might be some disagreement about how the end should be reached; but about the end there could be no disagreement.

A few weeks after I arrived at Bridgnorth there was an absurd storm in a teacup that almost landed me on a 'charge'. On the ticket above my bed I had stated that my religion was R.C. This meant that I did not have to attend church parades on Sunday morning. However, to a few acquaintances I had declared that I was a devil-worshipper. After lights-out in our billet someone asked me to tell them about devil-worship, and I talked for half an hour about imaginary rites. (I had probably found these in some volume of Montague Summers.) Everyone lay awake in the dark, listening and asking questions, and they were unwilling to let me sleep. One evening, while I was explaining some abstruse piece of diabolistic theology, the lights went on, and an Irish corporal from next door stormed in and told me that I was on a charge. Some frightened or offended Catholic had crept out and fetched him. When he saw the 'R.C.' on the card above my bed his rage was doubled; he swore that he would have me confined to camp for six months. The next day I had to appear in front of a Wing-Commander to explain why I had dared to try and corrupt the pure-minded youths in our billet. Not being a Catholic, he failed to see the point of the corporal's indignation; he also obviously felt that I might be 'officer material', and that we therefore had something in common; after winking at me, he told me to go away and sin no more.

I was shocked by the abuse of power in the RAF; I had never before seen such stupidity and sadism masquerading as protective authority. Boys who had been in the RAF for two months, who had taken a short course as drill instructors and been given two stripes, were then allowed to heckle and bully boys who were only three months behind them. I had read about the stupidity and brutality of the army, but had never imagined that it would be so much like a parody of itself. Still, I managed to stay out of serious trouble during my eight weeks at Bridgnorth. Long before the end I was bored again. Luckily, I did a great deal of running, and developed stiff muscles in both legs; I complained about this, hoping to escape a couple of parades, and was immediately taken into the hospital.

This was absurd; there was nothing wrong with me. Perhaps the doctor thought he would call my bluff. At all events, I spent a comfortable fortnight in hospital, reading all day and writing stories. To my delight, George Baxter, my old cycling crony from the Gateway, was also there, and we spent a great deal of time together. I also made the acquaintance of an orderly named Eric Huson, who told me that he intended to be a great painter. He lent me books on modern painting, and I introduced him to *Finnegan's Wake*.

I felt less triumphant when I came out of hospital and was told that I would have to be transferred to a different unit, since I had lost two weeks' training. But the time passed, and finally it was over. On our passing-out parade I remember feeling suddenly invigorated and happy as I watched the neat columns of men marching in the November sunlight, and listened to the brass bands playing. As we marched out, a new lot of recruits came in; I remember the feeling of superiority as we watched them file past, slovenly and apprehensive; the eight weeks between us seemed like years.

Back in Leicester, I revisited the Vaughan College, and saw Gerald and Millicent, and realised that things had changed more than I had believed they could. I even took a girl out to the theatre, but spoiled the evening by awkwardly kissing her goodnight.

After a few days' leave I was posted to Wythall, near Birmingham, to be trained as a clerk. This disgusted me; my period in hospital had convinced me that the ideal job for me would be that of a hospital orderly. Wythall was a dirty and uncomfortable camp, completely unlike the training camp, where everything shone. I resented being asked to memorise dozens of RAF forms. I also became keenly aware that all large institutions – particularly those run by the government – encourage the form of laziness and moral irresponsibility portrayed by Goncharov in *Oblomov*. Away from the strenuous atmosphere of the training camp, I realised that the RAF is simply another branch of the civil service; but without the pressures that demand a certain efficiency from a government department. The men who are in for long periods – perhaps twenty years – and who have found soft jobs, feel that they have cheated the social compulsion to work. There is a curious atmosphere of timelessness and emptiness, which I imagine to be the atmosphere of hell. They feel no necessity to answer to themselves – after all, it is the government they are cheating, and the government has relieved them of all moral responsibility.

I found this atmosphere stifling and rather terrifying. It made me aware that a man is a fool to accept any authorities that rob him of the agony of freedom. This became particularly clear to me towards the end of my stay at Wythall. To my disgust, I was placed on a charge for failing to polish the floor when I was billet orderly one day. I found this particularly absurd because our billet was a filthy shambles anyway, with broken window-panes, tattered linoleum, and moth-eaten blankets on the beds. I pointed this out to the Squadron-Leader who heard the charge, but he evidently felt that even if the place was falling apart morale must be maintained; so he sentenced me to a fortnight's C.C. I felt like a soldier who is shot by one of his own officers in a retreat, in a desperate attempt to maintain discipline. Confinement to camp involved reporting to the guardroom in full uniform, with pack and gaiters, about four times a day, at the most inconvenient hours possible, and doing various extra duties. During my second week I was sent to polish the floor in the billet of a warrant officer, whom I will call Tomkins. He came in while I was working, and started to talk to me. He seemed a pleasant and sociable man, with some knowledge of literature. He invited me to sit down. After ten minutes or so, he brought the talk around to the literature of sadism, and asked me if I had read various books on flagellation and other methods of 'self-chastisement'. We talked about these for another ten minutes – myself still suspecting nothing amiss. Then he asked in a roundabout way if I would consent to tie him up and beat him, or kick him around like a football. I was shocked, but tried not to show it; instead, I pretended to treat it as a joke, and told him that I had to leave to report back at the guard room. He was persistent: would I perhaps do it the following night? I avoided a direct refusal, but took myself off hastily. Luckily, the Christmas holidays were close; Tomkins went on leave shortly afterwards, and I succeeded in avoiding him. When I returned to camp after Christmas he was still on leave; and a week later, I left Wythall. The incident deepened the disgust I felt about Wythall; there was an atmosphere of slovenliness and lack of purpose about the place that made it the perfect background for any sexual perversion. This incident had later repercussions, as will be seen.

From Wythall, I was posted to my 'regular camp', Hucknall Torkard, near Nottingham. (I believe Wythall was closed shortly after I left.) This was the heart of the Lawrence country, with Byron's home, Newstead Abbey, nearby. Here, discipline was as relaxed as at Wythall. The camp was shared by the Army and the RAF, as well as by WAAFs. I did not, strictly speaking, belong to the camp, for I was the clerk of a small auxiliary anti-aircraft unit, which came under the jurisdiction of the RAF Regiment. There were only two other regular members, a corporal and the adjutant. We worked at weekends, when the auxiliary lads came in from Nottingham for their training, and had our 'weekends' at mid-week. This gave us a great deal of freedom, and also meant that we could ignore the guardroom as we walked in and out of camp.

At first the adjutant made rather a pet of me, imagining that I would be more efficient than his previous clerk, a lazy Scot. And I tried hard to live up to expectations. However, the relaxed discipline of the camp was against me. As at Wythall, the authorities were inclined to have sudden dive-bomber raids of discipline, when they would hand out weeks of C.C. with abandon and even rise to an occasional court-martial. After which the camp was allowed to sink back into its Russian-peasant lethargy. I detested clerking anyway. I also resented the lack of privacy, until I realised that I could return to the office in the winter evenings, and read with my feet up on the stove. Then I discovered a notice in the canteen asking for members for the Nottingham dramatic society, and went and joined. This was pleasant; we rehearsed Norman Ginsbury's *First Gentleman* twice a week; I played two tiny rôles.

After a month the adjutant made the discovery that I was inefficient, and began to nag me. I found this intolerable; he was a pleasant-faced, rather stupid public-school type for whom I felt no respect and not much liking. He was not content with occasional outbursts; being weak by nature, he fell into the habit of a womanish niggling and nagging, which reminded me unpleasantly of the physics master at the Gateway. The adjutant was also skilful in devising petty humiliations. There were times when the only courageous response would have been to hit him.

One week everything went wrong. I was unexpectedly informed that I would have to appear on parade – the adjutant's doing – and was there told that I would be placed on a charge for having dirty buttons and wearing my hair too long. A warrant-officer pulled me up for failing to salute him – I hadn't seen him – and made me clean out his billet for two nights in succession. Finally, the adjutant announced that he was going away for a few days; consequently, I arrived at the office half an hour late – and found him waiting for me with a smirk of triumph. He cancelled my mid-week leave, and awarded me extra duties.

The following day the adjutant began to nag me about some extra typing I had done. I had voluntarily stayed late to do it, and this fact added the final touch of injustice. When he waved the paper under my nose and shouted: 'Aren't you ashamed of yourself, Wilson?', I flushed and said: 'No'. He looked astounded. There were two other people in the room, so he sent me into his office to wait for him. I was in a violent mood, determined to spend the rest of my National Service in Bedford jail rather than submit to any more of this witless stupidity. I even contemplated throwing his inkwell through the glass panel of the door as he came in, and actually had it in my hand as he opened the door. To my surprise, he looked rather pleased with himself. Instead of calling for the guard, he asked me to sit down. No doubt he found the camp as boring as I did, and was grateful for the diversion I had provided. He explained that he could see I was 'different' and quite unsuited for the clerking job. I did my best to play up to his picture of me as a dangerous neurotic close to a breakdown, striding up and down the room, flinging back my hair and trying to make my eyes roll in a fine frenzy. He seemed impressed, and sent me along to see the Medical Officer, in the hope that he would certify me 'nervously unsuited' to clerking. Perhaps his delight came from the prospect of getting rid of me and getting a more efficient clerk. I agreed that I would prefer to be a medical orderly in a hospital, although in fact the whole business seemed to me a choice of evils.

The M.O. was very young; he seemed sympathetic enough, but was not convinced that my 'nervous instability' warranted a change in my trade. Faced with his refusal to be impressed, I considered how I might convince him of the urgency of my case. In quick succession, I rejected the possibility of claiming to have epileptic fits, hereditary syphilis, or homicidal tendencies. Another idea drifted through my mind. I had known in Leicester a youth who had been discharged from the army for an interesting reason. He was a homosexual, but no one seemed to mind this. But one day, on the rifle range, he was told: 'That target there is a man who is about to shoot you. If you don't get him first, you're as good as dead. Fire!' My acquaintance had flung down his rifle, rushed out on to the range, and screamed: 'Shoot me, shoot me!' He was immediately placed under continuous supervision in the guard-room; his knife and fork were removed after every meal, in case he attempted suicide; and a few weeks later he received his 'ticket'.

My rifle-range days were over, but I thought it worth trying to impress the M.O. that I was potentially as suicidal as my friend. So I began by confessing that my sex-life had been permanently warped since my mother had kept me dressed as a girl until I was nine years old, and that the real reason for my inefficiency was the emotional strain of living in close contact with so much male beauty.

To my amazement, I had to go no further. The suicidal tendencies were superfluous. The M.O. questioned me closely about my 'sex life' (which was actually non-existent), and I replied with all the text-book answers I had gleaned from Havelock Ellis and Stekel, with a few realistic details borrowed from the lives of certain acquaintances.

Half an hour later, when I returned to the office, I was convinced that my clerking days were over. The adjutant questioned me (I daresay the M.O. had spoken to him on the phone since I left his office); I repeated the sordid story; he was plainly delighted, and began to treat me with such big-brotherly solicitude that I began to feel ashamed of the deception. He promised that he would tell no one else, and told me to take the rest of the day off and go for a cycle ride. I cycled to Newstead Abbey; it was a bright spring morning, and I was chuckling like a madman. I felt as if the skies had opened. There was a definite presentiment of coming freedom.

The next day there were unpleasant repercussions. The adjutant had gone home for his weekend leave. I was informed that the Special Investigations Branch (S.I.B.) of the RAF police wanted to speak to me. Evidently my 'case' had been reported. They were anxious to know whether I could give them any information about homosexuality in the camp. This would have been easy enough; everyone in the camp knew that a certain sergeant, a certain cook, even a certain WAAF corporal, made no secret of their inclinations. But I knew nothing more about them than hearsay, and even if I had, would not have told him. When he mentioned specific names, I admitted that I was aware that the persons in question had the reputation of being homosexual, but told him I knew nothing definite. Then, to my surprise, he asked me about Warrant Officer Tomkins, the flagellant of Wythall; I admitted I knew Tomkins. (I was anxious to convince him that my knowledge of perversion was encyclopedic.) He then explained to me that Tomkins was now under arrest, having been charged with undue familiarity with subordinates, and sadistic cruelty to a cat – apparently he had put out one of its eyes with a penknife. If I would act as a witness against Tomkins at his court martial, the S.I.B. would overlook my own self-confessed transgressions. If not, I would be charged with immorality, and would probably spend the rest of my RAF service in jail.

I was sure he was bluffing, but found his persistence exhausting. He sent for me twice that day, and again the next day, becoming more threatening and angry. As soon as the adjutant came back I asked to see him, and told him what had happened. He immediately wrote me out a leave pass, and told me to go home to Leicester until he sent for me again. I could hardly believe in my luck. The episode of the S.I.B. had been a disguised blessing. For the next four weeks I stayed at home, returning to Hucknall (a mere 25 miles from Leicester) once a week to collect my pay. Eventually I was sent to Wendover to see a psychiatrist; he proved to be sympathetic, and told me that I would probably be discharged from the RAF. Later still, I came before a medical board, who could see that I was shamming; but I refused to admit it, even when they became abusive, and they had no alternative than to discharge me. At Hucknall everyone on the camp seemed to treat the affair as a joke (since I made no secret of it). Luckily this knowledge never reached the officers' mess. Six months after I entered the RAF I came out, having been certified 'nervously unstable' and altogether unsuitable.

As soon as I had committed the 'definitive act' that started the train of events – the act of losing my temper with the adjutant – the rest seemed to follow with complete inevitability. I was like a sleep-walker; there was no effort involved. The whole thing became a joke. Perhaps a better parallel to my state of mind would be drunkenness. My teens had been unusually hard; I had a sense that all my best energies were doomed to be wasted; my greatest efforts all came to nothing; I had no lucky 'breaks' at all; I had begun to wonder if I was another of the 'poètes maudits', doomed to live a completely unsatisfactory and frustrating life in order to create a few works of beauty. At seventeen I suspected that I would die at twenty-five, and be regarded as a twentieth-century Keats.

This fear vanished during my RAF period; the optimism that had been suffocated so many times in the previous three years had proved extraordinarily tough and durable, and was now in a thoroughly healthy condition. This was partly due to physical well-being, to sleeping heavily and eating ravenously. It was also due, in part, to Shaw and the *Gita*. Admittedly, Shaw's evolutionary optimism had convinced me when I first heard *Man and Superman*; but with the physical and mental strains of adolescence its grip on my imagination had been uncertain.

Now for the first time I seemed to see clearly, with my whole being, the answer to certain problems of existence. Not, admittedly, ultimate problems; but important ones nevertheless. The trouble with living was that our faces were held too close to the ground. We never possessed detachment until too late – except, that is, for sudden blessed flashes of happiness and wellbeing, of 'Yea-saying'. This, I could see, was the whole trouble, the only trouble. Destiny holds men firmly by the scruff of the neck, and makes sure that they never raise their eyes above the level of the dust they kick up. So all men are blinded, are kept deliberately blinkered, like horses in traffic. If this were not so, the unhappiest man would be the man who possesses nothing; and men would be happy in exact proportion to their 'blessings'. Instead, all men are like the old woman in the vinegar-bottle, never contented, never god-like and self-sufficient, always bowed under the appalling burden of being human.

The problem, then, was simply to out-manoeuvre destiny – or human nature. Man is not naturally contemplative. But ever since

I had heard Clifford Bax's play about Socrates (at some time during the war), I had been certain that contemplation is man's only escape from his limitations. Shaw and the *Gita* were in agreement about the superiority of the contemplative man over all other types. 'He who seeks in contemplation to discover the inner will of the world...' Since this seemed so self-evident it was amazing that all our civilisation should be built on the principle of hurry and non-stop physical activity. Plainly, the ancient civilisations of the East were wiser than we, since they held contemplation to be the highest form of activity. A similar tradition had always existed in Christianity, although I could find little enough evidence of it in our own century. But at least the poets had never deserted the great ideal. The poet was not, for me, the writer of verse (and I was contemptuous of most of the poetry written since Eliot); he was the man who was determined to live more fully than others. Pound had written: 'I am here a Poet, that doth drink of life/ As lesser men drink wine.'

I found the term 'original sin' of value in stating these convictions. It seemed clear to me that men live in a state that is analogous to sickness, in fact, *is* sickness, if those moments of detachment and illumination are taken as a norm of health. A man who suffers constant pain is incapable of delicacy of perception and apprehension, since his faculties are blunted by illness. And yet every poet – and perhaps every human being – wrestles constantly with the stupidity of his body, with the unconsciousness that is never far away, with the bluntness of his faculties. Occasionally, the sickness lifts; the stupidity rolls back; for hours or minutes the senses seem to stretch antennae out into nature; the mind is aware of new, subtle implications in every thought; man achieves something of the confident mastery of a god. Then the octopus regains strength; the tentacles wind round the heart and brain; the state of emergency is back; again the fight against suffocation.

If I suffer from a cold that makes my eyes burn and makes breathing difficult I at least know something about its causes – about cold germs, vitamin C deficiency, carelessness in forgetting to dry my hair after a bath. But this 'normal' thickness of the senses, this deadness of the nerves, heaviness of perception, seems to be a part of 'the human condition'. No human being, as far as I know, has ever cured himself of it, and most of us are not even aware of it. The sickness is born with us; the inner history of every life is a fight against it. Whether we call this state of affairs 'original sin', or prefer to invent some name for it (like Gurdjieff's 'kundabuffa'), its actuality is undeniable.

As I began to see this clearly, all the non-stop reading of my teens began to fall into place. (In 1947, I had intended to keep a list of the books I had read, but after noting down eighteen books read in January, I gave it up.) Shaw, Eliot, Hulme, Christian mysticism, Eastern mysticism, Dostoevsky, Tolstoy and Nietzsche and the rest ... all were saying the same thing in different ways. I began to plan some immense work on Outsiders, the men who were unfortunate enough to regard the struggle with the 'octopus' as the most important thing in life, and who were consequently out of place in our civilisation. For me, this constituted the bitterness and irony of the situation. Gurdjieff defined 'the organ kundabuffa' as an organ that causes men to perceive fantasy as actuality. It seemed that most men were wasting their lives chasing fantasies, while the few Outsiders were like the Dutch boy who found the hole in the dyke and realised that the whole country was in danger. But their cries of warning were taken for moans of self-pity, their attempts to avert the danger regarded as evidence of insanity.

The idea was to snowball for the next five years. (I had not, at this time, read Gurdjieff or Sartre, although Gerald had given me a copy of Wells's *Mind at the End of its Tether* for my birthday in 1948.) But 1950 was the year in which it first appeared to me in perspective; this was the reason for the optimism that carried me on a wave out of the RAF.

My immediate feeling was that I would never again submit to the frustrations and boredoms of 'safe jobs'. It might be difficult to adapt the Eastern idea of the 'wanderer' or God-seeker to post-war England, but with purity of purpose it could be done. My first step was to resign from the civil service (to my father's disgust). I was not sure what I wanted to do or where I wanted to go. I had at the back of my mind a vague ambition to go to the Aran Isles and live in a stone hut somewhere; but Synge's book on the Aran Isles hardly encouraged the idea; his islanders seem too solid and normal to take kindly to another invasion of 'saints', even though their ancestors must have fed the ascetics who gave the 'island of saints' its nickname.

The determination to become a 'wanderer' had come to me when I was down at Wendover seeing the RAF psychiatrist. I found I had a day to spare, and hitch-hiked to London. The name of Wendover brought Rupert Brooke to my mind; it was a sunny morning, and I was happy, and convinced that boldness was all I needed to achieve total freedom.

It is easy to feel like this in summer, when the weather is gentle. After a lot of consideration, it seemed to me that the best solution would be for me to become an actor. So a few weeks after my discharge I set out, wearing my old RAF uniform, hitch-hiking north.

First I called on the theatre at York; but was told that although they had a vacancy for an assistant stage manager they expected him to pay a premium of a hundred pounds. I tried Bradford and Harrogate, but still met with no success. Then, sick of the effort, I decided to visit the Lakes for a few days. (I have often thanked my good fortune for turning me away from the theatre; I might have enjoyed the life too much, and neglected writing.) My pack was heavy – it was full of books – Plato, the *Gita,* various Buddhist texts, and Eliot's *Four Quartets* and poems; my money was running low. Towards evening on a rainy and windy day I stood waiting for a bus somewhere near Bradford, and suddenly I felt an immense rage and indignation at my fate. It seemed stupid and unfair of destiny to throw me down into the world, and to omit to reserve a place for me, so that I should be forced to wander about with a feeling of homelessness. (I had quarrelled violently with my father about leaving the civil service, and knew that I would not be welcome back at home.) It struck me then that the idea of being a 'homeless wanderer' is not nearly as romantic as writers like Hermann Hesse make it sound – particularly not in England.

I spent that night at Catterick RAF camp (complaining that my official discharge had not yet been received), where I had a large supper and a warm bed. The next day I went on to Bowness, and later to Grasmere. In the Grasmere youth hostel I practised the 'yogic posture' for hours at a time, ignoring the other hostellers who wandered in and out of the dormitory and stared at me with wonder. Then I went home. The discharge papers had still not arrived, and the atmosphere lacked cordiality. I took a job on a building site to make some money quickly, and after two weeks set out again, this time making for Southampton, where I hoped to take a boat to India. I decided to spend a night at Stonehenge, and watch the sun rise over the altar stone – Stonehenge had always had magical associations for me since I first read Blake's *Jerusalem*.

I see in retrospect that this whole period was a kind of symbolic quest. India, Stonehenge, the Aran Isles – they were all symbols of an intensity that I sought. I knew in practise that Inishmaan or Khalighat would be a disappointment, as a child learns that it cannot grasp sunbeams; yet it seemed important to make the effort – as a symbolic gesture of rejection of 'ordinariness'. This also explains why I attached so much importance to the Church at the time, and thought so often of becoming a Catholic. Man needs symbols of the 'unseen' if he is not to become a slave of his own dullness. If I had learned of the existence of a society of Sun-Worshippers, I would have joined it; not because I think the sun a god, but because worship is the right attitude towards reality. Our moments of freedom are too rare; but in these moments, we become aware that mankind shares a common sin: the devaluation of life. Man has tried various methods of reminding himself of the insight that comes in the moments of freedom. One is writing poems and symphonies, or painting pictures like Van Gogh's. Another is the building of churches and cathedrals, whose steeples and stained glass windows assert that everyday reality is a liar.

The truth is that man is a 'calculating animal' in the best sense of the word. He does not live in the present, like all other animals; he tries to chart his future. For this purpose, he has developed memory and imagination to a degree unknown to other animals. The trouble is that he has not yet developed them sufficiently; they are too feeble to tell him the truth. They swindle him, offer him paste jewels instead of real ones. Man can recollect the taste of rum or whisky, but not the taste of freedom. So he is betrayed by memory and imagination; he sits still when he should be engaged in activity. So he writes poetry, builds churches, creates religions, for the same reason that he ties a knot in his handkerchief – as an attempt to remind himself of his highest purposes, and as a wry recognition of his fallibility. This also explains why I preferred the

Catholic Church to the Church of England. If your religion is an attempt to symbolise 'revelation', then it had better be as symbolic as possible. Every concession it makes to man's everyday nature is a step away from the basic insight into what man should be.

All this explains my state of mind when I sat on Stonehenge that night, in an icy wind, repeating stanzas from the *Bhagavad Gita*. It was not entirely pessimistic; at least, not about myself. It seemed a pity that the world I had been born into was such a mess; that all its values were so totally false. In that respect, my attitude was identical with that of *The Waste Land*. But it was something to have seen through it all, and to have rejected it. If I'd had a private income, it would have seemed no tragedy at all; I would have left the world to go to hell its own way. As it was, there were problems; my increasing hunger, and the cold wind.... In the end, I walked into Amesbury for a meal, then spent the night in a haystack, where the rats kept me awake. In the morning, I got up early, walked back to Stonehenge, and clambered over the barbed wire. But I was too late to watch the sun rise. And when it became light enough, I discovered that my clothes were full of tiny needles of hay, that refused to be brushed off, so that I looked like a wild man.

I decided to repeat the Catterick experiment, so I walked to the nearest RAF station, and again explained the situation about my discharge papers. They gave me two good meals, and kept me waiting in the guard room all morning. The officer I spoke to was irritable and rude, and it was a pleasure to be able to smile at him sarcastically, and know that he could do nothing about it. The RAF police contacted the civil police in Leicester, who called on my family to find out about me. My mother was frightened by the sight of a uniform at the door, and told the police to send me home immediately. It was all the same to me. I didn't particularly want to be anywhere. I didn't much like living. All the same, I got impatient with Gautier's *Mlle de Maupin* on the bus back to Newbury, and threw it out of the window. I was a romantic, but this kind of feeble wishful-thinking enraged me.

I was beginning to lose the sense of 'home'. In earlier years, whenever I had been away for any length of time, I had always been sentimentally delighted to be back in Leicester and with my family again. But now my family plainly felt I was a nuisance. They wanted me to settle down to a regular job; I found regular jobs hateful, and preferred to work as navvy or builder's labourer, for I could change these jobs as often as they became tiresome. I took another job on a building site, then got tired of that and worked on a fairground. By now it was midsummer, and in spite of my dissatisfaction I lived in a state of optimism. I was never without a copy of Nietzsche's *Zarathustra* or Whitman's poems. I had also found an excellent anthology called *The Pocket World Bible,* a condensation from *The Bible of the World* which I had discovered in the school library many years before, and which had had an immense influence on me – particularly the Tao Te Ching. I now no longer felt any conscience about not having a regular job; it was clear to me that all the 'world betterers' had felt exactly as I did and had not been afraid to burn their boats. For the first time in my life I began to read the Jewish-Christian Bible with interest, and concluded that it was the greatest book in our language.

My job on the fairground was hectic; it involved selling tickets for a gambling machine called a spinner. When all the tickets had been sold a great beam would spin round, and a light would flicker over a great bank of numbers; the spinner would stop, and the light would also stop on a number; whoever held the ticket of that number was given a prize. It involved shouting for hours, and I was always hoarse by the end of the evening. My parents were ashamed, for many neighbours saw me there and made unkind comments. It was a great come-down for the 'clever boy' of the street who had expected to become a scientist.

My boss on the spinner was well satisfied with me – I shouted so vigorously that strangers might have thought I had been born to be a race-course bookie. He offered to take me on permanently, so that I should travel with the fair, and I agreed enthusiastically.

This also came to nothing. One evening as I was selling tickets, a small, oval-faced child who looked about ten stood and stared at me, and finally asked me, 'Do you want to sell yourself?' Later, I walked her home and kissed her goodnight. (She was actually fifteen.) I agreed to meet her the next day and take her out to Swithland woods. It was a Thursday, and she would get the afternoon off, since she worked in Woolworth's.

I was altogether delighted with her. I gathered that she came from a large family, that her father was a dustman, and that she had left school at fourteen. She spoke with the most extreme version of the 'barbarous yawp' of Leicester, which seems to me the ugliest accent in England. But I also dramatised her as Eliza Doolittle, and myself as Higgins, and decided that I must educate her. So all the afternoon I talked to her about poetry; we became so absorbed that we missed the bus back to Leicester, and I decided not to go to the fairground.

When I went to the fairground the next day I was told that I was sacked, and that someone else had already been engaged in my place. I went to see Mary (this is not her real name) and discovered that she had also run into trouble. Her father always insisted that she should be home by half-past nine, and she had been half an hour late; in a fury, he had thrown her out of the house. She had run after me, but I had gone too far; she had knocked on someone's door, and a kindly bus-conductress had taken her in for the night.

Suddenly, I had 'responsibilities'. She asked me if I would marry her, and I said that I would if her parents refused to take her back. However, I called on her mother that afternoon – a worn-out, toothless old woman who was actually only forty or so – who was delighted to hear that Mary was safe, and told her to come home immediately.

I found a building job, and began to see Mary every day. Being completely inexperienced, I made no attempt to make sexual advances to her; but she had lost her virginity at thirteen – she told me she was raped – and soon made up for my inexperience. This seemed to be all that was needed to complete my feeling of entering a new life. I took another building job, and spent my days stripped to the waist in the hot sun, wheeling barrow-loads of cement. I was not in love with Mary – all my thoughts were now on the possibility of entering a monastery, or finding some other way of life that would give me freedom to meditate and write. However, I knew nothing of Protestant monasteries, so the first step seemed to be to become a Catholic. I began taking instruction from a Dutch priest at Braunston, and cycled several miles every Sunday morning to attend mass.

All the same, Mary produced in me a new sense of confidence.

Her total and unquestioning admiration was pleasant after years of self-doubt. It seemed to me that I would be able to do anything I set my mind to. At about this time I went into a coffee-bar with a friend who wanted to be a painter, and he introduced me to the scene-painter from the theatre across the road – a strange Irishman who was supposed to possess second-sight. The Irishman's first words were: 'You're going to be enormously successful.' I replied: 'I know.' I would be successful, not because I was destined to be, but because I had every intention of being successful.

Still, the problem of work continued. I had a few other acquaintances who seemed to be facing the same problem. There was a poet called Maurice Willows, a Yorkshireman who looked like Robert Louis Stevenson and had an adenoidal voice. He was married, wrote a kind of *vers libre* influenced by Spender, and worked as a factory caretaker or road-sweeper. I still saw a great deal of Gerald – who hated Mary, and tried to make her cry whenever he met her. At an evening class he had met an attractive spinster who offered to type his novel; she lived with her father, who was bedridden, and after a few months Gerald moved into her house. She felt that a brilliant young writer deserved to be encouraged and supported. I began to wish that I could find myself an attractive spinster who would support *me,* and I envied Gerald his undeserved security.

When I had tired of labouring jobs, I decided to try a government training scheme for farm workers. I was sent out to live at a farm at Newbold Verdon, where the farmer was paid by the government for training me. I had to get up at six in the morning and milk cows before breakfast (there were electric milking machines). Then, after a long day of haymaking or weeding cabbages there would be supper at about nine o'clock, and I would take a bus into Leicester to see Mary. Occasionally we quarrelled; she seemed to feel a necessity for emotional violence, and I found this very trying. After a particularly noisy quarrel she went off and got engaged to one of my friends who had always admired her. However, we met again a week later, and made it up; my friend found out, and broke the engagement; he also quarrelled with me.

The farm work bored me. After a few weeks, the farmer at Newbold Verdon recognised my lack of interest and sent me back to the

Employment Bureau. They sent me out to another farm near Melton Mowbray. I stayed there for about a month, quarrelling incessantly with the farmer's mother, whom I detested cordially, and then left. Finally, there were a few weeks on a farm at Houghton-on-the-Hill. I travelled there daily, and slept at home. September came, and I was tired of England. I decided that I would go to France. Mary and I went for a last holiday in the Lake District, and she spent most of the week in tears. When we returned to Leicester we said goodbye, and I set out for Dover – with half a crown in my pocket.

6
PARIS, STRASBOURG AND LONDON

THE TAO TE CHING SAYS: The further one travels, the less one knows. To me, this has always appeared axiomatically true. I have never liked travel, and have always believed that people who enjoy it must be empty-headed. When I was about ten I was taken to Doncaster to stay with my Aunt Ethel for a fortnight. Although she lived on the edge of the city – at Balby – so that I could have spent the time exploring the countryside, or learning how to milk cows on the farm next door – I preferred to sit in the front room with all the books and magazines in the house around me (to everyone's disgust). More recently, on a trip to Leningrad, I became so bored with travel that at Gdynia I refused to get off the boat; while the rest of the party went to see Danzig I stayed in my bunk reading science-fiction. The homing instinct is strong in me. I am happiest when I have long, empty days ahead of me, and I can sit in my own home, surrounded by books and gramophone records, with a typewriter conveniently near.

This means that I feel no strong compulsion to describe in detail what happened to me during the next two years. I travelled, and there were moments when I achieved some sudden intensity of insight that its worth recording; apart from that it was pointless movement.

I went from Leicester to Dover with a Northampton friend, and we worked picking hops at Canterbury, and earned a little money. I spent a week with Gerald picking apples at Marden, in Kent, and then we quarrelled, and Gerald went off to France alone. I spent a fortnight picking potatoes near Dover, sleeping in a derelict and floorless cottage. Then I crossed the Channel, reading Matthiesen's *Henry James, the Major Phase,* and envying James the financial independence that allowed him to spend his life as a detached observer. The first impact of France was pleasant and strange; I drank wine for the first time – I was puzzled that it was not sweet –

and ate onions with bread and cheese. I hitch-hiked to the Youth Hostel in Lille, where I became involved with two English girls, Birmingham bank clerks on holiday. A rather feeble confidence-trickster had fallen in love with one of them, and I found myself becoming involved with the other. The story is too long to recount in detail; we ended unexpectedly in Paris, where we spent a night in the police station in the Place de l'Opéra (not, however, under arrest), and I finally took the confidence-trickster back to Lille, where he promptly disappeared, with the police in pursuit. I now had no money left, and collapsed with an attack of influenza; however, I threw it off in two days, and returned to Paris (having left my shoes behind at the Youth Hostel as a pledge), light headed but determined to see my English girl. I was lucky enough to get a lift all the way with a chauffeur who was returning to Paris. The influenza had left me feeling strangely carefree – perhaps slightly delirious still – and I can remember the exhilaration of the straight, tree-lined French roads, sometimes ankle deep in brown leaves, and the thin autumn sunlight, and the feeling: There *must* be some other way to live, some way that gets to the heart of things and drinks their essence, instead of wasting time on material futilities. 'As for living, our servants can do that for us. . . .' In Paris, I hurried to the hostel at Porte de Chatillon, only to discover that my girlfriend had found herself a Danish boy in the meantime, and that I was superfluous.

I should be grateful to her; for her change of heart led to an insight that strikes me as the most interesting event of the whole French trip. I spent the night at the hostel, experiencing frequent twinges of rage and jealousy. It seemed a severe defeat, and I was afraid to think about it too closely, as one is sometimes afraid to examine a cut in case it proves to be deeper than it feels. As I left the hostel, I remember thinking: The next few days are going to be hell, trying not to think about her, and then suddenly remembering in an unguarded moment. . . . It was a fresh morning, but overclouded. As I turned into a wide avenue with trees, the sun came out. Quite suddenly, the sight of the autumn trees made me absurdly, ecstatically happy. There was a mystical explosion of sheer joy. Abruptly, the girl no longer mattered in the least. I wanted to laugh aloud.

The episode left behind a recognition of a world of reality and beauty that is hidden from us by our emotions. Kierkegaard was wrong. Truth is not subjectivity; it is *objectivity* – the sudden realisation that *other things exist,* that my suffocating world of dreams is not reality.

In Lille a Frenchman named Claude Guillaume had befriended me and lent me two shillings for the trip to Paris. I spent it on bread and sardines, and lived for several days on these and wild apples. In Paris – his home – he also offered me a bed for a few days, and I coached his wife for an examination in English literature. Then I learned of an old American named Raymond Duncan, who was known for his kindness to artists and musicians, and who would probably help me to find work. I went to see him, and discovered a strange old man dressed in a toga and sandals, with long white hair over his shoulders, who immediately, and very trustfully, offered me a makeshift bed in his house, and some kind of work in his printing shop. I was delighted; he even hinted that I should learn to print my own books. At this time I was engaged on the earliest versions of my novel *Ritual in the Dark*, which seemed completely out of tune with the do-it-yourself optimism that pervaded the 'Akademia Duncan' in the Rue de Seine.

However, I moved in and slept on a couch behind the stage. Duncan's house was large, with a courtyard in the French style, dark rooms, a kind of theatre, and various workshops. It was run by Mme Aia Bertrand, who dressed like a nun but explained to me that she was an atheist.

I spent several weeks there, learning to print, attending Raymond's lectures (which were delivered in atrocious French) and helping him to print his newspaper *New-Paris-York*. He preached a philosophy he called 'actionalism', a Whitmanesque idea with debts to Rousseau and Morris. Its basic tenets were that modern man is neurotic because he does not work with his hands, so that everybody ought to be capable of making his own clothes, mending his own plumbing, and building his own house. I found this reasonable enough – I have always enjoyed tinkering with machines, mending electric-light fittings and building bookcases. But Raymond did no writing, or very little; he spent his whole day making sandals and weaving cloth, or printing his newspaper. He also, I was told, owned a shop in New York that sold his home-made sandals (which he had invented in one night), and had been a millionaire three times, although he had given away most of the money. He gave concerts in the 'theatre', inviting young musicians and actors to come and perform; and took a group of musicians and painters to New York every year, where he hired Carnegie Hall for their use.

He seemed to me a saintly and vague man, astoundingly naïve, an atrocious writer of 'Whitmanesque' poetry – and altogether a weird and lovable crank. I found it impossible to take him seriously. He shared with his sister Isadora the belief that natural talent for self-expression means more than any amount of study and training. While this may be true for a dancer – even an actor – it can hardly be true for a man who makes it his business to handle ideas.

However, my stay at the Akademia came to an end after a few weeks. It was obvious that I lacked the attitude of an adoring disciple, and was not enjoying the printing lessons. Raymond, I think, would have allowed me to stay there indefinitely, but Mme Bertrand and the Greek cook seemed to resent my presence, and when one day a pen-friend wrote to me from Strasbourg asking me to go and stay with him, they gave me permission to go with obvious relief, adding that I would not be allowed to return.

I had been in correspondence with my pen-friend since school days, and he had stayed with me in England during the August when I left school. Now he sent me money to get to Strasbourg, and I set out to hitch-hike. The journey took me three days. It soon became plain that this was also a mistake. We had both changed a great deal since we were sixteen. I used to be inclined to defend the religious attitude, while he supported a vague agnosticism. Now he was a communist and a materialist, and we seemed to have no single point of agreement. I spent three weeks with him; then his mother indicated that they had had enough of me, so I borrowed my return fare from the British Consulate and came home.

My three months in France had taught me very little. I had not enjoyed it greatly, for I hated being without money, which entailed relying on the kindness of casual acquaintances. At all events, Leicester seemed less intolerable when I returned. I was so glad to be home again that I found myself an office job in a steel works at a mere £3 or so a week. Mary had found herself another boyfriend in my absence; my pride was hurt, but I was glad not to be involved again. However, I developed a flirtation with a nurse and began to spend most of my evenings in her flat, reading or listening to the radio.

The relief at being home soon disappeared, and I found myself bored and irritable as usual. I now felt almost perpetually as I had felt that rainy evening outside Bradford – that it was time Fate stopped treating me so badly and allowed me to do something I would enjoy doing. I was sick of being hounded by the need to earn a few shillings a week, sick of not being allowed to work at something I could enjoy. I wondered why England could not make some kind of government grant to young writers who show signs of talent. Sometimes, it has struck me that I was lucky to have to struggle for as long and hard as I did. A university grant at seventeen might have turned me into a totally different kind of writer. But I cannot believe that all the years of pointless struggle against circumstances were necessary. It is only limitedly true that work is 'ennobling'; beyond that point, it is degrading and stupefying.

By the new year, 1951, I had begun to feel that I would do something violent if I had to spend another day in the office. It was all a repetition of the boredom of the civil service – as if nothing had happened in the intervening years. So I gave up the office job, and took another job as a navvy for the Leicester Electricity Board. This was in every way preferable to the office, but it was still a bore.

One day as I was on my way to work seething with resentment at this series of hateful jobs that I could not escape, a solution came to me: I was being paid about twenty-five shillings a day, much more than I needed to live on. Supposing I could persuade the Electricity Board to allow me to work for only three days a week? This would be the almost perfect solution, for it would pay me enough money for my board at home, and would give me four days a week in which to do my own work. Once the idea had come to me I was amazed that I had not thought of it before. I went to see the Electricity Board, and they agreed. (I told them I wanted to study to take some exam.) But my workmates were resentful – in the typical moronic fashion of the British workman, whose only qualities seem to be selfishness and envy. They declared that I was being favoured

– although it could make no possible difference to them. The foreman phoned the Electricity Board, who withdrew their concession. I was so sick with fury and disgust that I walked off the job on the spot.

I now found a job that I unexpectedly enjoyed; this was with the Dalmas chemical works. My department made the sticky gum that goes on adhesive tape, and my job was to manufacture the basic constituent of this gum – a mixture of resin and lanoline. My immediate boss was a kind, easygoing man with a sense of humour; I had a great deal of freedom, and could slip out to the café over the road when I had nothing else to do. Sometimes I was sent out to help at various branches. At this time I was reading Mann's *Magic Mountain*, *The Brothers Karamazov* and James's *Varieties of Religious Experience* for the first time. I had also revived my interest in music. A friend had lent me recordings of Franck's Symphonic Variations and Rachmaninov's Paganini Rhapsody. I now spent part of my wages on records; 78 r.p.m. of course. I bought some of Stravinsky's *Firebird* music, and Flagstad singing the Liebestod from *Tristan*, and Falla's *Tricorne* suite, and the final dances from the *Rite of Spring*. I played these incessantly in the evenings, and whistled them all day. When I went to buy the *Leibestod*, and played it over in a booth in the record shop, I was so overcome with emotion that I had to stay in the booth for another ten minutes to recover.

At this point, it becomes necessary to state that I shall have to observe certain reticences about the next eighteen months. For this period, it ceases to be my story alone, and becomes that of myself and my first wife. For I married Betty – the nurse – in the June of 1951, and I left immediately for London to find us a home.

I stayed at the Youth Hostel in Great Ormond Street, and went to see the complete *Man and Superman* at the Princes Theatre half a dozen times in succession. It was appallingly difficult to find rooms. I seemed to spend my evenings in phone boxes, ringing up landladies who would say: 'Sorry, the room's been taken.' I found a labouring job at St Etheldreda's Church, Ely Place, which was being rebuilt after bomb damage. Betty sent me parcels of food and money, and came down to London for a weekend to celebrate my twentieth birthday. I found that, in spite of its problems, I was happy to be married. It was a relief to have somebody to love. Admittedly, there were times when I found myself looking at an attractive girl in some public library, and wishing I was free, but these were infrequent. The emotional security meant a great deal more.

Ultimately I found a small double room in East Finchley, and Betty moved to London. I took a job in a plastics factory in Finchley – Frazer and Glass – and enjoyed it. For the first time in many years, I was happy. I enjoyed marriage so much that I was surprised I had not thought of it earlier. I spent quiet evenings in our room, reading or writing, or listening to music on the radio; we went out for walks in the August evenings; I frequently got up early enough to attend mass in the Catholic church across the road. I discovered the Egyptian *Book of the Dead* in the local library, and began to wonder if I could not somehow use it as the framework of my novel, as Joyce had used the *Odyssey*. This novel, which had begun as a novella of 20,000 words, occupied most of my thoughts. It was to be a huge and ambitious thing into which I would pour all my obsessions, my belief about the need for intensity in a civilisation of weaklings. It was to possess the power of *Crime and Punishment*, and the length and technical complexity of *Ulysses*. I admired *Ulysses*, but thought it a pity that such a technical *tour de force* should have nothing to say; on the other hand, Eliot's *Waste Land*, while full of suggestions and implications about the spiritual state of our civilisation, was altogether too brief. But Eliot's vision was my own. If working in a bank had made Eliot see London as Dante's Limbo, with crowds of damned souls crossing London Bridge, my own years in dreary jobs had made me see our civilisation as Hell itself. I wanted my 'outsider' to walk through its trivialities and complexities possessed by some foreboding of judgement, seeing this world as the culmination of the agony of centuries. The most casual act – like buying a ticket for the Underground – would somehow echo strangely, a symbol of something much more important. I occasionally walked to the local branch of the public library, and would tell myself: You are walking in a city of damnation. The increase of neurosis and insanity was inevitable, for a civilisation that knows nothing of hell deserves to know nothing of heaven either; and all happiness must leak away until mankind recognises its responsibility, and is spurred to some enormous spiritual effort. At that time I was unaware that only 5 per cent are capable of any effort.

I suppose I attended mass for similar reasons. The Catholic Church at least stood for the world of the unseen, and declared that this world must not be taken too seriously. I took its truths to be symbolic rather than literal; and yet, like original sin, they shadowed the otherwise inexpressible.

A month before Betty was due to have a baby our landlady gave us a week's notice. She had warned us that we would have to find new lodgings when the baby arrived, but she suddenly became panic-stricken by the idea that it might be premature and her family be kept awake by its wailing. This gave me added cause for resentment against the tribe of landladies – I had already had trouble with my first landlady in Camden Town (where I had a room that later became the scene of most of *Ritual in the Dark*). Subsequent experience with landladies convinced me that becoming a landlady is the surest way to forfeit your immortal soul, for ninety per cent of them were incredibly petty and mean. In those days, there were moments when I dreamed of a dictatorship that would take all England's landladies, pack them onto ships, and send them away to some remote part of Australia, where they could torment one another with their malice and stupidity. Even now, after years of living without a landlady, my feelings about them are still as violent – if not as ill-founded – as Hitler's about the Jews.

The foreman at work had offered me a room in his house, and we were living there when the baby finally arrived – a boy whom we called Roderick. A few weeks after his birth our new landlady also gave us notice – she evidently found the baby's crying more than she had bargained for. Betty now returned to Leicester for a short period, while I moved into a room in Golders Green, with all our luggage, and the huge quantity of books I had accumulated. My new landlady ran true to form, and I never returned from work without finding an unpleasant note in my room. (Her first comment, when I moved in, was that she would not have let me have the room if she had realised I had so much luggage.)

By this time, I was sick of searching for rooms and moving from place to place, so I did very little to find a new home. But Betty advertised in a nursing journal, and got herself a job in Wimbledon that would allow us to 'live in'. When I went to see the house, it all seemed too good to be true. An old man named Penman lived in it alone; it was a pleasant semi-detached modern house in Queen's Road. I left my lodging in Golders Green, followed by wails and imprecations from my landlady, and we moved into Wimbledon in the spring of 1952. Mr Penman suffered from asthma, and wanted a nurse and housekeeper. He was a retired business man and seemed to be extremely generous; he told me that I could use his typewriter any time I wanted. As he spent most of the day in bed I very seldom saw him. I began to type *Ritual*, and spent every Saturday in the British Museum Reading Room – not because I wanted to do any special research, but because I wanted to write in a place associated with Butler, Shaw and Wells. I also spent a great deal of time in Whitechapel, looking over the murder sites, and began to use the scenes and circumstances of the Jack-the-Ripper crimes in my novel.

But the situation in Wimbledon proved to be less peaceful than I had at first expected. The old man seemed to be somehow jealous of me – he wanted Betty's attention all the time – and began to make a habit of keeping her up all night. He also lent the typewriter to a neighbour – obviously to prevent me from using it. Finally, it became too much for Betty, and she threatened to give notice. At this, Mr Penman's relatives arrived, and tried to dissuade her. The most powerful dissuader was a present of £20, and since we badly needed the money we decided to put up with the old man's tantrums and hypochondria. He also became rather more gentle and sympathetic after the disagreement, and consented to Betty's taking a fortnight's holiday. I also needed a holiday, since I had been travelling every day from South Wimbledon to North Finchley – an hour's journey by tube – and had very little free time left in the evenings. So we decided to go to Hayling Island, and to take a tent.

It was a delightful week, and seemed like a presentiment of a better future. We went to see Blake's cottage at Felpham, spent a day looking at Chichester Cathedral (where I discovered an excellent pamphlet by Eliot on the uses of cathedrals in England) and went to look at the *Victory* at Portsmouth. On Felpham beach I felt as if I could see Blake's angelic forms hovering over the sea.

At the end of the week we returned to Wimbledon, en route for Leicester, and discovered that Mr Penman had died of a heart attack. His relatives told us that we could stay in the house for a few more months, and I was given the typewriter.

The next months were peaceful and happy, since we were alone for the first time since our marriage, with no one to interfere and no landlady to nag us. If we could have continued like this, I have no doubt that we would never have separated. However, there was again the problem of where to live when we left Wimbledon. Betty advertised once more, and finally we decided on a house in Courtfield Gardens, Kensington. The trouble was that this would make it impossible for me to travel to Finchley every day, since there was no direct line. Reluctantly – for I had enjoyed working there – I gave up my job at Frazer and Glass's, and worked instead in a plastic factory at Wimbledon. However, it proved to be a difficult job, involving more manual skill than I possessed, and after a few weeks I was politely given notice. At this point, we moved to Kensington.

The next few months – the winter of 1952 – proved to be the worst ordeal of our married lives. I had no job, and jobs were scarce. The Fulham labour exchange could offer me nothing, so I went on the dole. Luckily, we paid no rent for our basement flat, so my dole money sufficed to feed us. Betty acted as housekeeper, combined with some nursing duties, to the woman who owned the house. She, unfortunately, was insanely neurotic, had never been able to keep a housekeeper for more than a few weeks, and had become so self-centred that she seemed to live in a solipsist universe in which other people were only shadows. When I first realised that she used to shriek at Betty I was filled with rage and stormed upstairs to see her. She declared that if we were not satisfied we could leave the house immediately. Since it had cost us all the money we had to move Betty's furniture down from Leicester to Kensington, this was out of the question; I was forced ignominiously to climb down and apologise. I went downstairs again cursing her with every drop of hatred in my composition, and invoking the gods to strike her dead. A few weeks later she was X-rayed in a hospital and discovered to have a cancer of the womb that would certainly kill her in a matter of months. This, no doubt, had been the basic cause of the insane rages.

For a few days after being told this news she was subdued and good tempered; then the fits of rage and suspicion returned. One day Betty got wind that she was about to be sacked; she forestalled this by giving notice; her furniture was put into storage, and she and Roderick went back to Leicester to wait until I could find another home for us. A few weeks later our ex-landlady died.

While we had been living at Kensington I had become involved with the London Anarchist Group. One day when Betty and I were in Hyde Park we heard a red-bearded speaker preaching anarchism. He seemed to be unusually intelligent and widely-read. I heckled him, asking him every question that came into my head, and his answers were witty, if not convincing. The following Sunday I returned to speak to him, and asked him if I might join the group. He replied that the group had no 'membership'. If you were an anarchist, then you belonged to the group. I asked if I might try speaking on the anarchist platform, and he seemed willing enough. So the following Sunday I went to Hyde Park, feeling weak and excited, to speak for the first time. I travelled by tube, and tried to get out of paying the full fare by claiming that I had boarded the train much nearer my destination than I had. The inspector asked me whether the station I had started from had had an escalator or a lift, and I was not able to answer; so I admitted that I had intended to swindle the London Transport. (He took my name, and in due course, I received a summons and was fined ten shillings.) This experience stimulated all my anarchistic inclinations, and I began my speech by telling my audience – a very large one, since other speakers had attracted it for me – exactly how I had been caught, and advising them on how to avoid paying their fares. This was a huge success; I found it easy to talk in the open air since I had to shout, and this prevented me from being nervous. I talked for half an hour and doubled the size of the audience. When I climbed down, several members of the group thumped me on the back, and hauled me off to Lyons's to celebrate on tea and sandwiches. One of them, Tony Gibson, seemed particularly enthusiastic, and we became firm friends. But when we rejoined the others I was told that my speech had not pleased the rest of the group; it might have been stimulating, but it was not anarchism. So I was instructed that I would have to spend a few months studying Malatesta and Kropotkin before I could be allowed to speak again.

The truth was that I thought the political theory of anarchism nonsense. One might hope for an increasingly democratic and intelligent society that would finally dispense altogether with authority, but it seemed obvious that in our present stage of political evolution we were not ready for it. On the other hand, I felt that the real aim of anarchism was to create a society of 'free spirits' who would help one another openly and generously. This was very close to my heart. It seemed clear to me that the disease of our civilisation was the self-interest and power mania of business men and politicians. I had worked for a while in a large toy factory in Wimbledon, and a few days there had been enough to make me want to destroy the place with dynamite; the workers were expected to work like demons for every single minute between clocking-in and clocking-out; there was no freedom of any kind, and to be a minute late was a serious offence. A week there had been enough for me. It seemed to me disgusting that this land of England, that had produced Sir Thomas Browne and Newton and Shelley, should have come to this: demoniacal, ruthless money-grubbing. And it was because this money-grubbing was a threat to me as a writer that I hated it so much. The aim of anarchism, as I saw it, was to create an England fit for men of talent, and a society whose aim would be the encouragement of talent.

However, the anarchists seemed to feel that my aims were somewhat too idealistic, and not nearly political enough. So I was banned from their platform. I then joined the North London Syndicalist group, who were glad enough to get speakers and allowed me to say what I liked on their platform. The matter of Sir Herbert Read's knighthood also caused some conflict within the anarchist group, which finally split into two factions.

My rather guardedly friendly relations with the London Anarchist Group came to an end when I offered to deliver one of the Tuesday lectures to a small group. I talked about the late Roman emperors from Tiberius to Nero, reading extracts from Suetonius, and ended by talking about Jack-the-Ripper. They all thought that I intended to draw the moral that power corrupts, but I was far more interested in trying to make them understand that there is an irrational element in human nature that will make the establishment of Rousseau's millenium impossible. I drew my text from Dostoevsky's *Notes from Underground*. Half my audience walked out, and the remainder attacked me violently; one of them said that I had used the lecture to get some sadistic compulsion out of my system. After that, I saw very little of the group.

However, after Betty had returned to Leicester I finally found work as a porter at the Western Fever Hospital in Fulham. The foreman arranged for me to 'live in'. Betty and I had parted on the most affectionate of terms; but as soon as we were two hundred miles apart we both felt the relief of sudden freedom from the strain of the past eighteen months, and almost immediately began to write each other recriminatory letters.

At first I enjoyed my job at the hospital. The work was easy, and we spent a great proportion of our time lounging around in the porters' room waiting for the phone to ring to summon us to the ambulance. Unfortunately, all the porters were dying of boredom, and spent their time quarrelling with one another or being thoroughly petty.

The place reeked of sex; it was the perfect atmosphere for incubating some future Jack-the-Ripper. Naturally, the job involved lifting half-naked women on and off stretchers, and walking in and out of wards where the female patients might be wandering around with very few clothes. The porters talked of nothing but sex, and a few of them pursued the nurses and maids with some success. One of the male nurses spent most of his wages on grubby hand-printed booklets of pornography obtained from some shop behind Leicester Square which were passed from hand to hand.

In *The Magic Mountain* Mann has portrayed his tubercular patients as interested in very little besides love affairs. My own experience of the T.B. wards confirmed this; but it seemed to be true of most departments of the hospital with which we came into contact. It may be due to the continually felt presence of death. This came home to me when I walked into the mortuary one day and saw a particularly attractive young girl lying naked on the slab. I had seen her alive a few days before; a few hours later I saw the body after the post-mortem, the brains and intestines piled on the end of the mortuary slab, all suggestion of a fellow human being having now disappeared. She was the mother of children, and happily married, and I found myself asking for the first time, with a real desire to understand : Why did she die? Could I die like that? Are we so unimportant to Nature? *Or did she die because she had no passionate desire to live, no real purpose?* Was Shaw right when he said we die because we are too lazy to make life worth living?

The anarchists had begun to produce a composite revue of the twentieth century just before the group was split by Herbert Read's action in accepting a knighthood. I had written parts of the revue myself. After the schism the idea was dropped; but I was unwilling to scrap my work, and decided to finish writing it myself and to find my own cast to perform it. The cafés and coffee houses were full of bored art students with no idea of how to kill time. A number of these I recruited for my revue. A young commercial artist called Jonathan Abraham let us use his room near Chalk Farm for rehearsal, and played us jazz and records of French cabaret. (He introduced me to the records of 'Bix Beiderbecke, who is still my favourite jazz trumpeter.) I continued writing the revue as we rehearsed it; 'rehearsing' meant reading it aloud, for we had no idea of how it could be staged. (Actually, it would have made an ideal production for radio.)

The member of the cast in whom I felt most interest was an eighteen-year-old writer named Laura Del-Rivo. She dressed and talked like a twelve-year-old, and yet her intelligence was impressive. I felt she was bored and unhappy, curiously 'at a loose end'. I went to Cheam to meet her parents; they were a Catholic family, and had an air of charm and innocence. I began to understand Laura's problem; it seemed that her teen-age mannerisms and twelve-year-old frocks were a kind of attempt to avoid the responsibility of adulthood. And yet she spent her evenings in the world of Soho, at parties where couples would 'neck' until they were obviously in a fever of excitement and then disappear to the bedroom; where sixteen-year-olds talked casually of abortions, and everyone smoked endlessly and drank strong tea. This world of pointlessness and boredom she was unwilling to enter, although it fascinated her.

One evening the two of us decided to get drunk. Neither of us had been drunk before. So we skipped a rehearsal of the revue and spent two hours in the Irish wine-bar in the Strand. We both felt sober enough when we left, but we took two bottles of burgundy with us, and drank it in the Festival Hall gardens, sitting on a seat overlooking the Thames. This did the trick. We wandered into Trafalgar Square, and Laura was suddenly sick into the fountain. A policewoman came over and was peremptory; we were causing a spectacle, she said. I looked around towards the National Gallery, and saw that, indeed, crowds of people were standing against the balustrade staring at us. So I took Laura into a coffee bar for some strong black coffee, and finally took her home to Cheam. On Putney Bridge Station at about midnight I was suddenly sick. The next day I felt awful; as luck would have it, I was given a hard job of window cleaning that lasted the whole day. I worked in a daze, swearing that I would never repeat the folly.

Finally, the revue came on. We hired a hall near Holborn – a large upstairs room of a café called The Garibaldi with a tiny stage. We had a large audience, and we read the revue, seated round a table; it went on for two hours, and was a fair success. We charged no admittance, but the money donated paid for coffee and cakes and covered the cost of the hall.

Afterwards the cast were gloomy; they had been rehearsing for months, and now felt the anticlimax. They urged me to write them another revue, and I began a play called *The Metal Flower Blossom*. This was far more ambitious, caused far more trouble, and was finally abandoned; but it served the purpose of keeping us all occupied throughout the summer.

Some of the cast were also working at selling subscriptions for a forthcoming magazine, to be called *The Saturday Critic*, edited by a young Welshman named Bill Hopkins. I knew nothing of Hopkins, except that Laura had once had a 'crush' on him; but I was told that he was probably the most brilliant man in Soho, and the most certain to make some immense future success. Naturally, I sought him out. At our first meeting I was disappointed. I had expected a man of calm and discipline, who had read as much as I had, and who had carefully calculated his assault on the literary bastions. Instead, I found a pale Welshman with a romantic idealism as innocent as Shelley's, who declared that he never read other people's books because he preferred to be completely original, and whose taste for rhetoric made it obvious that he was a compatriot of Dylan Thomas.

But there could be no denying the immense power of his personality. He seemed to be born to be a leader. His humour was so constant and individual that I found it exhausting after the first half hour or so. By comparison, I seemed brooding and sullen.

At our second or third meeting I lent him the uncompleted manuscript of an early version of *Ritual in the Dark*. For several weeks he was evasive about it, and I suspected, rightly, that he had not even opened it. But one day I went into a Cypriot café called the A and A, and found my manuscript waiting there for me, with a note enclosed that began: 'Welcome to our ranks! You are a man of genius.' He had apparently opened it casually, and had been immediately struck by the discipline of the writing.

On the other hand, I found his own writing disappointing when I first saw it. A short story was full of vague romanticism; it was about a soldier who is badly wounded in battle, and who has time to fall in love with a beautiful peasant girl before he dies.

The truth was that our standards of writing were completely different; I had 'trained' under Eliot and Hulme, and had been equally influenced by Shaw, Yeats and Hemingway. Bill was a completely self-taught romantic, writing in a tradition akin to that of Musset and Hugo. (The shade of Hugo seemed to haunt him, and he was once told at a spiritualist meeting – which he was reporting for a newspaper – that he was the incarnation of Hugo.) This immediately brought to my mind Gide's comment when someone asked him who was the greatest French poet: 'Victor Hugo, alas!' There were times when I suspected that Bill subscribed to Poe's dictum that the most appropriate subject for poetry is the death of a beautiful woman. A story he told me later was somhow completely typical of his character and of his approach to literature. In Paris he was asked to help in the search for a girl who had disappeared from her parents' home in Belgium, and was reported to be making for the Left Bank. He was given a photograph of an exceptionally beautiful girl, and told to comb the cafés of the Left

Bank. Understandably, he fell in love with the photograph, and spent weeks in feverish search for its original. Then he was told the search had been called off: the girl's body had been found buried near her home; a disappointed suitor had murdered her, and then reported that she had left for Paris.

Bill told me this story in connection with an episode in one of his novels (still unpublished at the time I write). A young and romantic German officer goes into a Polish castle that has been wrecked by shellfire. He enters a bedroom that obviously belongs to a girl; her photograph on the dressing table shows her to be exceptionally beautiful. But one wall of the bedroom is missing, and the bed is soaked with blood.

I am telling these stories – out of sequence – to illustrate the way in which Bill Hopkins's imagination works, and also to explain why it was that I found his short story disconcerting. His aim has always been to create a certain kind of intensity that has more in common with Hoffmann or Richter than with Hemingway. On the other hand, being Celtic, he is impatient of understatement and the long discipline of writing, so that the intensity often gets lost as he struggles with the boring technicalities of plot.

But the reason that I was immediately fascinated by Bill Hopkins was that he was the first man I had met who was as conceited and as assured of his future greatness as I was myself. Soho had disappointed me; I had expected to find a Murger-ish freedom of spirit; instead, I found the easily recognisable lack of self-confidence that I had thought to be the characteristic of provincial towns; after six months I had met no self-professed artist or writer who seemed to rise much above mediocrity. All seemed to be oppressed by some suspicion of future failure – the fallacy of insignificance. Moreover, I had never met anyone who seemed to be seriously determined to produce major work. (Laura Del-Rivo was, at this time, extremely modest about the value of anything she might produce.) Although we live in an age of specialisation, where years of study are required to become a technician or mathematician, most would-be writers seem to have no idea that their trade requires an equally long self-discipline.

It was true that Bill Hopkins also seemed to rely largely on native inspiration in his writing; but he gave the impression that he had never, in all his life, entertained a moment's doubt about his future eminence, and about the dignity that attaches to the destiny of being a writer.

It soon occurred to me that his main problem was simple: his immediate personal effect on people was so great that he might easily have spent his whole life dazzling a small circle of admirers (who would never cease to assure him of his genius) and never writing a line. The temptation was doubled because he comes of a family of actors, and he would therefore be only following the family tradition to rely on the spoken rather than the written word.

This came to me even more strongly when I heard him talk for the first time about the plot of his novel *Time of Totality*. As he told it, it was irresistibly dramatic. The romanticism was welded neatly with a plot that had the movement and economy of a Graham Greene thriller; listening to him, it was impossible to doubt that he had the material for a best-selling novel that would also be hailed as a unique expression of nineteenth century romanticism and contemporary psychological insight. And yet I had only to cast my mind back to the occasion when he had first outlined to me the plot of his novel *The Divine and the Decay*, and then to recall his years of effort in writing and rewriting it, to realise that there can be an immense gap between conception and execution. (I was, in any case, already aware of this from my own years of re-writing on *Ritual*.) In telling a story some difficult point is glossed over, some relationship made to sound more plausible than it will on paper. In writing, a conception that seemed water-tight and irresistible may appear more like a beggar's coat – more holes than cloth. There is no alternative but to work and re-work, until the original vision is no more than a distant memory.

However, in this digression I have left the story of *The Saturday Critic* suspended; and yet, when I first met him, it seemed to me – and to many people in Soho – that Bill Hopkins was about to become the new Frank Harris. If the magazine had ever appeared the legend of the Angry Young Men would have started five years earlier; for *The Saturday Critic* was to be devoted to violent demands for higher standards in all the arts, and ruthless condemnation of all that failed to meet these higher standards. (I have no idea of how he proposed to keep the good will of his advertisers.) His army of contributors were all pledged to make the fullest use of satire, irony, and downright abuse in their reviews.

Aware that confidence is most easily inspired by an appearance of success, he took an office in Southwark, close to the tavern from which Chaucer's pilgrims had set out, and had two telephones installed. Various publishers sent him books for review. Jonathan Abraham drafted a dummy copy of the first number, and this was printed with blank pages, and a violent editorial explaining the magazine's policy.

I learned that Bill Hopkins had worked in Fleet Street since his teens, and had at one time edited several North London papers simultaneously. *The Saturday Critic* seemed to have every chance of success. However, the problem was always money, and the free help and the few 'subscriptions' were not enough. As with the production of my *Metal Flower Blossom,* the whole scheme collapsed under its own weight.

But by the time it had collapsed I had moved to Paris. I had got tired of the hospital, and very bored – so bored that no amount of spare-time activity could stop me feeling as if I was rotting spiritually and mentally. Somehow, a mere five minutes in the porters' room could blot out all inspiration and reduce my thoughts to a repetitive channel, like a gramophone record with worn grooves. I made tremendous efforts against it; but it was no use; I stewed in my own apathy. At every opportunity I sneaked off to a room above the laundry, sat cross-legged on the dusty floor (breathing in a smell of dead mice) and tried to concentrate on the *Gita* and on freedom. I was haunted by an image from Cranmer Byng's *Vision of Asia,* a picture of 'Corea, the Land of Morning Calm' – an idea not without ironic implications in 1953 – and of three old men standing in a green basin in the hills, each tasting a jar of vinegar. Buddha finds it sour, Confucius is calm and indifferent, Lao Tse looks delighted; the brew, of course, is life. This image filled me with sick longing as I breathed in the dust, and then went downstairs again to hear the same conversation about football and sex, and watch the endless card games. It was history that had died for me. I had an unusual degree of freedom; the work was easy; I had many friends; but my mind was like a mouse in a bucket that cannot climb over the sides, and can only leap up and then fall back to the bottom.

At about this time the Christie murders were discovered, and the newspapers were full of photographs of detectives digging up the back garden of Rillington Place. These murders seemed to symbolise for me the sordidness and futility of my life in the hospital. I drove myself on by will-power; but I could not recover the delight and confidence of that summer of working on farms. I now often remembered a certain day of my last holiday with Mary, on a windy hillside in Derbyshire. We had been to the top of a tower on the hill, and the wind had blown away my beret; then it had rained heavily, and we had taken shelter in a wood, and lain under a ground-sheet cape, listening to the rain on the cape. Finally, walking down the hill, almost blown off our feet in the wind, and looking at the great circle of hills on the edge of Lancashire, I had been overwhelmed with a consciousness of power and freedom, with a sense that made the boredom of my teens seem negligible. It seemed that I had discovered a secret: never to quietly accept boredom and unfulfillment. 'If you don't like your life, you can change it....' With a knowledge of this secret, the future could hold nothing but triumph.

And yet here I was in a job that brought me constantly into contact with sickness, aware of the moral consequences of our stagnation in the porters' room, and making no real effort to escape. Part of the reason for this was that I sent Betty money every week. The work on my play and the Hyde Park speaking were also a consolation. And yet my mind was like a wet tinder-box, from which it is impossible to strike any spark. One day I met in Northumberland Avenue an old acquaintance from the Vaughan College in Leicester, who congratulated me on looking healthy and full of energy. I was interested in this observation, for I had been deliberately driving myself for many months, refusing to acknowledge exhaustion; yet I was aware of an immense listlessness inside me.

Two events led to my deciding to leave the hospital and go to France. The first was new quarrels with Betty. We had met in Leicester one weekend, and we agreed that we must make a joint effort to find a home for ourselves. I was not entirely happy about this; for while I loved my wife and son I had no particular wish to repeat the experiences of the previous year. But Betty borrowed money from her mother, I registered with an agency that offered to find us a flat for £5, and we started the search for a home again. The agency offered us a flat in Forest Gate, East London; I went to see it and liked it; they wanted £120 for 'furniture and fittings', but the rent was low: £2 10*s*. I immediately gave the agent a cheque for £50 as a deposit, and sent for Betty to come and see it.

She was reluctant – she thought the premium high and was suspicious of the terms of the agreement, and the lessors' refusal to allow her to take the agreement to a solicitor. However, she finally agreed to the price, and returned to Leicester. Then, later the same day, I received a telegram from her telling me that she had changed her mind, and wanted to call the whole deal off. I was furious. I had taken a great liking to the woman who offered us the flat – a plump Irish Catholic who was completely charming – and had told her that we would quite definitely take it. I sent her Betty's telegram, with a letter of apologies – she returned our £50 by the next post – and wrote to Betty saying that if she wanted a flat now, she could look for it herself. But I suspect I was also relieved that things had turned out as they had.

I had another reason for deciding to leave London. Exhaustion was bringing on attacks of the 'vastation' I had experienced years before in Leicester. One day in my bedroom (a kind of horse-box with thin wooden walls) in the hospital, I stood up and yawned. Everything dissolved; in a half-conscious state I groped about the floor, again aware of the curious trickling noise in my head and ears, and of separation from my body and all I called 'myself'. My identity dissolved; there was nothing left to hang on to; again I was 'conscious, but conscious of nothing'. Then my head cleared; but as I went downstairs to work, the 'ordinary world' had become a mockery, a pointless ritual of machines.

A few days later it happened again, on the deserted upper deck of a bus; I stretched and yawned, and became unconscious. I knew that this was because I was causing the blood to rush from my brain; but this was no answer to the sense of horror, the realisation that all human life was futile.

Again, I returned late one night, a little drunk, and lay in bed in the warm darkness; suddenly, I felt a sense of the absurdity of being there. It was suddenly very clear: I wanted to ask: Who am I? What am I doing here? What lies beyond life? We take this world in which we live for granted, as if it were the most ordinary and reasonable thing to be alive. What guarantee have we that we are not sitting in an execution chamber? For us, 'life' is all there is, but we are not afraid because there is always some alternative, some 'beyond' around the corner. But since we are living beings, what alternative is there to life? I suddenly felt like a rat in a trap, and it seemed that our stupidity and incomprehension was all that lay between us and some ultimate horror.

The great irony was that all these questions were irrelevant to my life. If the foreman said: 'Why are you looking ill this morning?', could I reply: 'Because I suspect that all life is false'? or 'Because I suspect you are a delusion of my brain'? We cannot live except as human beings, pursuing the human ritual; all we do must be 'human'; we must travel along our tram-line of time, and make time pass by various purposes that all relate to other people. We seem to be individuals; in fact, we cannot even breathe for ourselves; every act of self-expression of which we are capable is a human, a social, act. The only escape from our pain is by looking to other people or to some 'outside' help – to God or 'spirits'.

It seemed to me that I was like a slot-machine, standing on some corner and believing itself 'free', believing that it stands there of its own free will and disgorges each packet of cigarettes by an act of volition. Suddenly I had realised that 'I' was wholly mechanical, depending entirely on pennies, that therefore no act of mine was meaningful, that I could claim to be nothing more than an observer, a witness of life, consciousness trapped in matter but completely helpless, helpless even to observe except by the body's ironic grace, which might cut off consciousness at any moment.

Plainly, there is nothing to be 'done' about such a vision; but it saps the delusions that keep us moving. It seemed to me that the only sensible alternatives were suicide and leaving the hospital. Neither would be as sensible as simply not 'being', but since I 'was', I had no choice in the matter.

I sold all my books at Foyle's, collected together all the money I could muster, and wrote to Betty to tell her that I was on my way to France. (This meant that, technically speaking, I had 'left' her, although we had been separated for nine months by circumstances.) I spent a night sleeping on the floor of Bill's office in Southwark, and hitch-hiked towards Dover at a leisurely pace the next day. The following night I spent in a wood near Canterbury – in a sleeping bag, of course – and was up early the next morning to catch the first boat to Calais.

By midday I was back in France. This time, I had a little more money than I had had before – a few pounds. I went into a restaurant in a great barn-like place near the docks, and ordered a meal and some wine. I had not yet had breakfast. The wine soon made me drunk and happy; the place was decorated with paper streamers, for some reason, and the radio was playing Spanish music very loud. I was given an immense and tender steak. For the first time for a year – it seemed to be many years – the joy welled up in me, the strength of the power-house, as it had on the windy Derbyshire hillside, and I was certain I had made the right decision in leaving England. I felt that the gods were back with me again, and had sent me this glimpse of power as a sign of approval. I was in Spain and Calais and all over Europe at the same time; I could catch history like a bus.

Two days later I arrived in Paris, and went immediately to the room of Claude Guillaume in the Rue Bayen. He no longer lived there, but his mother kept the room on for her occasional visits to Paris. I had kept in touch with Claude and his wife (Marie had visited me while I was at the hospital, and I had 'showed her London'). The concierge had been told to give me the key; so I moved in.

The first problem was to find some way of making a living. It looked as if I might have found a solution on my first evening in Paris. I saw an advertisement for a new American magazine called *The Paris Review*. I went to visit the editor in his office in the Rue Garanciére; he proved to be a clean-cut young American called George Plimpton. George suggested that I should sell subscriptions for *The Paris Review*, keeping a large share of each subscription for myself. He supplied me with a list of Americans living in Paris, and a map of the city. It seemed an excellent idea; the subscriptions would be for a thousand francs each (about one pound in 1953), of which I would retain 400 francs. This meant that I could live by selling only one or two subscriptions a day. I went back to the Rue Bayen in a very cheerful frame of mind.

The next day I discovered that the work would be harder than I had anticipated. To begin with, the addresses on my list were often a long way apart; I would either have to pay heavily in bus fares, or walk. Secondly, very few Americans seemed to be interested in a new review. After a long day's work, and walking about twenty miles in oppressive heat, I had sold one subscription, but had spent about a thousand francs on cool drinks and bus fares. When the addresses were on the telephone, I tried ringing them up, but discovered that this method of approach was hardly ever successful; it was too easy for the potential client to refuse. One American told me to call the next day at his office. But his home address happened to be very close to the Rue Bayen, so I called there on the offchance of selling him a subscription on my way home. He came to the door, and when I told him my business, shouted: 'I thought I told you to come to my office! What the hell do you think I am! If you want to see me, you'll do it my way! Now get out!' He slammed the door in my face. I stood there, feeling the same hatred that I had once felt for the landlady at Courtfield Gardens, and invoking all the gods to bring on him the nastiest and messiest death possible. I went home wondering why it is that Americans can be the vilest and rudest people on earth (as well as the most charming on occasion).

After a few days I found various means of supplementing my income. The most useful was to sell individual copies of the review to possible subscribers who wanted more time to make up their minds. Many people were unwilling to part with a full year's subscription, but were happy enough to buy a single copy. As far as my job went, this was strictly 'illegal', but I had to live; and I felt that George Plimpton had misled me about the profits to be made.

About two weeks after I arrived Laura wrote to me to say that Bill Hopkins might be on his way over to look for a French printer for *The Saturday Critic*. I spent the next day in my room, hoping he might turn up. I was glad enough of an opportunity to spend the day reading poetry and Shaw's plays, for I detested my 'job'. But there was no sign of him, so the next day I went out and left a note on the door, saying I would be back at six o'clock. Still no one came; so the next day, I stayed in, and read all day. Towards seven in the evening there was a faint knock on my door. It was a London friend named Philip Veen, who told me that he and Bill had been waiting on the pavement downstairs all the afternoon. They had arrived at midday, seen my note (which I had forgotten to remove), and assumed I was not at home.

I was delighted to see them, for Paris had me in a defeated frame of mind. Bill, as usual, was a tonic. He also had no money. Philip had to return to London the following day; he had come for a weekend trip – and we discovered that we had just enough for his fare by clubbing together. Bill decided that he would stay on in Paris and sell subscriptions with me until we had enough money to return to England. Things would be different now, he said; a little fast sales-talk was all that was needed to make us rich.

In this he proved to be over-optimistic. We tried the address of every American in the Champs Elysées, sold half a dozen copies of the magazine, and took one or two subscriptions. But Bill was a non-stop smoker, and I ate large quantities of chocolate; so the money soon vanished, including George Plimpton's share of the subscriptions. We saw George that evening and explained to him that we had been forced to 'borrow' the money, and handed him the addresses of the new subscribers. We also saw the editors of the small English review, *Merlin* – and met Christopher Logue for the first time; we decided to add *Merlin* to our subscription drive, and equipped ourselves with a large armful of copies of the magazines. The *Merlin* subscriptions, like those for *The Paris Review,* had to be impounded to feed us; but we did not starve.

We shared the room in the Rue Bayen, taking it in turns to sleep on the bed. Bill is a night-worker; he would often type (on his *Time of Totality*) until three in the morning, and then wake me up and insist on taking a walk round the empty boulevards. In the long discussions on our temperaments and methods that continued for days on end each of us was frank about his low opinion of the other's approach. I felt, with instinctive resentment, that Bill was patronising me. Since I had worked for years on the assumption that I was the only writer of genius living in Europe this astounded me. I was glad enough to acknowledge him as the only potentially great writer I had ever met; but to be aware that he did not regard me in the same light was irritating. Consequently, I was as candid as I could be about the defects of his own writing, about his lack of serious discipline, and the time he wasted on trying to influence people directly – either by conversation or in the magazine – instead of concentrating on creating major works. He in his turn declared that I was too subjective and introverted; and that this revealed my fear of having my conviction of superiority shattered by contact with other people. We wrangled for days, and ended in some kind of agreement, both acknowledging partially the justice of the other's criticisms; we also agreed that a new phase of modern literature had begun when we decided to form an alliance. Certain misunderstandings were also aired and cleared up (there had been an unfortunate business of a communist girl in London – she figures distantly in *Ritual* – who had rather played us off against each other and left us both with a certain mistrust of the other's intentions). All this left us feeling optimistic; and we often celebrated a long day of selling subscriptions with a few bottles of cheap wine at the expense of *The Paris Review*.

Still, all this did nothing to advance the fortunes of *The Saturday Critic*. (Bill had come to Paris hoping that French printers might be cheaper than English.) So after several weeks of working on our respective novels and spending a great deal of time drinking with the *Merlin* crowd in the Café Tournon, we decided that the British Consulate must once again be called upon for 'repatriation'. It was a hard decision; I had come to Paris with every intention of living there. Logue and the rest of the *Merlin* writers managed to make a thin living from teaching English, and they offered some helpful advice. (When Claude Guillaume arrived unexpectedly at the Rue Bayen one day, Bill spent the following night sleeping – or trying to sleep – on Logue's floor, and listening to helpful advice and sonnet sequences until dawn; this, I think, hastened the decision to return to England.)

So in late November, after a mere two months in Paris, I returned. I had no heart for London, and in any case, had no money to find a room. I stayed for a few days with a Hungarian acquaintance, Alfred Reynolds, who had recently moved into a house in Dollis Hill; Reynolds ran a kind of humanistic political group which he called 'Bridge', and preached a gospel of absolute tolerance to a group of young men once a week. I stayed long enough to attend one meeting, decided that this kind of tolerance had nothing to teach me, and went on to Leicester. The Labour Exchange directed me to Lewis's, the big store in the centre of the town; they needed temporary salesmen for the Christmas rush, and I was allotted to the carpet department.

I had come to Leicester hoping vaguely that fate might have changed its policy towards me. It seemed to me that I had been a dissatisfied wanderer for as long as I could remember, either enduring futile jobs, or drifting at a loose end. I felt myself a perpetual misfit. And yet it was not because I had the temperament of a drifter or a 'bohemian'. It would appear that fate had no intention of allowing me to relax. I had made various bids for independence. The last one had been in the autumn of 1952, when I had tried to set up in the woven-rug business with Betty, and had spent days walking round London's big stores trying to find a market for the rugs that Betty could weave on a loom. It seemed I was destined to go on working for other people and giving up every job after a fortnight.

However, working in Lewis's was not disagreeable. The manager questioned me for half an hour on the morning I applied for the job. He established that I was not 'respectable', but still seemed sympathetic. He even stretched a point about my lack of a suit, and allowed me to start work in the carpet department on a temporary basis. I enjoyed it for a while. The Christmas rush kept us busy. The loudspeaker blared Christmas carols all day, and I liked the others in my department. On my first day there I met a man of my own age who had just left the army – he had been an officer in the Tanks – and we did some drinking together. His name was Halliday – nicknamed Flax – and he also had the rolling-stone temperament. He was intelligent, but no intellectual, and cared mostly for sport and beer. The basis of our liking was problematic. To begin with, I think, he was a friendly person who missed the companionship of the officers' mess, and who took trouble to make himself agreeable to me. But he was also possessed of a curious physical will-to-power, and preached a kind of gospel of power that interested me. He had noted that certain officers, sons of rich or titled men, seemed to give orders without effort, and were obeyed mainly because they *expected* to be obeyed. One such officer had shouted across to him once: 'Halliday, get some more drink', and he had been on his way back across the room with the drinks before it struck him that the form of the request had been hardly polite, and that he ought to be offended.

Flax's will-to-power became apparent in other ways, particularly when he was drunk. On the first evening, I went back with him to his flat; he showed me his army revolver. He then asked me casually to pick up something at the side of my chair. As I leaned over, there was an explosion, and the wood near my nose splintered. I picked up the object – a pipe, I think – and handed it to him as if nothing had happened. 'Hmm, your nerves are good', he commented, peering into the smoking revolver. He talked with a certain admiration about officers he had known who played Russian roulette, or who would offer to prove they were not drunk by spreading their fingers out on a table top and stabbing between them at incredible speed with a sharp stiletto. He told me that one of them had missed, and pinned his hand to the table; he said this with admiration. I told him of a German girl I had known at the Western Hospital; during the war she had been a troop-leader in the Hitler Youth, and had adored the Führer; she confessed that life seemed intolerably insipid since the end of the war. Flax obviously sympathised deeply with her, and we had a discussion on Hitler that ended with Flax presenting me with a copy of *Mein Kampf* inscribed briefly: 'Halliday to Wilson'. He reminded me of certain officers described in Russian fiction of the nineteenth century – Pushkin's Hermann, Tolstoy's Dologhov, or Lermontov's Pechorin.

I introduced him to other Leicester friends – to Gerald (whom he instantly detested), to Maurice Willows, and a recent acquaintance named John Crabbe. Crabbe was my age and looked at least forty, with a small moustache and the mild eyes of Wells's Mr Polly. He loved music – especially opera – and had many gramophone records. I quickly took advantage of his collection, and spent whole evenings listening to the complete *Meistersinger* or *Bohème,* or ancient 78s of Patti and Galli-Curci.

There were other diversions in Leicester. I was soon bored with the carpet department, and decided to start a drama group to try to produce a Christmas concert. The idea of producing my *Metal Flower Blossom* was vetoed by the manager when he read the script; but he agreed that *Man and Superman* was unexceptionable, and I decided to do the first act, and to complete the concert with a few sketches and any 'turns' I could get together from the talent available in the store. Rehearsals went on at the Capital T, a temperance club in Granby Street. I, of course, played Tanner, and since I had seen Clements act the part a dozen times I think my performance was finally good imitation-Clements. Anne was played by one of the trainee sales-managers, a slim girl called Joy Stewart; she was a friend of Flax's current girlfriend Pat, so I saw a great deal of her apart from rehearsals; the four of us did a great deal of drinking together. We had two excellent comics, who finally saved the show, and the usual floating cast who might or might not turn up for rehearsal. After several delays the show finally went on in early January, a few days before I left Lewis's. The man who was playing Octavius dropped out at the last moment, and his part was taken at short notice by the Leicester poet Barry Hipwell, who had to read his lines from the script. The audience were a little bewildered by Shaw – particularly as I acted the part dressed in a white polo-necked sweater – but cheered up when the comics came on, and became almost enthusiastic towards the end of the evening.

Now that I was back in Leicester I saw Betty again; she was living with her mother and had not yet found a job. I was able to help her, and for a time there were suggestions that we should live together again. But the old problems were unsolved: where to live and how to live? I had no desire whatever to return to the old routine of snarling landladies and boring jobs. It was bad enough living like a bum, drifting from job to job and city to city; but at least I was responding to my basic dissatisfaction by moving on.

During all this time I had never ceased to write, and to study the books that seemed to me to be somehow the basis of my projected novel. For Christmas in 1953 I bought myself *Seven Pillars of Wisdom*, Hylton's *Ladder of Perfection*, and *The Cloud of Unknowing*. The novel was becoming a complicated mass of cross-reference and allusion, which attempted to carry out my design of combining the techniques of *Ulysses* and *The Waste Land*, using the ground-plan of the *Book of the Dead*. I had rewritten it continually, and it was still a mess.

This, and various other dissatisfactions, made me decide to leave Leicester. My two months there had been unexpectedly amusing, a series of parties and night-long discussions. Flax had persuaded me to climb the steeple of a nearby church with him and to take a fourteen mile run out to Great Glen and back; Maurice Willows and I had agreed to start a contest to see which of us could find a publisher first. (In this, he was successful; a Leicester firm brought out a book of his poems called *Late Days*.) John Crabbe had introduced me to operas I had never heard. I had acted in *Man and Superman* and had to some extent compensated for my earlier failure to produce *The Metal Flower Blossom*. I had also seen a great deal of Joy Stewart. She was a graduate of Trinity College, Dublin, and intended to go to Canada to marry the following spring. Her gentle personality fascinated me, and the interest deepened when I discovered that she knew a lot of Yeats by heart and had read *Ulysses*. Most of the attractive girls I had known had been definitely un-literary, and the literary ones had been unattractive. Even Betty, who was intelligent in a practical and down-to-earth way, had never really shared my interest in literature and ideas. So Joy seemed too good to be true. I set about trying to make her change her mind about marrying.

I left Lewis's in January, 1954, and spent the next fortnight helping Joy to decorate a flat that she and a girlfriend had rented from Flax Halliday. Then I took another temporary job, this time in a shoe factory. It involved standing at a machine all day long, and polishing the soles of shoes at the rate of two hundred an hour. The pay was good; I stayed for a few weeks, then decided it was time to return to London. I spent a last evening drinking with Maurice Willows, and feeling unexpectedly satisfied with my stay in Leicester.

This is perhaps the point to say something more about Maurice. I was to see him at intervals over a period of years, until, a few years ago, a letter from his wife told me that he had died of an overdose of sleeping-tablets. I took the volume of *Late Days* off my bookshelf, and some of its poems seemed to me exceptionally fine.

There was something curiously unprepossessing about his appearance. He had a thin, consumptive looking face, although he was not consumptive, and he spoke with an adenoidal Yorkshire accent; altogether he gave an impression of weakness that was deceptive. (When Flax taunted him with being afraid of heights he shinned up a church steeple like a monkey and stood balancing dangerously on top – there was some scaffolding to help him, but wind and rain made it a difficult feat.)

There was a certain sloth about him that I found infuriating; he lacked the drive of a man determined to succeed. When I first knew him – in 1949 – he seemed to me to be a typical provincial amateur writer whose only qualifications were an amorphous culture, a vague dissatisfaction, and a half-hearted desire to be a poet. My own optimistic idealism seemed to have some influence on him, and this naturally flattered me into studying his own work more seriously. It was then I realised that, in spite of the lack of discipline, he was undoubtedly a poet. In that winter of 1953 it seemed to me that he had increased in stature as a writer. We spent whole nights in talk. One evening we went out together to buy another bottle of wine – cheap Spanish burgundy – and I said (perhaps with the intention of flattering him – 'selling him the confidence trick', as Bill Hopkins calls it) : 'You know, Maurice, you'll probably become known long before I am. You've got a far more practical approach to writing.' To my surprise, he answered seriously : 'You're probably right...'

Some of his 'practical' devices pained me; he would sketch out second-rate plays on 'popular' subjects (I recall one about a man who won the football pools) and post them off to the BBC or various theatres; they were always returned. But in 1954 my belief in his ability to succeed seemed justified. In that year he wrote an essay on 'The Fool in Lear' that won some prize, and ultimately gained him a scholarship to Cambridge. He was then in his late twenties, but had spent his adult life in uncongenial jobs – like myself – and felt that university life represented total freedom. After a year at a college in Birmingham he went on to Cambridge; but he was soon bored and disillusioned. I visited him when I was writing *Ritual in the Dark* in a cottage belonging to Angus Wilson; he had separated from his wife Freda, and was living with the girl who later became his second wife. He was morose and irritable about Cambridge, which he called 'a menagerie of adolescents' and described as incredibly superficial and tedious. Finally, he gave up the university, after doing only one year of a three-year course, and became a chicken-farmer. I saw him again after *The Outsider* had been published, but by then it seemed that he had grown tired of writing poetry. However, I insisted on looking at the poems he had written during the past year, and offered to send two of them to Stephen Spender for *Encounter*. They seemed to me to lack the old skill, and parts of them were downright clumsy; so after some deliberation I made a few verbal changes before I posted them off. I enclosed a letter asking Stephen, in the event of rejecting them, to return them to me, and not direct to the author. I reasoned that *if* they appeared in print Maurice would forgive my alterations; if not, he need never know. Unfortunately, Maurice wrote to *Encounter* enquiring about them after a few weeks, and by some error they were posted direct to him. I never heard from him again. Two years later his wife wrote to tell me of his death. A psychiatrist had prescribed sleeping-tablets. 'Whether this was intentional or accidental,' she wrote, 'I shall never know, but the coroner returned a verdict of misadventure.' She also spoke of 'the sense of failure which had always dogged him'. She confirmed my belief that the episode of the *Encounter* poems had stopped him from getting in touch with me. (I had had no idea of his address latterly.) It seems to me now that I could have prevented his death had I kept in touch with him and perhaps tried harder to help him to find a publisher. Then I think about the thousand miles of void that exists between all human beings, and wonder if all my efforts could have made any ultimate difference.

7

LONDON AND *THE OUTSIDER*

W. B. YEATS who, like myself, was thoroughly superstitious about matters of 'fate' and destiny, once wrote about men of ascetic temperament:

> 'They are plagued by crowds until
> They've the passion to escape.'

When I returned to London early in 1954 it seemed to me that I had been incessantly plagued by crowds since I was sixteen; but the means of escape still eluded me. And at that precise moment fate applied every kind of spur to force me to devote all my attention to the problem of escaping.

My first six months in London were the worst I had yet experienced. I found myself a room in the Archway district (N.19), in a house run by an incredibly stupid Scotsman. I had hoped that a landlord (unmarried) might be preferable to a landlady, but I was soon disillusioned. I went to the labour exchange in North Finchley, and was directed to a job in a laundry. It was heavy work that involved loading wet laundry into half a dozen spin-dryers, and unloading it fifteen minutes later. I handled tons of wet laundry a day. Joy wrote to me regularly, and finally agreed to come to work in London. She was a quiet, easygoing girl who seemed to wander around in a dream – or a daze, although she gave a superficial impression of efficiency. To be honest, she was extraordinarily like Betty in many ways – but then, some wit has said that men who marry twice usually marry the same girl, so this is only to say that she was basically of the same type as Betty. Possibly there was even a perverse desire to dissuade her from getting married, merely for the sake of influencing her. (I suspect that most men at twenty-one have a little of Constant's Adolphe in their composition, and more than a little of Julien Sorel.) However, things seemed to take a more serious turn when her parents discovered that she no longer intended to marry, and that she meant to come to London. There were family quarrels. I received a visit from her indignant father, who left more indignant than he had come, prophesying that I would 'end in the gutter'. However, things were smoothed over eventually.

In the meantime I was having trouble with my landlord. The gas fire seemed to be blocked; it frequently went out. I dismantled it, and asked my landlord to get it repaired. When the workman came he told the landlord that a dismantled gas fire could be dangerous. When I returned from work that evening the landlord gave me notice. I pointed out that to look at a faulty gas fire is hardly a crime; but he had the temperament of a timid old woman, and refused to reconsider. He asked me how soon I could leave, and I demanded a fortnight's notice. However, I felt so indignant that I found myself a new room two days later, in North Finchley. I kept this fact to myself; and on the Saturday, when my rent expired, I told my landlord that I intended to leave immediately. Now it was his turn to be indignant. He had turned away an inquiry for a room only that morning, he claimed, and had told the man to return the following Saturday; he was therefore losing a week's rent. I said I was delighted to hear it. He threatened to keep my luggage unless I paid the rent; so I went to the local police station, explained the situation to the sergeant on duty, and was told that the landlord would have to sue me if he thought he had a grievance. I returned to my room; the landlord was out, so I left him a letter, giving him my new address, and saying that I would expect to hear from his solicitor. I never heard from him.

I worked at the laundry for about a month, and found it exhausting. My new rooms were excellent; I had the upper floor of a council house, with hardly any furniture, but at a rent of thirty shillings a week. I decided to change my job; and in spite of my resolution never again to work in an office I applied at the local exchange for an office job, and was directed to a large garage near Finchley Central station. I was taken on as store-room clerk, and my job was to keep a check on thousands of spare parts, and to issue them to garage repair-men. As I had never looked under the bonnet of a car the various names were Greek to me; after a fortnight, the firm sacked me. I then found a job with the Victoria Wine Company; but this was even more boring. The Scots clerk with whom

I worked had a curious belligerence; he seemed to regard it as a personal insult that a 'bohemian' should occupy the next seat to him (the word 'beatnik' had not been invented then), and argued all day. (In 1960, I met him by chance in Stockholm; his first words to me were 'You know, I'm far more of a genius than you are' – he had been stung by some Swedish journalist's description of me.) After a few weeks, the Victoria Wine Company sacked me too. I was not sorry.

In any case, I was beginning to feel goaded in many ways. I received a letter saying that Betty was suing me for maintenance. This seemed to me one more attempt to tie me down to a respectable job and turn me into a 'husband and father'. However, she dropped the idea when I promised to send her an allowance in the future. There were also minor irritations about my lodging. The old lady who rented the house lived off National Assistance; she had a daughter in her mid-thirties – a large, owl-like girl – and a fat grand-daughter. The daughter soon made me her confidant, explaining that her husband had left her and that she supplemented National Assistance with a little street-walking. I did not in the least object to the street-walking, but I found it tiresome to discover in my bedroom unmistakable signs that it had been used to receive her male friends. The girl herself seemed to have a curious preference for eating fish-paste sandwiches in bed, and I often had to remake the bed to remove stale crumbs and fragments.

Next I found a job in a plastics factory at Whetstone, and for a few weeks I enjoyed this. Then one morning (a Saturday when I was working over-time) I had a quarrel with the foreman, and walked out. On the Monday, he gave me notice.

By now it was June, and I was in a perpetual state of irritation. It came to a head on the day I was given notice at the factory; my landlady told me she objected to Joy visiting me so often, as it might lead to gossip among the neighbours. Since I had been carefully preserving the secret of her daughter's spare-time occupation (the old lady was luckily deaf and almost blind) this struck me as completely ironical; so I gave her notice at once.

It seemed that I was being called upon for a bold decision. I had had four jobs in as many months, and had been sacked from three; I had changed my rooms twice. I cycled to work brooding on the problem. The trouble, it seemed, lay with modern civilisation, which permits no leisure. I wanted to be a writer; but the novel on which I had spent four years seemed as far from completion as ever. I thought about Joyce working for years in banks and schools while he wrote *The Portrait* and *Ulysses*. I had no desire to work in a bank. Left to myself, there might be some possibility of earning enough to keep alive while I went on writing; but I had a wife and son. According to books like Hesse's *Siddartha,* it was all much easier in the East. It might have been easier in England a few centuries ago, when monasteries offered a refuge. But in modern England, one can become neither a 'tathagata' nor a monk. (At least, the difficulties seemed insuperable.) I began to wonder if it would not be possible to buy a tent, and to live somewhere in a field. There must be places out beyond Barnet...

The more I thought of the idea, the more practicable it seemed. I could probably live on a pound a week. I had been given a fortnight's notice from the job, and could save a fair amount of money before I left – ten pounds or so at least.

I put the plan into operation immediately. Jonathan Abraham had given me an old bicycle; he also recommended me to buy a waterproof sleeping-bag, which would cover an ordinary kapok sleeping-bag. I bought an immense ex-paratroop rucksack, and a groundsheet. When my week's notice in my lodgings elapsed I still had another week to work in the plastics factory. I left my books and other belongings with Joy, who had a room near Chalk Farm, and started to sleep on the edge of the golf course at Whetstone. After the first night I slept well enough. I tried a night on Hampstead Heath, but from there it was too far to cycle to work. However, when I had finished work at the plastics factory, the Heath seemed the best idea. I could now put into operation my plan to spend my days in the Museum reading room. Besides, the Heath was conveniently near Joy's lodging. I knew of a bus-men's café at Chalk Farm where I could buy bread and dripping very cheaply; I went there every morning for breakfast. I would then cycle down to the Museum, and leave my rucksack in the cloakroom. (The attendant obviously regarded this as an imposition, and threatened to complain to the Museum authorities; but nothing came of it.) At once I began to work hard on rewriting *Ritual in the Dark*.

This new routine was infinitely preferable to working every day in an office or factory; but it was by no means ideal. I was mentally exhausted by the wear and tear of the past two years; leading the life of a tramp in London did nothing to ease the strain. When I told Bill Hopkins that I was sleeping on the Heath and writing in the Museum during the day, he said enthusiastically: 'That's the idea, Col, build up the Wilson legend!' But one cannot live on legends. By all normal standards I had become a bum and a drifter; I had done no regular work for a year, and was living outdoors to avoid paying my wife maintenance. And yet I still had the totally subjective temperament of my childhood; I wanted to be left alone with a pile of books in a room of my own. I hated this business of living outdoors, of never being able to sleep deeply and soundly because some tramp might stagger over me in the dark, or a policeman order me to move out of the radius of London. (A policeman had told me that it is illegal in England to sleep without a roof over your head.) In the mornings I would wake up to find the sun shining on the damp grass, the sky bright blue; the Heath empty; it ought to have been poetic, but I had no capacity for enthusiasm; I saw it all through a grey mist of exhaustion.

In the reading room I had met Angus Wilson, who was then known as the author of two volumes of short stories and of *Hemlock and After*. I had read *Hemlock* and disliked it intensely; but the author himself seemed to be a friendly and pleasant man. With his high, fluting voice, he was well-known to everyone in the reading room. In spite of his position as a well-known author and a rather exalted Museum official, he seemed always ready to be helpful to readers. I asked him one day if he knew where Eliot's essay on *Ulysses* could be located, and he came back several hours later with the volume, having spent the morning searching through the catalogues for it. We got into conversation, and I told him I was writing a novel. He said that he would like to see it when it was finished, and that if he liked it he would show it to his publishers. I took this very seriously (although, having myself said the same thing to many young authors, I now realise that it may not have been too seriously intended). After that I saw him occasionally, but we never exchanged more than a few words.

Joy had now decided to become a librarian; her first job was at

Stanmore, so she moved to lodgings there. She was given some kind of a grant, from which I borrowed when my money ran out. August was approaching, and I wanted to leave London for at least a few weeks. This meant finding another job. I was told that there were many well-paid temporary jobs in dairies; I made inquiries, and was directed to a dairy out on the Great West Road, near Osterley Park. The pay was good, but the work was monotonous and hard. It consisted of lifting crates of milk bottles on to a moving belt all day, at the rate of twenty a minute. The day started at seven in the morning, and I could, if I liked, work until seven in the evening. I found a field only a few minutes away from the factory, and slept there. Close to the field – on the Great West Road – was a workman's café called The Better 'Ole. (It has since been pulled down to make way for a garage.) I spent most of my evenings there, since it was too far to go into town for a few hours. I repaid Joy the money I had borrowed (part of which had been spent on a copy of *The Gospel of Sri Ramakrishna*), and had soon accumulated enough to take a fortnight's holiday in the Lake District with my brother Rodney, who was then twelve; and then another fortnight in Cornwall with Joy. This was my first visit to Cornwall; curiously enough, we camped in a field that is less than half a mile from the house where I am now living (I discovered this only after I had moved in here). The West country delighted me; we brought Norway's *Highways and Byways in Devon and Cornwall* with us, and followed Norway's route, reading aloud to one another legends of giants and fairies, or stories of the Spanish Armada. The trip to the Lake District was less memorable, except for an exhausting experience of climbing Helvellyn one afternoon. There was a gale on top, and a heavy mist, and Rodney found it all terrifying; it took us until after dark to find our way down, and then we had to walk back to Bowness in heavy rain over the Kirkstone Pass, a distance of ten miles or so.

Back in London, I took a job at the Lyons Corner House in Coventry Street – this time as a kitchen porter. It was pleasant enough; I was glad to have my meals supplied, and began to put on weight. I continued to sleep on Hampstead Heath, always choosing the same spot under a tree on a slope. When the weather became colder I decided to look for a room again, though it was not the cold that bothered me, but the rain. For some reason I chose south London, and found myself a room in Brockley, near New Cross station. My landlady was the best so far; she had a large family, and had better things to do than nag her tenants.

Towards Christmas I bought for £7 a second-hand typewriter from a friend of Bill Hopkins, and started to type out the first part of *Ritual*. Although this version had very little in common with that finally published, its first part ended, as in the published version, with Sorme's vision of Austin Nunne as Nijinsky. I completed this just before Christmas, and spent Christmas Day in my room revising it. I had been told that Angus Wilson intended to leave the Museum and devote all his time to writing, and I wanted to show it to him before he left.

I had left Lyons's before Christmas; now I applied at the local labour exchange, and was directed to another laundry. This job was even harder than my previous laundry in Finchley. We worked in shifts, starting at seven in the morning. My job was to load rusty tin baths full of wet clothes on to a moving belt. My hands were soon covered with cuts from the baths. It started to snow heavily, so that it was difficult to cycle to work. Since it was dark when I set out I could not see where the snow was passable and where it had piled into drifts; it was easier to walk, pushing the bicycle. The laundry was in Deptford, close to the docks. This was probably the most unpleasant job I have ever had, and the hardest; however, things were about to improve. One day the laundry became too much for me. My journal had been stolen from my pocket while I worked, and it covered the past two years. This so disgusted me that I gave in my notice on the spot, and went to look for another job. A friend had told me that a new coffee house was opening in the Haymarket, and that they would need staff. I applied, and was given a job as washer-up in the basement.

I found this in every way a relief after the laundry. The surroundings were clean and pleasant to look at. The food was excellent. The staff was made up mainly of young out-of-work actresses, or RADA students. I liked everyone there, and found the work easy. The washing-up was done by machine.

At about the time that I started work at the coffee house I planned *The Outsider*. Stuart Holroyd, whom I had met at 'Bridge' meetings, had decided to write a book about poetry and religion. At that period he had been strongly under my influence, and the book naturally echoed many of my ideas. As soon as I saw its first chapter, I decided that it was time I wrote my own critical book. It had, of course, been in my head for many years; I had written about 'Outsiders' in my journal ever since I was sixteen. I may have discovered the word in Shaw (in the preface to *Immaturity*), but I am not certain. In half an hour I had sketched out a plan in my journal; the book was to be called *The Outsider in Literature,* and would be a study in various types of Outsiders, ranging from 'weak' Outsiders (Fitzgerald's Gatsby, Oblomov, Hamlet) to the Outsider philosophers – Gurdjieff, Nietzsche, Kierkegaard, etc. Its purpose was simply to demonstrate that a man who begins by feeling 'out of place' in modern society may end as a mystic or a saint.

Once I had the idea I wrote very quickly. I cycled to the British Museum one morning – I did not have to be at work until 5.30 p.m. – and planned the opening chapter in my head. I recalled a book by Barbusse, mentioned in the preface to the Everyman edition of *Le Feu,* in which a man looks through a hole in the wall at the people who come and go in the next room. In the Museum, I traced the book – *L'Enfer* – read it in a morning, and then started my own book by simply copying out a key sentence on a sheet of paper : 'In the air, on top of a tram, a girl is sitting...' Then I wrote an account of Barbusse's book, and immediately went on to write about Wells's *Mind at the End of its Tether.* I finished the first chapter a few days later, and took it to a writer-friend, Hugh Schonfield (for whom Stuart Holroyd was then working as a secretary) and read it to him. He said he liked it, but that the book needed a beginning, and that Barbusse, Wells and Sartre needed to be connected more obviously. That weekend, as I hitch-hiked to Stratford-on-Avon with Joy, I thought out a beginning for the book, and 'connecting links' for the first chapter. T. E. Hulme had intended to write a book to prove that humanism is superficial, and that any deep thought leads inevitably to a religious attitude – that is, to the recognition of 'the greatness and littleness of man' and the need for God. (Many of the men I was writing about – Sartre, for example – would acknowledge the need, but deny that it proves anything.) Hulme was killed before he could write his book; I would therefore write it for him. The book as I then planned it would begin and end with Hulme. (Later, at the suggestion of the publisher, I dropped the introductory chapter.)

In retrospect, I have one major criticism of *The Outsider* : it is too romantic. Its mood of world-rejection, of disgust with civilisation, is too absolute. Now it seems to me that the distinction I then made between religion and humanism is a false one. I knew that I sympathised with Eliot, and agreed with him that 'civilisation cannot survive without religion'. I knew that I had no patience with the anaemic, university-trained humanism of Kathleen Knott in *The Emperor's Clothes*. The truth is that the basic position of the book *is* humanistic. I had been divided for years in my attitude towards religion. I was in total intellectual agreement with the 'dynamic' religion of the saints (to use Bergson's terminology), but had no sympathy for the 'static' religion that develops from it. By temperament I was not fitted to be a member of any group or congregation. I was irritated by the pessimism of 'religious intellectuals' – Eliot, Greene, Marcel, Bernanos, Kierkegaard, Simone Weil. I was equally irritated by the shallowness and intellectual laziness that I found in Russell and Ayer. I felt no hesitation in choosing between the two. My mistake was in supposing the choice was necessary, for I had as little – or as much – in common with Kierkegaard as with Russell. I should have asked myself the question : which would be easier : to deepen philosophy until it includes the insight of religion, or to somehow 'humanise' religion? As it was, I rejected Kierkegaard's dead-end pessimism about philosophy, and stuck to my Shavian evolutionism, without seeing that this made me a humanist. It is a pity that I use the word 'humanism' in *The Outsider*; I should have risked inventing a word like 'Russellism'.

I wrote every day in the Museum, went to the coffee house in the evenings, and cycled home to New Cross in the early hours of the morning. For the first time in years, I was happy, and no longer had a sense of being backed into a corner.

Later that year, I decided to change my lodgings to a house behind Grays Inn Road, where I had a room with an Irish family. However, I made the mistake of taking a Soho bum back with me one night and allowing him to sleep on my floor, and my landlady gave me notice next day. The manageress at work – a delightful Rabelaisian character called Gabby – short for Gabriele – told me of a basement room near Baker Street where the landlady could be relied upon not to make a nuisance of herself. The rent was higher than I could afford, but I took it. This was altogether more convenient for the Museum and for work, and Joy could reach it easily from Stanmore. The landlady, a friend of Gabby's, did not seem to mind whom I brought home, provided they were not noisy. I made a habit of taking friends back with me after midnight, and talking until four in the morning.

I found a publisher for *The Outsider* accidentally. I had bought a remaindered copy of Victor Gollancz's anthology of mysticism, *A Year of Grace*. There were many things in it that I disliked; its conception of religion seemed to me sloppy and humanistic, with too much emphasis on 'loving your neighbour' and too little on the individual need to fight for a spiritual discipline. Joy and I had a violent quarrel in Canterbury Cathedral one Sunday because I was fulminating about Gollancz's humanism, and she felt that my language was unsuitable for a cathedral.

However, it struck me that a publisher who had himself compiled an anthology of mysticism might well be interested in *The Outsider* (or *The Pain Threshold,* as it was then called.) One day I typed out the introduction, and a few pages from the middle, and sent them to him with a letter giving a synopsis of the book. He replied within two days, saying that he would be interested to see the book when completed. Encouraged, I began composing direct on the typewriter instead of writing it by hand first.

By this time I had found myself a day-job that entailed very little work. Maurice Willows, who was then in London, had been working as a telephonist for a firm of builders; he had to sit in an office for a few hours a day and answer the phone; the pay was good, and there was no work, apart from sitting there. When he left, to go to Cambridge, he offered me the job. I needed the money, so I transferred my typewriter into the office, and settled down to typing *The Pain Threshold*. But although I liked the manager of the firm, the foreman was an unpleasant and petty person. I had taken a gas-ring to the office, to make myself tea during the day.

He objected to this, and turned off the gas at the mains. I found the switch and turned it on again. He hid the kettle; I brought one of my own. One day our feud flared up into a violent quarrel; he told me I was sacked. I could have replied that I preferred to wait and speak to the manager, but I preferred to get up and walk out.

Luckily, I had by this time typed out all the parts of the book that I had so far written by hand. On the day I quarrelled with the foreman I heard from Leicester that my mother was seriously ill. Our family doctor, an incompetent who had killed my grandfather and grandmother, had diagnosed appendix trouble as a stomach complaint; the appendix exploded, and my mother was rushed into hospital suffering from peritonitis. I delivered my half-finished manuscript at Gollancz's; a drawling young man told me that Mr Gollancz never looked at unfinished manuscripts, but I prevailed on the typist to let me leave the manuscript with a letter. Then I rushed up to Leicester to see my mother. She seemed very weak, and complications had set in. It looked as if I was going to lose her just as I was about to prove to her that I was not a layabout. I stayed in Leicester for several days, and then returned to London. The first operation was unsuccessful; so were a second and third. It began to look hopeless. I had lost all heart for my book, and stopped writing. Even an enthusiastic letter from Angus Wilson about the first part of my novel failed to cheer me up. However, a letter arrived one morning from Gollancz's. He liked the book, was willing to publish it, and urged me to go on and finish it. I sent a telegram home: 'Book has been accepted', and went back to work harder than ever. After months in hospital my mother seemed no better and no worse, and it seemed likely that she might recover if she could keep on resisting for long enough.

August came. Joy and I travelled to Cornwall again, this time on bikes. I was bursting with optimism, and seemed to have good reason for it. I had told Angus Wilson that Gollancz was interested in the Outsider book, and he had suggested that I show it to his own publisher, Fred Warburg of Secker and Warburg. 'No harm in getting two offers.' Warburg seemed unenthusiastic when I took the manuscript in, but twenty-four hours later he rang me up in great excitement to say that he thought the book excellent, and would give me an advance for it immediately, as well as a contract for my novel. I was doubtful, since Gollancz's had offered to publish it; but I decided not to make a hasty decision. So on our Cornish holiday I felt that I had at last received some recognition, and had begun my career as a writer. Two years before I had decided that there was no point in worrying about publication and recognition. If the general public was unable to read your work, then the best thing would be to ignore the general public and get on with the work. I had even written in my journal that I was prepared to wait for recognition until I was fifty; I promised myself that by that time I would have a cupboardful of books ready for publication. Now it seemed that such stoicism would not be necessary, and I was already straining at the leash, planning the works to be written immediately after *The Outsider* and *Ritual*.

I finished *The Outsider in Literature* and showed it to Gollancz, who seemed pleased with it. (I had been secretly afraid that the second half might disappoint him.) Next, I showed it to Warburg, who renewed his offer, but wanted some changes made in the book. He liked the chapter on Lawrence, Van Gogh and Nijinsky, and thought it ought to be twice as long. I disliked the idea of re-writing, particularly since I was satisfied with the book. So I asked Gollancz for his views; he said he would be happy to print the book as it stood, and I signed the contract.

In the coffee house I had been taken off washing-up, and was transferred upstairs to serve the coffee. I liked this less, on the whole. I had enjoyed working on the washing-up machine; I could spend hours day-dreaming about the publication of my book. But at least there was no chance to be bored, particularly on Saturdays. When the rush started, a queue of a hundred or so would wait to be served; the four coffee-urns were inadequate; it depended on split-second timing and cool-headed planning to make more coffee as fast as the urns were emptied. When we finally closed the doors, at eleven o'clock, we felt like a defending army that has just repelled a heavy attack. We all seemed close together as we changed out of our white coats. Then I would cycle back through the empty streets, arriving home at half past midnight.

Still, in spite of my preference for the job over any other I had worked at, I basically disliked working at anything but writing. So when Gollancz offered to let me have an advance of £25 immediately (with another £50 to follow before publication), I accepted it, and persuaded the manageress to allow me to work three days a week only. I now settled down to completing *Ritual*. Christmas came; I spent it in Leicester. My mother was now home, looking ten years older, but slowly recovering after five operations. I could now go into the Coleman Road Working Men's Club with my father and be introduced as 'an author'; my position was no longer ambiguous.

After Christmas I decided that it was time to change my lodgings again. This time I had no complaint to make of my landlady, who had treated me very well and put up with my friends at all hours of the day and night. But fifty shillings a week was more than I could afford when I had only a few pounds to last me until publication day the following May. I saw an advertisement on a notice-board in Notting Hill, and rang the number. A girl with a pleasant voice invited me to go and see her. The house was in Chepstow Villas, W.11, on a corner, and was completely dilapidated. It had stood empty for many years, but its owner had now given it to her daughter, Anne Nichols – my potential landlady. She thought of making a living by renting rooms, but since the house was in appalling condition, with peeling wallpaper and shattered windows, she needed someone to help her get it into a state of repair. I explained my need – a very cheap room – and she made me an offer. I could have the upstairs bathroom for a pound a week (it had no bath, only a disused lavatory) if I would help her to get the rest of the house into order. I agreed, and moved in immediately. Bill Hopkins also was interested; he was at this time working as a night editor on *The New York Times*, and wanted to be closer to his office.

It was a freezing January, and I had no furniture. I slept in my sleeping-bag on the bare floorboards of the bathroom, and cooked on a small electric ring. House-decorating was hardly in my line, but I worked hard at it. Anne was a painter, and all kinds of weird Soho characters drifted in and out.

In February Angus Wilson offered to lend me his cottage near Bury St Edmunds, so that I could finish *Ritual* undisturbed. I accepted the offer gratefully, and cycled there on a windy day, with a portable typewriter, borrowed from Laura Del-Rivo, on my bike, and the usual library in my haversack. The cottage stood in the middle of a field, and had no electricity; the gas-mantles worked off calor gas. The day after I arrived it began to snow, and soon it was difficult to get in or out of the place. I worked hard, and managed to finish *Ritual* in two weeks; but I was dissatisfied with it. This was not the novel on which I had worked for so many years. Admittedly, the writing of *The Outsider* had made me feel that I need not pack all my ideas into a novel, so I dropped the Ulyssian system of cross-reference and allusion, and tried to write a more straightforward narrative. It was immensely difficult, for a reason that will be immediately apparent to any novelist. I had written and rewritten it all; some pages had been retyped a dozen times. The final manuscript was barely seventy thousand words long, and yet I had probably written half a million words over five years. All this meant that I could not approach the task with a fresh outlook; I had lost my critical sense completely about some of the older passages. It was like trying to rebuild a house that you have pulled down twenty times, using a mixture of old and new bricks. (In fact, when I came to begin the published version in Hamburg two years later, I found it necessary to forget all earlier versions and write a completely new book.)

However, it was finally finished, and submitted to Gollancz, who declared that he could not print it. The subject – a sadistic sex-killer – was bad enough; but the unending sordidness of the scenes had a profoundly depressing effect on him. He told me that he suspected I was not a novelist, and advised me to begin another philosophical book. Angus Wilson's opinion of the book was more cheering. It had many faults, he said, but he would certainly recommend Warburg to publish it if I would try to correct its structural faults. Warburg agreed to this, and advanced me a badly needed fifty pounds.

When I returned to Chepstow Villas I discovered, to my disgust, that a lavatory in full working order had been installed in my room. My books and other belongings were strewn all over the floor. Anne explained that the sanitary inspector had threatened to throw everyone out unless a lavatory were put in. I moved all my belongings down to a room on the ground floor, and agreed to pay an extra ten shillings a week for it. On the whole, I doubt whether it was worth it – any more than the bathroom had been worth a pound

– but total freedom from the usual landlady interference was important, and I would have been sorry to leave the house. The ground-floor room was slightly larger than the bathroom, so Bill was able to move in too. He was being well paid by *The New York Times*, and I borrowed from him while I waited for advances.

This was a pleasant period. I saw a great many people, spent whole nights awake talking with Bill, and even went to a few parties. I worked at odd jobs spasmodically, when the cash shortage became too serious: a few weeks in the Northumberland Avenue coffee house, a few weeks for the Students' Association, making flags for their flag-day.

Finally, publication day approached. Gollancz told me that a journalist from the *Evening News* wanted to interview me, and I cycled around to see David Wainwright, who had been told about my book by John Connell. David, a quiet, rather shy young man – not at all what I expected for a journalist – was delighted when I told him about Hampstead Heath, and said it was a 'natural' for a story.

Saturday came; I saw a notice in one of the evening papers that mentioned that I could expect a review in *The Observer*. I bought an *Evening News*, but could see no review. I took Joy to the cinema. When we came back, I discovered that my bike had been stolen from outside the house. This seemed inauspicious. That night I woke up and again experienced the 'vastation' feeling – the total absurdity of life, the possibility that all life is only an escape from the horror of death, that human relations are a temporary deception to make us forget the horror. It seemed that each human being is alone; our human companionship is no more protection than the companionship of sheep against the butcher.

The next morning I hurried to the corner and bought *The Observer* and *Sunday Times*, then rushed back home without opening them. I gave Joy the *Sunday Times*, while I read *The Observer*. Philip Toynbee's review was splendid, comparing me to Sartre, and saying that, on the whole, he preferred my style and method. Joy read aloud bits from Connolly's review in the *Times*; it was as good as Toynbee's. At this point someone from downstairs came up to congratulate me on my review in the *Evening News*. Incredulously, we searched through the *News* again, and now found a paragraph by John Connell with a headline: 'A Major Writer – and he's only twenty-four'.

The man from the basement shouted that I was wanted on the phone. It was a friend, ringing to congratulate me. No sooner had I returned upstairs than it rang again; another friend.

The phone rang steadily for a week. The following day – Monday – an immense pile of letters arrived for me; it seemed that every friend I had ever had had decided to write and congratulate me. The *Sunday Times* rang and asked if I would like to do regular reviewing for them at £40 a review. I gasped at the sum. The BBC and television rang and asked when I would be available to make recordings. On Monday evening, David Wainwright's article appeared – a full page, with photograph. Reporters were arriving at a rate of four a day. I had my second expensive restaurant meal with Godfrey Smith of the *Sunday Times* – the first had been with Victor Gollancz.

By a coincidence John Osborne's play *Look Back in Anger* appeared at the Royal Court Theatre the same week that *The Outsider* was published. The *Sunday Times* wrote about the two of us in 'Atticus', and J. B. Priestley wrote an article on us in *The New Statesman*. *The Times* used the phrase 'angry young men' about us, and suddenly a new cult had started. Kingsley Amis and John Wain were added to the list of 'angries'; another young playwright, Michael Hastings (who was only eighteen) had his first play presented at the New Lindsay theatre in Notting Hill Gate, and he too was enrolled by the press into the angry young men. The *Daily Express* approached Hastings, Osborne and myself to contribute to a series called 'Angry Young Men' and to explain why we were angry. I wasn't in the least angry – except about my years of struggle; and now that I was recognised, even this hardly applied. But the *Express* was paying well, so I agreed to write for them.

One thing puzzled and worried me – that in spite of all the praise, I seemed to arouse a violent hostility out of all proportion to my ideas. One evening I joined a group of new acquaintances in a restaurant for supper; we had all been at a party given by Margot Wamesley of *Encounter*. Opposite me was sitting the novelist Constantine FitzGibbon. Margot asked me my opinion of Dylan Thomas, and I replied that I disliked most of his work intensely –

that it was all sound and no meaning. To my amazement FitzGibbon went purple in the face, and began to shout at me and invite me outside for a fight. 'You bloody young upstarts who think you own the world because you've had a lot of publicity...' Margot finally calmed him down, but he glowered sullenly at me for the rest of the evening. I gathered that he had known Thomas, but this was hardly relevant to my criticism of Thomas's poetry. Two evenings later he poured a pint of beer over a friend of mine who was defending me in a Soho pub. This friend, Dan Farson, had written an article about me for the *Daily Mail*, and later began his TV career by interviewing me.

I had grown used to the absurd distortion of my ideas, and to being treated by admiring journalists as if I were an electronic brain. I hated this, for it was like seeing my face in a distorting mirror. After years of thinking of myself as the heir of Eliot and Joyce – both men who belonged to the 'esoteric' tradition and worked quietly in isolation – I now found myself being treated like a film-star, an intellectual prodigy, a boy wonder. It was undoubtedly more satisfactory than being unknown, but it was also a tremendous drain on my energies. Besides, I was flattered by all the offers of lectures that poured in, and accepted them all, travelling in quick succession to Oxford, Cambridge, Eton, Northampton, Leicester and even Glasgow.

In all this, Bill Hopkins played something of the part of a Machiavelli. Like me, he had always admired the combative older-generation of writers, from Victor Hugo to Wells and Shaw. He believed, as they did, that a writer ought to be prepared to be a national influence. He was even more contemptuous than Milton of 'cloistered virtue'; his ideal was a kind of writer-politician, foreshadowed by Shaw in Undershaft. One day a female journalist came to see me when Bill was present; he joined in the arguments with enthusiasm, and expressed a violently anti-feminist point of view. Her article, when it appeared, was scathing; but it quoted all Bill's opinions as if they were mine, and made no mention of Bill.

My success filled Bill with determination to join in the battle. He began writing like a steam-engine on his novel *The Divine and the Decay*, which was immediately accepted by a publisher. Stuart

Holroyd had now finished his *Emergence from Chaos*, which had been accepted by Gollancz.

My own financial success had been considerable. Gollancz had printed a first edition of five thousand copies, but this sold out within a few days of publication. After that, impression followed impression in quick succession. The book went on to sell forty thousand copies in its guinea edition. An American publisher – Houghton Mifflin – accepted it, and published it in September. *Time Magazine* brought out a full page interview with me shortly before publication, and the book quickly became a best-seller in America too.

8

THE SUCCESS PROBLEM

BEING caught up in a 'popular success' is a vertiginous experience, and one that nobody would wish for twice. Of course, every writer dreams of success. But what he dreams is quite different from the reality. I used to read biographies of every writer I could lay my hands on in the local library, and I always galloped through the early pages to get to the moment of break-through; the more spectacular the break-through – Carlyle with *The French Revolution,* Dickens with *Pickwick,* Haggard with *King Solomon's Mines* – the more I read and re-read it, to get its savour. But my success was like nothing I'd imagined. I suppose this was inevitable; for if a book like *The Outsider* became known to a wide public it would have to be for the wrong reasons. This was why success was such an unsatisfying experience. I had always been obsessed with the problem of the meaning of human existence. When I suddenly became clearly aware of this problem – at about thirteen – it seemed to me that no other human being had ever recognised it. Then I discovered an awareness of it in Shaw and Wells and Eliot, and grew excited, and wanted to plunge into the discussion, and it seemed intolerable that it might take years to get into print. When I read Auden and Spender and MacNeice, I raged because it seemed they had betrayed literature to the stupidities of politics. Before I published *The Outsider,* I re-read the manuscript until I knew it by heart, and thought: '*This* should liven things up'.

And then suddenly I was in television studios under arc lights, being encouraged to quarrel with Wolf Mankowitz; or at the opening of an art exhibition in Soho, drinking champagne with a lord whom I was encouraged to call by his Christian name; or at a party in Putney, being pointed out to the guests as a kind of natural curiosity; or being attacked by the television columnist in the *Daily Mirror. What had all this to do with 'The Outsider'?* The book was about Nietzsche's vision on a hill called Leutsch, and the 'vastation' experience of William James, and Nijinsky's 'God is fire in the head', and Van Gogh's 'Misery will never end', and Ivan Karamazov's 'It's not God I reject; I just want to give Him back the entrance ticket.'

It was incredible; it was stupider and madder than anything I could have imagined; it had no relation at all to anything I was interested in. It was a grotesque parody of success. At first, I thought that something might be salvaged from it. I was often asked to lecture: sometimes to adult audiences, sometimes at schools. It ought at least to be possible to find a small group of friends whose interests were the same as my own. I recalled a story of Berdyaev's with nostalgia – of how a group of friends in St Petersburg talked all night, and then when it was proposed that it was time to go home, someone said: 'No, we can't go home yet; we haven't decided whether God exists.' Surely there ought to be a few others of my way of thinking, who believed that Blake was fundamentally right and logical positivism fundamentally wrong?

It seemed not. Lecturing was interesting enough. University audiences were responsive, and a group at Eton kept me talking half the night. But when it was over, it was over. There was no follow-up. And about eighty per cent of the letters I received about *The Outsider* were from cranks, or from people who told me to trust in Jesus, or from people who felt that society was rotten because it didn't think them very important. I actually began to feel revulsion for the themes of *The Outsider,* and wanted to groan when I heard Nietzsche or Dostoevsky mentioned.

No one, I think, has ever found success quite so irrelevant. I felt this was pretty unfair. I've never been much disposed to self-pity – my basic cheerfulness gets in the way – but it *had* been a bloody long struggle from the textile warehouse in Leicester to the publication of *The Outsider*. I'd always been bothered by the suspicion that the struggle *could* end in defeat because the odds were too heavy. Shaw was right when, in *Back to Methuselah,* he defined the basic ailment of the 'short livers' as discouragement. Eight years is not a very long time, but looking back on them, they now seemed half a lifetime – much longer than the ten years that have passed since then. On that Sunday morning when the first reviews appeared,

I thought I'd won; I'd made my point. Then, as the weeks of publicity went by, I realised that whatever else I'd done, I had *not* made my point. The battle had merely been transferred to a new front. I began to recognise the truth of Sartre's statement: Hell is other people.

All this no doubt gives a false impression of what actually happened in the second half of 1956. I didn't go around scowling and muttering 'Morons' under my breath. I went to parties, had friends around to supper, and began *Religion and the Rebel*. I encountered a certain amount of hostility and a fair number of people whom I felt to be morons; but I suppose I liked far more people than I disliked.

All I am trying to convey is that it had nothing whatever to do with *The Outsider*. It was pure waste of time. It would have been a waste of time even without the swing-back, the general decision that *The Outsider* was a grossly over-rated book by a young man with a gift of ready quotation.

For this, in fact, is what did happen. A fortnight after the book appeared, *The Sunday Times* published a note in the gossip column to the effect that Gollancz was log-rolling the book to fame by exaggerating the number of copies he had sold; the size of a Gollancz impression, it said, was something of a joke in the book trade. The writer added that he had no doubt that most of the book's sales were 'furniture sales' – that is, it was bought by people who wanted to leave it around their sitting rooms to show that they were up to date with the intellectual fashions.

What surprised me about this was that *The Sunday Times* had signed me up as a reviewer the day after *The Outsider* appeared. The initial agreement was that I should do six reviews; but after number two, the idea was dropped. This second review contained an attack on logical positivism, and on Ayer in particular. It was an aggressive review, and ended with a deliberate mistranslation of Wittgenstein: 'When you've nothing to say, you'd better keep your mouth shut.' Ayer promptly countered with an acid review of *The Outsider* in *Encounter,* in which I was compared to a dancing dog. The shots were flying and – inevitably – I was getting the worst of it.

What was more disconcerting were the unprovoked attacks. One evening at the Royal Court Theatre I took part in a debate on the modern theatre; Kenneth Tynan was the chairman, and others on the panel were Arthur Miller, John Whiting and Wolf Mankowitz. Within a few minutes of the start of the discussion, Mankowitz suddenly described *The Outsider* as an anthology of quotations; this raised a laugh. Encouraged, Mankowitz kept up this line of attack throughout the evening. The following day, a report in a London evening paper declared: 'Mankowitz played with Wilson like a good natured lion with a mouse'. The next day, I was asked to appear on television to argue the point with Mankowitz. I did, and the discussion was heated but not downright rude. Afterwards I asked Mankowitz who had written the piece in the London evening paper; he reddened, then scowled defiantly and snapped 'I did.'

I was asked to address some kind of a spiritualist society at a Knightsbridge hotel; when I arrived, I discovered they were mostly mild old ladies. A reporter from the *Daily Express* approached me, winked at me, and asked me to come and have a quiet drink. He intimated that we were fellow conspirators among a lot of old tabby cats, and asked me to 'have a go at the old bitches'. I said I couldn't do that – they were my hostesses – but we went on drinking on friendly terms. In my speech after the meal, I said that I was tired of being described as a spokesman of the younger generation; I represented no one but myself. *The Outsider* was a personal statement, and I felt a fraud when it was taken to be an expression of a new anti-establishment attitude.

The next day, the *Daily Express* appeared with a headline: 'Colin Wilson admits he is a Fraud'. I was quoted as saying '*The Outsider* was written with completely false intent...' Two days later, Gollancz's solicitors managed to induce them to print an apology; but I got the feeling that a great many people would be only too happy to dismiss the book as a fraud. In fact, when *The Observer* published, in its Christmas issue, a page by well-known writers stating what they thought to be the most interesting books of the year, *The Outsider* received only one mention, by Arthur Koestler. It read: 'Bubble of the year: *The Outsider*. In which a young man discovers that men of genius are prone to *weltschmerz*.'

Six months after its publication, it was the general opinion among

English intellectuals that *The Outsider* had been a craze that had died a natural death, and that I should now be returned to the obscurity from which I had accidentally emerged. I subscribed to a press cutting bureau, but the cuttings were almost entirely depressing; I got the feeling that every journalist in England wanted to throw his stone on the cairn that covered my dead reputation. The Americans also joined in the fun. No country is more eager to hail celebrity; none more delighted to see its downfall. At a party in London I had met a fat and pleasant-voiced American called Dwight Macdonald, blessed with an attractive wife and a pretty daughter. We got on excellently. One morning, my press cuttings brought me a copy of a review from the *New Yorker* that amounted to a long and vigorous attack on *The Outsider,* signed by Dwight Macdonald. I remained friendly with Macdonald, but I didn't like the way that his review was taken as a general signal for a radical re-estimation of *The Outsider* by his countrymen. It seemed to indicate that even highbrows have a secret hankering after the pleasures of the lynching mob. Soon after the book came out, the American impresario, Sol Hurok, had written to me asking me to do a lecture tour in the States; I refused; I'd had enough of lecturing. But the attacks on *The Outsider* made me consider that it might be an idea to make money while I could; I wrote to Hurok asking him to arrange a tour for me. After a few weeks, he replied that he couldn't raise enough interest in me now to justify the tour. The cairn seemed to get larger daily.

The interesting question presents itself: Why was there such a reaction against me? *The Outsider* is not a fraud; neither is it superficial. It attacks a real problem – one that has poisoned European culture for nearly two centuries – and comes closer to solving it than any similar book (for example, *The Romantic Agony* of Mario Praz). The reason, I think, has nothing to do with the book, and very little to do with me. It has simply to do with what the 'success mechanism' did to me. There is a basic hatred of success in all human beings. It is twice as strong in intellectuals as in other people. We take an irrational delight in seeing the successful toppled from their pedestals. If there existed some magical means of bringing down disaster on successful people, most human beings would seize on it with delight, and mutter incantations against the Beatles, Peter Sellars, Brigit Bardot, John Osborne, J. D. Salinger, Tennessee Williams, Truman Capote... Luckily, most success is built on a secure foundation. There is not much you can do against the Beatles while the fans go on buying their records. But my own success had almost no foundations. There are as few people really qualified to understand *The Outsider* as to understand quantum theory. So when the few 'intellectual' reviewers – Connolly, Toynbee and so on – decided to back out, the book had no court of appeal. It was like declaring a Roman holiday complete with Christians and lions; except that I am not a Christian, and the critics are not lions.

I had noticed one curious thing about most of the successful writers I had met: the more successful they were, the more they seemed to suffer from a persecution complex. I now began to understand why. There is a necessary assumption among intellectuals that all success is achieved by fraud or compromise. One can be very comfortable in England with a moderate reputation and a moderate-sized public. Poets are respectable – provided they are not, like John Betjeman, also fashionable. A novelist who is also a don or a regular reviewer is well liked, because it is clear that he cannot live by writing alone. But the 'successful' are never quite respectable. Even T. S. Eliot's reputation took a downward swing when he became the commercially successful playwright of *The Elder Statesman*.

Inevitably, the result of widespread attacks is to make any writer feel 'insecure'. It cannot be otherwise, unless he is eighty years old and can take the detached view of an adult in a nursery.

I think I had had some training in detachment in the years before I wrote *The Outsider;* but it was not enough to make me feel indifferent to this general view of me as a kind of literary confidence swindler. My resentment was reflected in the early pages of *Religion and the Rebel*: 'The Outsider... lives in a world of apes, whom he detests. He is told that religion consists in loving your neighbour as yourself and in practising the virtues of patience and charity. The most the Outsider can say is that he dislikes his neighbour just a little more than he dislikes himself. Most human beings strike him as so stupid that they might as well be dead...'

The reaction to the attacks is also reflected in the material of

Religion and the Rebel, which goes even further than *The Outsider* in placing the emphasis on mysticism and world-rejection. No doubt this was the reason that certain Catholic journals predicted that I would eventually find myself in the church.

Yet although my position as a writer with a tarnished-tinfoil reputation struck me as absurd – in Camus's sense – I now see that it makes good sense. *The Outsider* was an attack on certain values that are generally held in our society; I thought that the book would place me in the position in which Nietzsche found himself after publishing his *Birth of Tragedy* – that is, of universal rejection. This, in fact, is what happened – but in a roundabout way. And what, in the nature of things, could be more fitting? The epigraph of *The Outsider* is a quotation from *John Bull's Other Island* in which the following exchange takes place:

> KEEGAN: You feel at home in the world, then?
> BROADBENT: Of course. Don't you?
> KEEGAN (from the very depths of his nature): No.

It would have been even more of an absurdity if the reception of *The Outsider* had had the effect of making me feel more at home in the world on which the book is an attack. In that case, *Religion and the Rebel* would have been a hopelessly insincere book. As it was, its sense of world-rejection is stronger than that of *The Outsider*. And I deliberately began the book with an analysis of the career of Scott Fitzgerald to make the point that in the modern world, success can alienate a man as thoroughly as neglect – and perhaps destroy him more efficiently.

I decided that the answer was to get out of London. A correspondent called Hugh Heckstall Smith offered me the use of two rooms in his house near Totnes, Devon, and this seemed a reasonable solution. I had never met Heckstall Smith and knew nothing about him, except that he had been a headmaster, and had written text books on physics for schools. Bill Hopkins decided that he would come with me for a few weeks, and we set off in November. But although Hugh Heckstall Smith turned out to be the soul of amiability, and one of the most interesting and original minds I had encountered, the idea didn't work out. Perhaps it was the cold and damp of November; perhaps it was living away from Joy – not to mention books and music. But after a week or so Bill and I returned to London. I had managed to get well into *Religion and the Rebel* in a fortnight, and Bill had written a chapter of *The Divine and the Decay*.

I have just mentioned music, and I should now add that the one wholly pleasant consequence of 'success' was to be able to afford to buy a gramophone and long-playing records. It took me some months to decide to buy a gramophone; I doubted whether I could afford it. Although *The Outsider* went on to sell some forty thousand copies, both in England and America – which represents about £4,000 in royalties – I never seemed to see any money in a lump sum; every week or so I had to write to Gollancz to ask for another £50 from royalties. A good gramophone would have cost about this sum, so I put off buying one. One day Dan Farson offered me his own picnic-size model for £10; I could afford that. Then I found a bookshop in Notting Hill Gate that sold second-hand records. At about 27/6 each, they seemed a reasonable outlay. I started off buying music I already knew and enjoyed: Mahler's ninth symphony, Brahms's third, Bruckner's fourth, Beethoven's Pastoral, Franck's Symphony, Stravinsky's *Firebird*, Puccini's *Bohème*. I also bought music I didn't know but had always wanted to know – Beethoven's late quartets and the sonata opus 111, Franck's sonata, Shostakovich's piano quintet. Inevitably, I began buying simply for the pleasure of discovery. (At the time of writing, my record collection is in the area of 5,000 LPs, which includes some 300 complete operas.)

I mention all this because the atmosphere of hostility towards me made music an important safety valve. Poetry I find only moderately satisfying, because I am too aware of the poet's personality, and, in most cases, of his weaknesses. One of the penalties of knowing what one wants is a certain lack of patience with poets who complain that the world is too much with them. They declare that life is fundamentally tragic when what they mean is that they prefer self-pity and gentle melancholy to standing up and fighting. A poet should be something of a scientist; if he sees the world as problematic, he should recognise that the peculiar glory of the human mind is its capacity to solve problems. Unfortunately, most poets find that defeat makes better poetic copy than analysis. For this reason I have never been able to share Eliot's admiration for Baudelaire and Mallarmé, and I find it hard to keep patience with Shakespeare. Music, on the other hand, is less explicit about its creator's personality. No one would guess from hearing Bartók's music that he was a neurotic self-betrayer, or from Bruckner's great sweeping symphonies that he was a frustrated little man who made sheep's eyes at servant girls.

So the world of music made a welcome change from the world of Sunday reviewers, and I bought records every other day, until Gollancz explained to me that I would soon have to take a job if I kept on spending money at this rate. Again, I brooded on the idea of moving to the country – I thought the Outer Hebrides would be a good idea. (I have seen them since, and am relieved that it never came to that.)

The move was precipitated by a sudden irruption of publicity. Joy had now moved into my flat in Notting Hill, although she kept on a small room somewhere in the area to which her family could address letters. In early 1957 she went home to Bedford to have her tonsils removed. I went up to see her, and while I was at the hospital her sister picked up a journal I had left on the hall table and opened it casually. Some impatient remarks about her parents aroused her interest, and she read on. There was an entry about a homosexual friend who had talked to me about his problems, and a great deal of discussion of the sexual problems that are the main theme of my *Ritual in the Dark*. Altogether, I think she had an interesting half hour. When I returned I thought she looked at me oddly, but I paid no attention. The storm broke about a week later, when Joy and I were in the Notting Hill flat, giving supper to Gerald Hamilton (the original of Isherwood's Mr Norris). The door burst open, and in strode Joy's mother and father, brother and sister. They announced that they had discovered that Joy was living with me, and then told her that I was a homosexual and had several mistresses. (I am not sure how they reconciled these two statements.) When I discovered that my journal was the source of the trouble, I found it and told them to go ahead and read it. But they were not to be pacified, and Joy's father produced a horsewhip. This was not actually used, for by this time several other tenants, attracted by the uproar, had rushed in. Joy was dragged halfway down the stairs – they had decided to take her home by force – and I hung on to her other hand, trying to pull her back. This tug of war was abandoned when the other tenants joined in on my side, but the uproar went on. Eventually, I rang the police, who arrived quickly, and explained to Joy's parents that since she was over 21 they could do nothing about it, even if I was a potential Jack-the-Ripper. Finally, everyone left except the two of us; but even the peace seemed ominous. Five minutes later, the first of the reporters turned up at the front door – I presume their arrival was somehow associated with Gerald Hamilton's disappearance halfway through the scene. I saw them at the front door and told them the story briefly. Ten minutes later, more reporters arrived, and several cameramen. We rang up Tom Maschler, who lived nearby, and sneaked out of the back door. He put us up overnight, and gave us a chance to discuss the problem quietly. What bothered us most was that her parents might make another attempt to drag her off, perhaps meeting her on her way back from work. She kept repeating: 'They're so innocent.' We decided that we had better leave London for a few days. The next morning we took a train to Devon, and went to stay with Negley Farson, Dan's father.

No doubt this was a mistake; the story would have otherwise died a natural death in a day or so. Only a few newspapers carried small paragraphs about the horsewhipping attempt. But our disappearance drew headlines about 'runaway lovers'. Joy's father handed over my journal to a daily newspaper, which printed brief extracts without my permission. I decided to let another newspaper print long excerpts, to correct the impression given by the previous quotations. (I later used this situation in a novel called *The Man Without a Shadow*.) The press discovered our whereabouts and turned up in droves. We moved on to Ireland, but by this time a few reporters had caught up with us and stuck like limpets.

P. T. Barnum once said that there is no such thing as bad publicity. No doubt this is true if one is running a circus or freak show; but it certainly does not apply to writers. A week of heavy publicity wrecked any remnants of serious reputation that I had left. When I returned to London it was obvious that it would be stupid to delay finding a home in the country. The poet Louis Adeane lived in the room below us, and told us he had a cottage in Cornwall. He had been hoping to return there when he made enough money in London, but the day still seemed far ahead; so in the meantime, we could rent it from him at thirty shillings a week. We went down one weekend to see it. I was not entirely happy about the prospect, because there was no electricity. But a sight of the place changed our minds. It was about two miles outside Mevagissey, a fishing village on the south coast, and had to be approached down a long and bumpy farm track. The cottage was at the bottom of a valley, at the end of which the sea was visible. A noisy stream ran close to the front door. The door of the cottage was surrounded by a trellis covered with dog roses. There was no other house for half a mile. I found myself wondering why I had taken so long to discover that London was intolerable. We left an electrician friend installing a second-hand generator (which we had cause to regret later) and hurried back to London to pack our belongings.

9

AFTER THE DELUGE

ONLY a year before, this would have been my idea of the idyllic life. A cottage within five minutes of a private beach, a wooden hut to work in, with a stream under its window, a small income – adequate for this kind of life – and hundreds of books and records. On sunny mornings, when I worked in the hut with the windows wide open, and the smell of its wood hot and slightly tarry in the sun, and the stream making a noise like heavy rain – so that we could never tell when it was raining – it seemed perfect.

But there was another side to it. My press cuttings were now uniformly hostile. When I had written *The Outsider* I had re-read every page with satisfaction, feeling that this was something that might change the complexion of modern literature – or at any rate, relieve the general atmosphere of brainlessness. Writing *Religion and the Rebel,* I no longer had any reason for optimism. That it would be misunderstood and attacked amounted to a certainty. For years I had been driven by the usual ambition, the desire for success and recognition, to feel oneself a living influence on literature. Now the success had come and gone, and I felt like someone who has missed a train and has the prospect of a night in a waiting room. So the sense of having a home of my own was compensated for by a deeper insecurity. I had always believed that if I could say everything that was in me, recognition would be automatic. Now I'd said it, and I seemed farther than ever from the goal. Obviously, new tactics were demanded. To demonstrate that I was not a flash in the pan, I had to create an immense structure of serious work. It did not enter my head for a moment to doubt that I could create a larger and solider body of work than any writer since Shaw; it seemed obvious that there was no rivalry. Joyce, Wolfe, Hemingway, Mann, Eliot, Greene – all essentially minor figures, crushed by the magnitude of the problem: how to be a great writer in an 'age of anxiety' and neurosis. Of contemporary figures, only Sartre interested me greatly, but his pessimism proved that, for all his intellect, he was another victim of the 'age of defeat'.

The problem was time. How many years would it take – ten, twenty, thirty? It brought on the sense that Wolfe used to get – a feeling of the need to work obsessively, day and night; then I remembered what had happened to Wolfe, and tried to curb my impatience.

The episode of the Royal Court Theatre deepened this sense of pessimism. George Devine, its director, had invited me out to lunch in 1956 and asked me if I would like to write a play. He explained that the Royal Court was the ideal opportunity for a writer like myself, because it was willing to 'nurse' its dramatists; if a play was bad, he would get a few actors to show me why it was bad, and how it could be put right... This was in the period of early success that followed *The Outsider*. On subsequent visits to the Court, I sensed an 'atmosphere', and my friend Sandy Wilson confirmed that there was a general feeling that the Court shouldn't become a showcase for the fraud Wilson. One day, I got a good idea for a play – it seemed tailor-made, a sheer gift – so I invited Devine to lunch and outlined it to him. He told me to go ahead and write it. I finally settled down to writing *The Death of God* at Old Walls – our cottage. Then I sent it to the Court. A month went by, then the play was returned with a printed rejection slip – not even a letter. I wrote to Devine an aggrieved letter, and read it aloud to Bill Hopkins, who was staying with us. Bill's brother Ted was working at this time on the now defunct *News Chronicle,* and Bill asked me if I would allow the *Chronicle* to print my letter as 'an open letter to George Devine', since much of it dealt with the policy of the Court, which I felt to be narrowly left-wing and aggressively anti-intellectual. (Kenneth Tynan made the same point in reviewing a Wesker play, when he said that there could be no doubt that the New Left Wing had its heart in the right place; what worried him was its tiny pin-sized head.) We dictated the letter to Ted over the phone, and Bill phoned it through to some other newspapers, arguing that it should be made as public as possible. What we should both have realised was that the main publicity angle of the story would be that I had had my first play rejected. This is what happened, and one newspaper quoted Ronald Duncan, who had been on the board that rejected the play, as saying that it read like a child's TV serial, and that I ought to be a soap advertisement salesman. (When I met Ronald Duncan some months later we became friends immediately, and he subsequently lost a regular reviewing job by refusing an editor's instruction to 'slam' my second book.)

It seemed that it was impossible for me to receive any good publicity. It was at about this time that Lord Beaverbrook launched a magazine called *Books and Art*. While staying with Negley Farson I had made a recorded interview with Dan, mainly by way of testing out a new tape recorder. A few hundred words of this interview were offered in the first issue of *Books and Art* under a headline 'Colin Wilson talks about: MY GENIUS'. (Dan later claimed that he was responsible neither for the headline nor for the selection of material.) The exchange that justified the title went somewhat as follows:

> DAN: Do you believe that you're a genius?
> MYSELF: I think every writer should work on that assumption. It may prove to be wrong; but without it, no one can produce major work.
> DAN (blandly ignoring my qualification): Are there any other geniuses in England at the moment?
> MYSELF (naming Dan's particular aversion): Bill Hopkins.

A Sunday newspaper carried a paragraph headed 'England's Other Genius', which concluded: 'What has Mr Hopkins published so far? Absolutely nothing.'

So that first year at Old Walls was not entirely happy. I used to walk up to the farm to collect my mail on sunny mornings, and observe with interest that the charm of the countryside completely failed to work for me. For all the pleasure I felt, I might as well have been walking through Manchester on a rainy morning. It was largely, I think, a kind of emotional exhaustion, similar to that which I used to feel when I woke up on Hampstead Heath. There was also a strong ingredient of an ailment I seldom experienced in those earlier days: people poisoning.

In the autumn of 1957, *Religion and the Rebel* finally appeared. On the Sunday morning before publication day – and just about 18 months since my last – I hurried out to buy the newspapers. In Mevagissey *The Observer* was sold out, so I drove ten miles into St Austell. I had been expecting the worst, so it was not as bad as it might have been. In *The Sunday Times,* Raymond Mortimer said mildly that my first book had not been his cup of tea, and that therefore he was hardly qualified to judge my second; having said which, he proceeded to damn it. Philip Toynbee was evidently anxious to redeem the faux pas he had committed in hailing *The Outsider,* and described *Religion and the Rebel* as a rubbish bin. (Another critic who had helped to launch *The Outsider* had already explained to various acquaintances that he had not actually *read* it, but thought it deserved a good review on the strength of its blurb; the acquaintances took care to pass this back to me.)

There was a kind of consolation in all this. My reputation had quite clearly touched rock bottom. It could go no lower. This did not necessarily mean that it now had to rise; but at least it could not fall. So when a newspaper reporter called that afternoon to ask me how it felt to be damned by the critics who had once praised me, I replied truthfully that it was flattering to be the object of so much attention at my age, and that it was something of a relief to be down off the pedestal.

It was very quickly clear that Toynbee's change of heart was regarded by the popular press as a final proof that 'the Wilson phenomenon' had definitely come to an end. The Americans followed suit gleefully, led by *Time,* which described me as a 'scrambled egghead', and quoted Nancy Spain's statement : 'We are sick of the Boy Colin.' About a week after the publication of *Religion and the Rebel* Gollancz asked me to come and see him in London. His advice was that I should simply stop writing for a year or two, and take a job. Whether the attacks on me were reasonable or not, it was obvious that they would go on for a long time. The only thing was to 'vanish' until it was all forgotten. He went on to tell me gloomy cautionary tales about other writers who had started with immense success, and then found themselves unable to live up to it – Ernest Raymond with *Tell England,* Alec Waugh with *The Loom of Youth;* he also told me stories about writers he had published who had started with novels of promise, then published a bad second book and been forgotten. One in particular had been sensible enough to take a job as a schoolteacher, and was willing to spend ten years on his next book if necessary...

After my eight years of factories and offices, all this was as unwelcome as it could be. I had spent too long working for nine hours a day at half-a-crown an hour to even entertain the thought of going back to it. Sometimes I had nightmares in which I could not find a publisher for my next book and had to work in a factory again. So I told him firmly that, whatever happened, I would never take a 'regular job' again. And I went on to see T. S. Eliot at Faber and Faber's, to talk to him about getting Ezra Pound out of gaol (a project upon which Ronald Duncan and I collaborated). He also told me that he thought talent had to be carefully nurtured, and that nothing could be deadlier to it than hasty publication for money. When I left for Cornwall a few days later I was more thoroughly depressed than for the past year. I could see Gollancz's point. In *Religion and the Rebel,* I admitted that I could not see any practical and immediate solution of the 'outsider problem', and ended that book by declaring that it would be my last philosophical book for some time. I had written a play that had been rejected, and had no further ideas for plays. (Although a journalist later plagiarised the main idea of *The Death of God* in a play that reached the West End.) Gollancz had rejected the earlier version of *Ritual in the Dark,* and was obviously disposed to believe that I could not write a novel. Admittedly, *Religion and the Rebel* would probably make a small amount of money – perhaps enough to live on for another year. But then what? You can't live on writing philosophy.

Luckily, there was a diversion. I had been invited to lecture to the university literary society in Oslo. The day we were due to leave was publication day for Bill Hopkins's *The Divine and the Decay.* On the way to the airport I bought a copy of *Books and Bookmen,* which included a two-page extract from the novel and, I seem to remember, a photograph of Bill on the cover. An article on Bill by Dan Farson was less than kind, but on the whole, it was clear that *Books and Bookmen* expected the novel to be a runaway success. I felt a twinge of envy, and vowed to make a really determined attempt on *Ritual in the Dark* the moment I returned from Oslo.

Oslo proved delightful. I was surprised when newspaper reporters asked me about my work and ideas, not about my private life. The hotel was opposite the theatre with statues of Ibsen and Bjornson. There was a feeling that literature was here a subject for excitement, that ideas might be a real influence on the future. The atmosphere was incomparably different from London's. Here, being a writer seemed to involve all the things I used to dream it involved before I published a book: a sense of intellectual vitality, of participating in literary history. I lectured in a vast hall, and the students sat at tables and drank beer as they listened. When I had finished, there was an interval, during which a string quartet played Brahms and Nielsen. Then the discussion started; students went up to the stage and made speeches in which they set out their own views and their objections to what I had said.

But at this point, I should give a brief outline of my lecture, for the ideas that I then developed contained the seed of all I have done since.

I began by summarising the philosophy of Sartre and Heidegger, explaining how their existentialism was essentially static and pessimistic. This was because both of them laid the central emphasis on the idea of *being*. They look at the world around them. It just *is*. They scrutinise it as I might scrutinise the face of a man with whom I am playing poker, to find out what kind of a hand he holds; but, like a good poker player, the world is inscrutable.

This leads Sartre to the view of consciousness as a *nothingness*, a pure observer. I always assume I possess a 'soul' and free-will, particularly if I am a man of action, because I think I can *see* my free-will in action. But if I am left completely alone, without anything to stimulate my vanity or sense of purpose, I quickly sink into boredom. My 'free-will', in fact, is mainly a matter of stimulus from outside; I am an elaborate penny-in-the-slot machine. Once I realise this, I begin to realise what Sartre means when he says that consciousness is a 'nothingness', an emptiness, a mere passive observer. It can do nothing but watch the penny-in-the-slot machine working. For example, if I am alone in a big city where I know no one, I become merely a pair of eyes and a set of senses looking outward at *things*; I feel my emptiness. Admittedly, there are many moments when I feel like slapping myself on the chest and saying 'I *am* somebody.' But if I am honest, I will acknowledge that this is mostly vanity and self-flattery. If I look at myself in a mirror and ask 'Who am I?', I know that the answer is: Merely a face looking at itself, plus a 'history' that has been *given* to me by the circumstances of my life.

This, in summary, is the existentialist position on consciousness and 'being'. I went on to expound briefly Sartre's 'bad-faith', and Heidegger's categories of authentic and inauthentic existence.

But, I went on, my own experience of the world does not agree with this existentialist position. Admittedly, it agrees 99 per cent. But it is the odd 1 per cent that is important here. I have moments – and I think this is true for most healthy people – when I am overwhelmed with a sense of *meaning* outside me, a meaning which is hidden from me because of the dullness of my senses and the extreme complexity of my mechanisms. It may happen on a spring morning, or in listening to music, or even in reading philosophy. I am a philosopher because philosophy gropes at the universe, treats it as a problem that *can* be solved, and that therefore makes me feel that life is inherently more meaningful than I feel when I scrutinise its poker face. Even reading Sartre and Heidegger induces this sense in me. Therefore their final conclusion that the universe is 'meaningless' strikes me as self-contradictory. They feel there *is* a point in groping for meaning, otherwise they would not be philosophising. The centre of my philosophy is *meaning,* not Being.

At this point, my lecture took a new direction, stimulated by the reception of *Religion and the Rebel*. As I observed the attentive faces of my audience, I was aware that what I was now saying was one of the most important issues that human beings could ever face, and that I was grappling with this issue in a way that brought the possibility of a solution into sight. So what did the morons mean about 'woolly minded generalisations' and the rest of it?

One of the strangest things is that a large percentage of human kind seem to be unaware of these issues. Shaw thought so, anyway, when he made Shotover ask: 'What then is to be done? Are we to be kept forever in the mud by these hogs for whom the universe is nothing but a machine for greasing their bristles and filling their snouts.... There is enmity between our seed and their seed. They know it and act on it, strangling our souls. They believe in themselves. When we believe in ourselves, we shall kill them.' And when Hector objects that the 'hogs' are too stupid to use their power, Shotover replies: 'They do use it. We kill the better half of ourselves every day to propitiate them. The knowledge that these people are there to render all our aspirations barren prevents us from having the aspirations.' (I found myself thinking very clearly of certain critics at that moment.)

Whether this distinction between the children of light and the children of darkness is a genuine one or whether, as is more likely, all men are moving in the same direction but at different speeds, is beside the point. In our society, it is a practical distinction that has been very clear since the time of Blake. In our own time, it reappears as the 'outsider problem'. The Boss Mangans (of whom Shotover was speaking) find the materialistic philosophy derived from science much to their liking, and in our own time it has become the philosophy that underlies totalitarian politics and big business — fascism, communism and capitalism alike. Positivistic philosophy also takes it for granted. And since it is difficult for an intelligent man of today to take the church very seriously as a vital force, existentialism remains the only philosophy that tries to get things into perspective, and to emphasise that there *is* a problem of being and a problem of meaning connected with human life. But existentialism spikes its own guns by declaring human life to be meaningless. The positivists can at least claim to take a practical and optimistic view of society. The only hope for a cultural renaissance, as far as I can see, is therefore through a revitalised existentialism that throws firmly out of doors this nonsensical vision of the meaninglessness of human life and the nothingness of human consciousness. Human consciousness is only a 'nothingness' because we are only aware of its top layer. But moments of intensity, whether they come through art, nature, religion or sex, reveal that the real problem is to learn to reconnect ourselves to a *meaning* that is never entirely absent from the world — even for a man suffering from a bad hangover or Sartre's 'nausea'.

This was the essence of my lecture, and I felt aware that I was on the brink of something important. The trouble was that I still couldn't answer the question 'What do we *do* now?' that one of the students threw at me. The 'Where next?' still eluded me. I could only say vaguely that existentialism would have to be revised from the foundations upwards. They asked – very reasonably – how that could save a civilisation faced with the hydrogen bomb and the arms race, and an ideological war based upon misunderstanding. The church had at least once provided a principle of unity.

I could only say that to me is seemed that the worst part of the problem was our cultural bankruptcy. This might seem an unimportant element in the face of such realities as the Hungarian revolution and the H-bomb tests. But what had started as a tendency to mild despair among the intellectuals had now become a torrent of nihilism, neurosis and noisy self-pity.

The discussion went on endlessly. When I had made my reply to questions, I was invited to a students' party at which dons were not allowed to be present unless specifically invited. I had hoped to relax and drink, but instead they sat me in the middle of the room, found chairs or cushions for themselves, and kept on firing questions. I returned to my hotel at four in the morning, feeling mentally exhilarated but physically exhausted, and with the feeling that I was on the point of catching a father and mother of a cold.

The next day, it had me by the throat – the worst cold I'd had in years. I stayed in bed for three days, my eyes streaming and my voice inaudible, reading paperbacks that Joy brought me from the bookshop next door. At the end of the three days, I got up and croaked out a lecture to another society.

Bill wrote to us from Hamburg, where he had gone to write his second novel *Time of Totality* (which was later destroyed in a fire). We decided to break our flight back to London at Hamburg to see him. We found him depressed; his publisher had promised him £10 a week while he wrote the novel; so far, nothing had arrived, and he hadn't eaten for twenty-four hours. We decided to stay overnight, and took him out for a meal. Afterwards we sat in a café in the Stefansplatz and drank hot grog with lemon, and listened to sentimental German music, and quite suddenly felt so happy that we decided to stay on in Hamburg for a further week or so. I suppose the truth was that I was secretly unwilling to return to London. So we booked a room at Bill's *pension* in the Heimhudestrasse, paying for a month in advance, and I settled down to read *From Here to Eternity*.

Bill's girl friend in London had not yet sent him any reviews, and I had only seen *Books and Bookmen*. The morning after we arrived, Bill came into our room for tea, and told me that I let the attacks on *Religion and the Rebel* affect me too much. It was to be expected in an age when success had become associated with film stars, etc. No one had had my kind of overnight success since Byron woke up on the morning he published *Childe Harold* – and look what they did to Byron...

There were letters waiting for him downstairs, but he decided not to open them until we got to the café where we intended to breakfast. On the way there Bill continued in the same vein. One should be strong enough to laugh at attacks... He opened a letter, and pulled out some press clippings. For a moment or two, he read in silence; then his face reddened, his eyes opened wide, and he suddenly exclaimed, in a voice that startled everyone in the café: '*The bastards!*' A moment later, he saw the funny side of it and joined in our laughter.

But the reviews certainly were not funny. Kenneth Allsop has remarked in *The Angry Decade* that in this case the critics seemed to have ignored the tacitly recognised rule that an author's first book should be treated with a certain amount of gentleness. All this was very clearly the result of the 'England's Other Genius' publicity. The critics went in with knives and knuckledusters.

This was not completely unprecedented. Stuart Holroyd's *Emergence from Chaos* had appeared earlier in the same year. A week before it came out a journalist interviewed us both, and then ran an article warning the public that they were about to be subjected to another 'Messiah of the milkbars', who was also a friend of mine; the public was advised not to allow itself to be taken in again. Gollancz, with a kind of miscalculation unusual in him, had stated on the jacket that readers who had enjoyed *The Outsider* would also find this book stimulating; it had, in fact, been started before *The Outsider*...

Emergence from Chaos was not badly received, but this should be qualified by saying that it was hardly received at all. One of the 'posh' Sunday papers ignored it completely; the other commented satirically on Mr Gollancz's propensity to cradle-snatching (the blurb mentioned that Stuart was even younger than myself) and was dismissive about the book. In *Encounter* Maurice Cranston said that it was a better book than *The Outsider* (this was inevitable) and in the popular press there were a few speculations about whether *The Outsider* had inspired *Emergence* or the other way around. *The Guardian* stated baldly that this book revealed that I was Holroyd's disciple, not vice versa, as many had assumed, and did not print a letter from me giving the actual facts about the two books.

Stuart's second book was a kind of autobiographical credo called *Flight and Pursuit*, and it came out some time after *Religion and the Rebel*. Gollancz still hoped for success and promised to make it one of his 'red star' books of the year. The reviews soon made it clear that there was nothing to be done with it. This time the gloves were off. Most reviewers seemed to feel affronted that a man of twenty-five was offering a kind of autobiographical book; the reviewer in *The New Statesman* also found its religious existentialism offensive, and produced a review that deserves to become a classic of destructive criticism, a 'razor-job' of near genius. Hardly any reviewer mentioned the book's ideas; no one attempted to deal seriously with them.

Authors tend to be a self-pitying bunch; but I think it can be taken as a strict statement of fact that few authors ever recover from really destructive attacks early in their career. Strindberg is a case in point. The facts, in any case, speak for themselves. Bill Hopkins published *The Divine and the Decay* in 1957, and has published nothing since; Stuart Holroyd published *Flight and Pursuit* in 1958, and has also published nothing since. Both have become successful in other fields – Stuart Holroyd as head of a language school, Bill as an expert on antiques.

It was a pity. There can be no doubt that both were victims of my publicity. I am glad they bear me no grudge for this. In my own opinion *The Divine and the Decay* is an important and exciting novel, in spite of some faults; there can be no doubt, I think, that if it had been published in 1955 instead of 1957, it would have been regarded as the work of an exciting, if rather off-beat writer, as much an 'original' as the author of *Lord of the Flies*. I have explained my reasons for these views in an appendix to *Beyond the Outsider*.

We stayed in Hamburg until Christmas – about a month in all. The alienness of foreign towns used to produce in me a sense of loss of identity; in the autumn of 1957, I was glad to lose my identity for a month.

10
STARTING AGAIN

BACK at Old Walls, nothing had changed, except that the damp had got through a wall and ruined the covers of a set of *Britannica*, and rats had found a way into the place under the kitchen sink. (The rodent operator disposed of them with bran mixed with arsenic.) Before I left, I had felt punch-drunk and dazed; now I felt ready to start all over again. Once again my optimism came to the surface. The new conditions – notoriety and hostility – had taken a lot of getting used to; but the inoculation had 'taken', and the swelling had gone down. Besides, Bill had given me an excellent idea for *Ritual*: to lay the opening scene in Richard Buckle's Diaghilev exhibition, which I had seen twice in 1953, and to use Diaghilev's curious scent, Mitsouko, as a kind of motif in the novel. As soon as I started, I knew that I had taken the major step; the book was 'moving' this time. What was more important, the whole idea of the book began to unfold in my mind, with all its implications, which led on to other implications. The 'creative urge' was back; I had not felt it truly since I had written *The Outsider*. It requires a sense of undivided attention upon the object, and while I wrote *Religion and the Rebel* I was constantly aware of critics breathing down the back of my neck.

We did little in 1958. I stayed quietly at Old Walls, went on writing *Ritual,* and kept out of the news.

I should say something here about this new version of *Ritual*. It had little resemblance to the book as originally conceived. The fundamental ideas were the same, but my natural optimism was beginning to change all the emphases.

The attitude of the modern writer to his world tends to be one of hostility. Dickens obviously loved the world he lived in, in spite of the Gradgrinds and Squeerses and Scrooges. But then, Dickens was no realist; his people often seem to be no more than shiny, beautifully-painted puppets. With Lawrence and Joyce the note of aggressive hostility creeps in; in any book of Lawrence's we are aware of Lawrence the disgruntled outsider, hating about fifty per cent of what he writes about. *Ulysses* makes it equally clear that Stephen Dedalus was a disgruntled outsider, and reaches a climax of violent rejection of everything and everybody in the Night Town scene. But the point to be noted is that *Ulysses* was a tour de force, and the night town scene is its climax; after *Ulysses,* Joyce was no longer the rejected misfit; he had become Europe's foremost novelist. And in the same way, Eliot became the foremost poet of his time by expressing 'the disgust of a generation'.

This lesson was not lost on their contemporaries. Faulkner began as an imitator of Aldous Huxley, trying to write wittily of the arty set; in no time at all, he had made 'gloom and doom' his stock in trade. His novels are as unrealistic and melodramatic as Dickens's, but the melodrama is now used to express life-hatred. The same is true of Graham Greene. Today, this attitude has been taken to a certain limit of absurdity by writers like Genêt, Beckett, and William Burroughs.

Now there is nothing wrong with pessimism and life-hatred, provided it is honest and perceptive. At least it is a sign of seriousness. (The other night, I read fifty pages of *The Naked Lunch* and dropped it in disgust; then I read a few chapters of Noel Coward's autobiography, and found myself looking at *The Naked Lunch* with positive sympathy.) But I think it is significant that many of these pessimistic writers, when examined closely, prove to be curiously undeveloped personalities. Dickens was a man of affairs with a strongly practical side to his character; once, when he was involved in a train wreck, he took charge of the rescue operations. Faulkner spent a great deal of his life drunk; most of the anecdotes concerning him emphasise his tremendous capacity for whisky. The same is true of Hemingway, and again of Dylan Thomas and Scott Fitzgerald. Every book about Lawrence emphasizes the spoilt-child streak in him. People who met Joyce were also surprised by his curiously un-adult character; he lived in the past and told jokes that dated back to his childhood. William Burroughs makes no attempt to hide that *The Naked Lunch* was written under the influence of drugs.

It seems to me that pessimism and world-rejection is a natural stage in the development of any serious writer; even G. K. Chesterton went through such a phase in his teens. But if these attitudes stay around for a lifetime, then it is a sign of lifelong adolescence. (No one who has studied De Sade, for example, can doubt that he was still fifteen when he died at the age of seventy-four.)

This has certainly been my own experience. In my early teens I was influenced by Shaw, Chesterton and Dickens, and thought Anatole France's *Thais* the greatest novel ever written. By about the age of seventeen, the optimism was flagging badly – the expectation of fame, admiration, disciples, triumphant first nights. One night, I read a long, Jamesian story to a literary society, and they yawned and chattered all the way through it; so I went home and wrote a sort of bitter nightmare fantasy in the manner of Joyce's Night Town scene. From then on I worked in the spirit of a dynamiter – in short, in the modern spirit. I learned my Eliot, Joyce and Faulkner by heart. I particularly admired a story called *Christ in Concrete* by Pietro di Donati, which describes the collapse of a building and goes into detail about the agonies of the people being slowly crushed to death. (At the same time, I noted that Donati had never written anything else of any interest. His contribution consisted in this one symbol of modern violence.) The early versions of *Ritual* were all darkness and violence, and its Jack-the-Ripper theme was only introduced at a fairly late stage as another symbol of violence.

After the RAF I had already found my attitude changing; Eliot's poetry no longer struck any deep chord in me. I scrawled in my copy of his poems 'Of honest mind but of low vitality' – patronising and absurd, no doubt, but still fundamentally true. And rather against my will, *Ritual* got cheerfuller and cheerfuller. I also began to find that I enjoyed story telling – I enjoyed a plot for its own sake, quite apart from its 'symbols'. Its first completed version shocked Victor Gollancz – and my agent Curtis Brown – because it was still too full of determined attempts to take the reader by the throat. But the second version was begun after the success of *The Outsider,* and by this time my natural optimism was back at full strength, and I felt no inclination to take the reader by the throat and shake him. I enjoyed telling the story, I enjoyed developing the ideas; and if the style still owed rather much to Hemingway and Joyce, this was inevitable, considering that it had been under way for nine years.

Friends have occasionally protested that my novels after *Ritual* lost a certain obsessional quality. I know this to be true, and feel it is as it should be; they express my natural attitude. The obsession with ideas is still there, the obsession with the 'question of being', the *lebensfrage*; but the desire to paint the world black has vanished. Gollancz said of my second novel *Adrift in Soho* that it had 'the *perpetuum mobile* quality of a Viennese waltz', while a puzzled reviewer said of *The World of Violence* : 'It seems in places to be intentionally comic'. The generally optimistic atmosphere of *Necessary Doubt* so baffled American reviewers that they assumed it to be a deliberate parody of the classical British detective novel. (In fact, it owes less to Conan Doyle than to Dürrenmatt.)

But to return to 1958. Another project occupied me on and off at intervals, a book to be written with Bill Hopkins and Stuart Holroyd on the subject of 'the vanishing hero'. Bill proposed to deal with the political aspect, Stuart with the religious aspect, and I with the literary aspect. Then Negley Farson introduced me to David Riesman's book *The Lonely Crowd,* whose theme is that the 'inner directed' man is vanishing from American society. I saw its connection with my Outsider theme, and wrote *The Age of Defeat* in a few weeks, even though writing it seemed a waste of time when our bank account was nearly empty. Something important had struck me : that what I was trying to do was to create a new existentialism. The existentialism of Heidegger, Sartre and Camus is no more than a philosophical statement of the *social* problem that is expressed by Riesman in *The Lonely Crowd,* by Galbraith in *The Affluent Society* and Whyte in *The Organisation Man.* Now no one would expect a sociologist to come up with solutions to the problem; he is mainly an observer. But existentialism *can* be accused of shirking its responsibilities. It is an attempt to create some kind of replacement for the religious faith that has been undermined by the age of science; but in fact, it offers no kind of comfort. 'It is meaningless that we live; it is meaningless that we die', says Sartre. Now I have never subscribed to this view. In spite of 'vastations', I have always regarded life as fundamentally meaningful. The trouble is that man seems somehow cut off from the source of 'power, meaning and purpose', and his problem is to find out why. It followed that my own existentialism is optimistic in nature; and yet writing about how Sartre and Camus had reached their negative conclusions, I could see no way to avoid them. My problem was to think out my own existentialism in detail.

I sent *The Age of Defeat* to Gollancz to read over Christmas, and went back to *Ritual*. In the New Year, he wrote to say he liked the book, and to ask if I would be willing to publish it on its own. By way of an inducement, he offered me an advance of £500 – just about five times what I had expected to make out of it – and pointed out that my American publisher would almost certainly offer the same. I asked Bill and Stuart their views; neither had even begun their essays, so they both advised me to accept the offer.

The year began inauspiciously, in spite of this. When we moved into Old Walls, Louis Adeane – who rented it from the farm – had told us that we could have it for two years, and that if his situation was unchanged at the end of that time, then we could stay on. Now Louis wrote to remind us that our 'lease' would be up in a few weeks. I sent back a letter by return, reminding him that he had provisionally agreed to an extension. But he is a bad letter writer, and when we had no reply after a week, we decided we had better start looking for somewhere else. Or rather, I should say, we decided that Joy should start looking for somewhere else. The idea of house-hunting somehow aroused dormant neuroses in me. No doubt this was really the motive behind the decision to look for another house. After years spent in lodgings where the landlady was likely to leave unpleasant notes out on the table, I had become thin-skinned, and the least breath of insecurity was enough to make me contemplate violent upheavals. Within a week, Joy had spotted the house in Gorran Haven. As she described it to me, it sounded too good to be true: standing on a hill above the sea, with a view of about fifty miles of horizon, and approached by a long drive – which meant that we would be almost as isolated as at Old Walls, without the disadvantage of three farm gates and deep mud in the winter. A retired couple had had it built only three years before; but they were town dwellers, and found the quiet of the countryside too much for them. I looked over it and liked it. The price was more than I thought we could afford, but some unexpected royalties arrived, and together with the advances on *The Age of Defeat,* these made up the necessary sum.

It was still a gamble. *Ritual* was now finished, but I knew that Gollancz was inclined to be prudish about books dealing with sexual violence; if he rejected it, it might be difficult to place. However, we moved in, and invited my parents to live with us – as I have related in the first chapter. The day after we moved in, Gollancz rang me to say that he had read *Ritual* straight through, thought it excellent, and would pay me an immediate advance. We all heaved a deep sigh of relief. Admittedly, he wanted certain things cutting out. The book is about a sadist, but he thought this should be played down. I was so relieved to have the book accepted that I would have agreed to anything. I am now sorry that I allowed the cuts. They were small ones, and were not particularly hair-raising; most readers would not have noticed them. But they made clear the central idea of the book. When I wrote a preface to the Norwegian edition of *Ritual,* showing its relation to the ideas of my 'philosophical' books, I found it necessary to mention the 'censored' material to show exactly what I was trying to do.

I was not looking forward to the publication of *The Age of Defeat.* It had been two years since *Religion and the Rebel* had been hatcheted to death, and in that time I had managed to avoid publicity. But there had been no noticeable change in the tone of press-cuttings. My name still got mentioned if someone needed a symbol of intellectual pretentiousness, or unfounded generalisation, or an example of how hysteria can make a reputation overnight. I concluded – rightly, I think – that the public does not bother to change its views once it has someone comfortably pigeon-holed. I felt *The Age of Defeat* to be a good book with some important ideas; but then, so were *The Outsider* and *Religion and the Rebel,* and it hadn't made any difference to them. They could still be dismissed as pretentious rubbish by popular journalists who would find Joad's *Guide to Philosophy* intellectually fatiguing.

On publication day, I realised there was no cause for nervousness – and none for rejoicing either. Reviews had lost the edge of violence; they tended to be polite and dismissive. Cyril Connolly, who had praised *The Outsider* and avoided reviewing *Religion and the Rebel,* gave it a full-length review, but was obviously unable to stifle his boredom; he described it as a kind of literary sight-seeing tour. There seemed to be an unstated feeling that the 'Colin Wilson story' should have ended after *Religion and the Rebel,* and it was tiresome to get another chapter. But *The Times* reviewer remarked that I was obviously 'here to stay'. I muttered: 'He's damned right I am.' Whether they liked it or not.

But it would be wrong to give the impression that I had developed a chip-on-the-shoulder attitude about the critics. I've always been contemptuous of writers who let the critics affect them to the extent of raging in public. Even Shaw, I think, would have been well advised to keep back his 'First aid to reviewers' introduction to *The Intelligent Woman's Guide to Socialism.* It reveals an inability to see in perspective. If a writer's work is going to survive, his readers of the next generation will find this bickering tiresome anyway. Besides, it shows that the writer's attention is in the wrong place: on the public and the effect of his books instead of on his own development.

I personally feel that the story of what happened after the publication of *The Outsider* is at least as interesting as what went before it. I have tried to tell it accurately. I must admit that during the 1956–1958 period I felt badly treated. On the other hand, I've always had an optimistic temperament, a basic feeling that the gods mean well by me, as well as several years' training in getting on with the work in hand and ignoring other people. In retrospect, I'm not sure that what happened after *The Outsider* was not the best thing that could have happened to me. It has often been said that the success of *The Outsider* was a fluke, since a book of that sort could hardly be expected to have a general appeal. I don't agree. There have been equally unlikely best sellers – Galbraith's *Affluent Society* and Koestler's *Act of Creation,* for example. Secondly, *The Outsider* was bound to make me some reputation. Whatever its faults (and I personally don't think it had many) it was bound to make an impact as a lively and controversial book; and since its author was unknown, it *had* to have the effect of making him known. If it had simply been quietly and favourably reviewed, and sold three thousand copies, I would have remained *persona grata* with the establishment, and would almost certainly not have felt the need for the self-searchings that produced *Religion and the Rebel* and *The Age of Defeat*. As it was, the few weeks of approval that followed publication of *The Outsider* seemed to paralyse my impetus. When I read the following paragraph from Emil Reich's book on Hungarian literature, I understood exactly what he meant:

> 'Charles Hugo ... is one of the numerous Titans of the Hungarian capital who cannot do anything halfway creditable unless they fail to gain reputation. No sooner do they become "famous" than they cease to be interesting or productive. Hugo's *Banker and Baron* had not only a great, but an extraordinary success. Not only incense was strewn before the poet, but, to use Lessing's phrase, the very censer was hurled at his head. The enthusiastic crowds carried the author bodily from the theatre to his favourite café. This unhinged poor Hugo's mental equilibrium. He considered himself a second Victor Hugo; and so never wrote any other great drama.' (p. 216.)

Well, I was never carried shoulder high to my favourite café, but I think that the full battery of attention of the press, television and radio must produce an approximation to the sensation. Writing is a delicate internal mechanism, like digestion, and it is easily upset by self-consciousness. On the whole, I think things worked out well. The feeling that no one much cared about what I was doing led me to give my full attention to the task of creating a new form of existentialism.

Ritual in the Dark appeared in 1960, and sold a great deal better than anything since *The Outsider*. This was partly due, I think, to an excellent review in *The Sunday Times* by Dame Edith Sitwell, who had also praised *The Outsider* before its publication.

There were signs that some of the hostility was dying down. I was asked to talk about the book on a television programme compèred by Jack Lambert of *The Sunday Times*. When I arrived at the hotel in Birmingham I was slightly dismayed to discover that I was to be interviewed by Christopher Logue. I have mentioned meeting Logue in Paris in 1953, when he put himself out to be helpful to myself and Bill Hopkins. After *The Outsider* came out I met him in London, and was surprised to find his attitude completely changed – he seemed irritable and hostile. In a letter to the *New Statesman*, he described me as a 'filthy fascist beast'; since he included T. S. Eliot and Graham Greene in this category, I think it meant mainly that he associated an anti-humanist attitude with Franco and Salazar. Later, when Stuart Holroyd presented a rather bad and pseudo-religious play called *The Tenth Chance* at the Royal Court (in a Sunday performance), Logue was involved in a disturbance in the theatre and a subsequent quarrel with myself and Stuart Holroyd in the pub next door – about which I shall not go into detail, as it is best forgotten.

So I didn't feel particularly cheerful to find that Logue was due to interview me. However, I was disposed to sympathy because the rest of the television team (I have forgotten who they were) were so clearly prepared to dislike Logue even before he arrived. His reputation as a left-wing fire-eater who modelled himself on Brecht was by this time well-known. As soon as Logue arrived, he sensed this hostility, and reacted accordingly; he spent the evening wearing a slightly sneering 'I don't give a damn for the lot of you' expression. Remembering his kindness in Paris, I put myself out to show myself sympathetic, and he became appreciably less irritable. The next morning, we rehearsed the programme. Logue asked me if I was satisfied with the book. I said no; it wasn't anything like my original conception of it, and in certain ways I thought it was awful. As soon as the rehearsal was over, Logue gripped my arm and said fiercely: 'Now listen, you're not going to say that stuff about the book being awful. It's not. Anyway, even if it was, it would affect your sales to say so on television.' So I dropped the self-criticism, and felt the revival of a certain affection for Logue.

But although *Ritual in the Dark* sold fairly well, and was the first of my books to go into paperbacks, the reviews continued to be hostile – with the exception of Dame Edith's. Before publication a film company had expressed interest in it, and a sum of £25,000 was mentioned. It would have enabled me to work at my 'new existentialism' for the next ten years without bothering about publishing. I think the dismissive reviews discouraged the film company; to my disgust – and that of my bank manager – the deal collapsed.

This business of money was a considerable nuisance. Nothing is more difficult today than to live by writing, unless your name is one that automatically leaps on to the best-seller charts. A novelist who churned out a novel a year might reckon to make anything between £100 and £1,500 a year. The latter sum is adequate; but as most writers are extravagant by nature – they hanker after good food and comfortable travel – it is certainly not enough to allow complete freedom of mind. As to myself, I find travel a bore, but have an enormous appetite for books and music, which are quite as expensive when bought in quantity. I also enjoy good wine, and like to be able to offer it to my friends when they come over to listen to records. A book like *The Age of Defeat* might, with luck, make a thousand pounds; a novel like *Adrift in Soho* perhaps twice that, but probably less. A writer who produced a book every three years (as many writers do) would obviously make less money than any navvy or dustbin man. And this is provided he has enough reputation to guarantee a minimum sale. Otherwise he may make no more than the £100 advance on a novel. It can be seen why there is no reason for anyone to envy a writer – even a relatively successful one.

Luckily, I enjoy writing. The more one develops a philosophy, a line of thinking, the wider its implications become, just as the largest countries have the most neighbours. *Ritual in the Dark* was a book about meaning and the search for meaning; it was about the paradox that man's greatest driving force is the need for freedom, yet he doesn't know what to do with it when he has it. The hero of *Ritual* is obsessed by the feeling that there *is* meaning in human existence, and that it is accessible to the mind – if only the mind knew the right way to go about finding it. One of the commonest 'meaning experiences' comes through sex, and therefore sex makes a valuable *starting point* for the search for meaning. (I italicise 'starting point' because it seems to me that nothing can be more futile than sex carried on as a kind of vocation – as by Casanova or Frank Harris.)

In a more recent novel, *The Glass Cage* (written in 1965), I try to take the problem a stage further, deliberately constructing a plot that parallels that of *Ritual,* but with a Blakeian mystic in the place of Gerard Sorme. The idea came to me as I was walking along the Portobello Road, thinking about the 'nude murders' along the Thames – the sixth victim had just been found. It suddenly struck me that Sorme made one fundamental error of logic. He assumed that his strictly rational and empirical attitude towards experience is the only one possible for an honest thinker. But the strictest rationalist lives upon certain unstated assumptions. The most important of these is his assumption of continuity. He assumes that he will not only breathe out the breath he is now breathing in, but that he will be alive tomorrow and in a week's time. You might reply: 'Why not? The odds are high in his favour'. But that is not the point. He is not calculating on odds. His forward-drive is based on a kind of intuitive *certainty,* that goes beyond the possibility that he might die of heart failure at any moment, or even the knowledge that he undoubtedly *will* die of old age within fifty years or so. Is this just blindness and stupidity? A 'pure rationalist' would say Yes; a mystic would say No. It could be animal stupidity – or an evolutionary purpose that goes beyond conscious knowledge.

Besides, it *is* possible to have some knowledge of the future. My friend Mark Bredin, a brilliant pianist, was once driving along the Bayswater Road in a taxi after a concert. While still a hundred yards from Queensway, he suddenly knew, with absolute certainty, that the taxi would collide with another taxi at Queensway. But the idea of warning the driver seemed so absurd that he sat still. At Queensway, a taxi tried to rush the lights, and hit them side-on, exactly as he had known it would happen.

I have never had any similar experience. But I have experienced vague certainties at odd moments, and they have always been justified. My only 'premonition of disaster' came one day when I intended taking some friends out for a run in a speed boat; an hour later, trying to land on a beach, the engine cut out, and before I could start it, we were caught by a breaking wave and thrown on the rocks. No one was hurt, but the boat was almost a write-off.

So I am inclined to believe that our sense of continuity is not an illusion; it is the result of the operation of a kind of mental radar. For most of us, the sheer triviality of our lives, our preoccupation with the immediate, deadens its operation. In sketching the character of Damon Reade in *The Glass Cage* I wanted to show a man who has developed his 'radar' by simply concentrating upon what he considers to be the underlying reality of experience, and working upon the assumption that the universe means well by him. Reade knows intuitively that the human will is something deeper than personal self-assertion or calculated effort. It is the invisible part of our total being, like the part of the iceberg below water, and is inaccessible to ordinary conscious demands.

I enjoy writing novels. They are far more satisfying to write than philosophy. When I try to analyse this satisfaction, I realise that it is based on a kind of self-assertion. All young writers are inclined to put their friends and relatives into their fiction, because it flatters the ego to pin down acquaintances like butterflies. There is a very similar – although less egotistic – satisfaction in pinning down experience in the same way. Basically, and at its best, it is a kind of god-like sensation. The painter takes pleasure in capturing something of nature; if he could, he would create matter out of empty air; painting is a second-best. Writing poetry or novels is another way of 'permanising' the passing moment, universalising your unique individual experience. I find that true whether I am writing a personal, semi-autobiographical kind of novel like *Adrift in Soho* or *The World of Violence,* or total fantasy, as in *Necessary Doubt* or *The Mind Parasites.*

For me, there is another, and even more basic, reason for writing novels. They are also a manner of philosophising. I do not mean this in the obvious sense – of introducing ideas into a novel. Ever since Hamann, existentialists have been dissatisfied with reason as an instrument for grasping the nature of existence. Words conjure up concepts, and concepts often libel reality as a bad photograph might libel a beautiful woman. It is easy to stumble into the pessimism of Kierkegaard, into feeling that philosophy is the intellectual's favourite way of lying to himself. But then, Kierkegaard was a very bad novelist. Philosophy may be only a shadow of the reality it tries to grasp, but the novel is altogether more satisfactory. I am almost tempted to generalise and say that no philosopher is qualified to do his job unless he is also a novelist. Whitehead knew that philosophy has to throw off the tyranny of concepts, and try to break through to the reality of *all* experience, 'experience drunk and experience sober, experience religious and experience irreligious...' And yet this is precisely what Whitehead's stiff and abstract language fails to convey. Shaw once said he would have given any dozen of Shakespeare's plays for one of the prefaces he ought to have written. I would certainly exchange any of the works of Whitehead or Wittgenstein for the novels they ought to have written.

I have spoken of *The Glass Cage* at this point because it marks such a considerable change in my outlook.

I first became clearly aware of this change in 1961, on a lecture tour of the United States. I did this tour mainly because I needed the money. I hated the idea of leaving Joy and my year-old daughter for three months. I am a bad traveller. People bore me; change of scenery stimulates me for a short time only, then I want to lock myself into a hotel room with a pile of books and writing paper. I get no immediate pleasure from the presence of an audience either. So for the first week or two of my tour, I was bored and depressed. Then I began to find that the challenge of compressing my ideas into a forty-minute lecture was acting as a stimulant. The ideas began to emit a kind of light of their own. And then, one morning, I suddenly realised that I had 'broken through'. William James has described the feeling: 'We have a thought, or we perform an act, repeatedly, but on a certain day, the real meaning of the thought peals through us for the first time...' I was suddenly able to see my ideas as a whole. And I realised that I had solved the problem – that I had held the solution all the time. I was no longer in the *cul de sac* of Sartre and the existentialists.

In an odd way, my break-through frightened me. I suddenly felt like a bank messenger carrying a million pounds in notes. It was clear that what I had to do was to hurry home and get this all down on paper as quickly as possible.

But when it came to it, it took me four more years to get them on to paper. For it was a problem of compression – of presenting an outline so clearly that it would be impossible to escape its conclusions. *An Introduction to the New Existentialism* was rewritten half a dozen times before its appearance in 1966. (Typically, it was largely ignored by the British press; none of the 'posh' Sundays bothered to review it.) It seemed to me as I wrote it, that it represented a turning point in the stream of western philosophy. I reread it the other day – two years after completing the final version – and this still seemed true. For a quarter of a century, western philosophy has been divided between two negative attitudes: Logical empiricism and existentialism. Logical positivism declares that it is meaningless to ask questions about the meaning of human existence. Existentialism says the *question* is not meaningless, but existence itself is meaningless. So the choice lies between two forms of pessimism. My work has shown that there are radical errors in existentialism, and that it is loose thinking that has led to the pessimism of Sartre, Heidegger and Jaspers. I have produced the only acceptable alternative to these two unacceptable philosophies.

Since the 180 pages of the *Introduction* took four years to write, it is obviously impossible for me to offer a 'summary' here. All the same, this book would be incomplete without some attempt at a sketch.

A personal approach might simplify this. Obviously I have always been preoccupied with the problem of the 'two worlds' – the world of everyday experience, and the world of the mind. I have always been obsessed by Axel's 'As for living, our servants can do that for us.' I do not particularly like 'living'. It bores me.

The romantics felt the same. But they jumped to the conclusion that to reject 'living' means to choose death. This is careless thinking, of the kind that Ryle attacks in *The Concept of Mind*. In the strictest sense, there are not two worlds, but two viewpoints. The worm and the eagle see the same world, but from such different angles that it is convenient to speak of a bird's-eye view and a worm's-eye view as if they were different worlds.

Man is an animal; but he is an animal with his foot already in a different world. A tiny percentage of human beings, the evolutionary spearhead of the race, reject mere 'living' – that is to say, the collective life-world of human society. This 'animal world' is somehow futile and circular. It won't *take* man's sense of purpose, any more than a five volt wire will take a hundred volt current. If your main interest is money, you can have an interesting time becoming a millionaire; but after that, you have reached a dead end. It doesn't make any difference whether your income is a *thousand* pounds a week or ten thousand pounds a week; you can't do any more with it. If you are a lover of food, you are in the same situation. Once you can eat twice a day in one of the world's best restaurants, you have reached a dead end. The room can be piled up to the ceiling with food, but you won't want to touch it. If you are a Casanova-type, you reach your limit with a dozen or so mistresses. There is no point in raising your score to a hundred, because there's nothing more you can do with them. It is the problem of Alexander crying for fresh worlds to conquer. The 'animal world', like the earth we live on, is circular; go far enough, and you arrive back where you started.

Our experience of the world of the mind gives us a completely different intuition. Once you enter the world of science or mathematics or philosophy, endless plains open around you. The more you learn, the more fascinating the whole thing becomes. The same is true of the world of poetry or painting or music. Operating in this sphere, the mind is capable of achieving a steadily mounting intensity. There is no limit. As Wells said, the brain is man's true domain, just as water is the fish's and air the bird's.

Here the problem arises, the problem that defeated the romantics, and then the existentialists; the problem summarised in *Faust*. After an hour or so in this world of the mind, man is exhausted and defeated. You can see this if you simply try to finish a long book before going to sleep. It is not only your eyes that get tired. You feel a sort of spiritual indigestion, a deterioration of the will, *a sinking of vitality.*

Julian Huxley once declared that, just as there is an 'absolute' gap between dead matter and the lowest living animals, so there is an equally absolute gap between 'animal matter' and 'human matter'. In other words, you might compare dead matter to a straight line, which possesses length but no thickness – existence, but no freedom. A worm could be compared to a square, for it has this extra dimension of freedom, of life. Yet a worm's 'freedom' is extremely limited, almost non-existent; it is little more than a self-reproductive machine. Man has this extra dimension again, this dimension of the mind. An animal is stuck firmly in the present;

it has virtually no past or future. Man's mind can 'contemplate the universe', search for truth, devote itself to mathematics.

I cannot agree entirely with Sir Julian. Man *does not yet* possess this third dimension. The 'Dark Room' experiments prove this conclusively. Place a man in an entirely black and soundless room, and he goes to pieces in a matter of days – sometimes hours. He still belongs 99 per cent to the physical world, and needs its constant stimuli to keep him 'up to the mark'. If he were truly a creature of the mind, this would not be true; he would welcome the Black Room as an ideal opportunity to devote himself to exploring his mind and the endless universe of ideas.

We *know* that the inner-world of the mind is as vast as the external universe. We have only to take a dose of mescalin to realise this. One day, man will be able to travel as freely in this world as he now does in the physical world. But for various reasons, this inner-world is largely inaccessible to him at present.

Now these conclusions are the basic reason that existentialism has ended in a *cul de sac*. Man is a slave of contingency, says Sartre – of this physical world. His freedom is real, but extremely limited, and cannot be increased. So the best he can do is to aim at universal justice, love his fellow man, and pray for the extermination of the *bourgeois*.

But is it true that man's freedom cannot be increased? The romantics despaired because their moments of freedom seemed to come and go without reason. If this is so, then the human predicament is paradoxical and tragic.

Consider this from another angle. The scientists of the 19th century were swept away with enthusiasm for the power of the human mind. They declared: 'Man's reason has overcome all obstacles. If he continues in this way, he cannot fail to become perfect one day – perhaps even a god'. The romantics – and later the existentialists – replied with justifiable contempt: 'You are ignoring the major problem. Man's reason cannot be applied to his most important problem: himself. Man is bored, war-like, self-contradictory, hopelessly confused. Thought may be all-powerful, but he is a mere thinking reed, faced continually by the facts of his pain, his weakness and his ultimate death'. And Goethe, in Faust, created the classic symbol of the insufficiency of knowledge.

There, indeed, is the problem, and this is how the question has stood for nearly two hundred years. But anyone who has ever known the ecstasy of discovering the tremendous halls of science *cannot* accept that it is all self-delusion. To begin with, science itself is only the most highly organised form of the basic drive of all life: that striving to conquer. To deny science is to deny life itself; for the moment life appears, it proceeds to struggle, to try to assimilate dead matter. The only really logical denial of science is the view of the Buddhist, that life itself is evil, and that the best thing would be for the universe to return to nothingness.

And so, we must take the most difficult step ever taken by the human mind: the decision that the weaknesses and imperfections of the human mind can be remedied, just as we can remedy the faults in a sewage system. This is difficult – almost impossible – because of our deep-seated habit of taking ourselves for granted. We divide the world into subject and object. Objects can be examined, explored, acted-upon; but the subject is the explorer, the actor, and can no more examine itself than a football can scratch itself. It *can* act-upon itself in an indirect way, through objects; it can stimulate itself with cigarettes or alcohol; it can forget itself in a book or film. It can even 'raise itself' morally by 'living up' to some religious or idealistic standard. But for all these processes, the external world is an absolute necessity. It cannot act upon itself directly.

But is this *always* true? How about the moments of freedom, of poetry? These cause an actual change in consciousness – yes, in *consciousness,* the very thing you take for granted as the basis of your existence. It is synonymous with being alive.

If my car goes wrong, I can repair it by a series of acts which are basically acts of thought. Supposing I could affect my consciousness by acts of thought? At present, I can change it by drinking a glass of whisky, by taking mescalin, by taking a holiday when I am run down. But consciousness seems to have no power to change itself. If I feel run down and depressed, 'taking thought' is almost useless. The more I think, the more I get involved in the tangled net of my mental states, and the tireder I get. I reach out for the whisky bottle, or switch on television. And this is an admission of defeat, of abdication, of my ultimate slavery to the physical world.

Before I sketch my own 'answer' to this problem (perhaps I should say, my method for arriving at an answer), let me approach it from a slightly different angle.

When I learned to use this typewriter, I did it slowly and painfully, with many mistakes. But after a long time, the knowledge of how to type was passed on to a useful robot in my subconscious mind. He now does most of the work, while I can concentrate on thinking. He almost speaks French for me (rather badly) and drives my car.

Unfortunately, he interferes with my pleasures. If I hear a symphony that moves me deeply, or read a poem, the robot begins to feel left out. And after I've heard the symphony half a dozen times, it is no longer me who is listening to it. It is the robot. If I go for a walk on a spring day, the robot comes with me and listens to the birds for me.

When I was a child, the robot wasn't nearly so efficient, so *every* spring day was a delight, and my senses were ten times as alive. But I was also a great deal more miserable. Without the robot to protect me, living was exhausting work, and small problems seemed overwhelming.

When I took mescalin a few years ago, it had the effect of putting the robot out of action, and sensory impressions again became as vivid and meaningful as in childhood. But it also made the world as disturbing and alarming as when I was a child – a continual explosion of emotional states. It also impaired my efficiency as a thinker. My best moments occur when my thinking goes beyond normal clarity, and becomes a kind of vision, a lightning flash of insight. This would have been totally impossible under mescalin, which amplified all my feelings and crippled my rational intelligence.

So mescalin is no answer. But then, why does my thinking occasionally take on this quality of pure freedom, and become a kind of vision? It is because years of discipline, of learning the techniques and short-cuts of thought, enable my thoughts to achieve an unimpeded velocity that was impossible when I was sixteen. It is because the robot has grown, in some respects, steadily *more* efficient. One has to go *forward*.

In short, the robot is largely responsible for the Faust problem, for the 'St Neot margin'. But this is because he is not yet efficient enough. His machinery is too crude.

T. E. Lawrence describes how he set out early one morning with the Arabs, 'when the senses wake up before the intellect', and how everything seemed beautiful and vivid because the world was not 'filtered through or made typical by thought' (i.e. by the robot). Lawrence, like most romantics, felt that this situation could only be altered by putting the robot out of action. This is the central error of romanticism, and it reappears in a new form in existentialism (i.e. the talk about commitment).

What I have tried to do in the above paragraphs is to show the problem naked, so that we can see exactly what has to be attacked. I have also clearly implied the method of attack. Man has reached his present point in evolution by the aid of certain habit patterns. Now some of these patterns must be broken, and restored to the realm of conscious activity. The problem of consciousness must be attacked by consciousness. The mind must gain a new power of manoeuvrability, a power over consciousness itself, if philosophy is to continue. At present, it is like a car with a locked steering wheel, so that it can only go forward in a straight line. Hence the absurdity of all 'systems', from Platonic idealism to logical positivism; the car always ends up in the middle of a field.

I must speak again in personal terms. In my teens, I was keenly aware of the Faust problem. There were times when a poem or an idea provided me with the key to the locked door of my mind. Suddenly, the external world became a thing of no account. It receded to its proper place, as a mere back-drop to my real life, to the exercise of my freedom. There would be an overwhelming feeling of having the 'answer' to the problem of what life is all about. *This* is what life is all about – those vast unexplored countries of the mind, whose landmarks are Schumann and Einstein, Plato and Michelangelo, Wordsworth and Darwin and Newton and Shaw.... But the real world seemed to get jealous of being treated as a background, and after a while, the vision would be lost. And the next time you tried to escape into the country of the mind, the real world would grab you by the collar and say: 'Oh no you don't....' And instead of being able to pass cleanly into the second world, you found yourself stuck half-in and half-out. And it was a debilitating sensation, like a jealous woman poisoning a love affair by continually making scenes and writing poison pen letters....

But as I brooded about this problem, I had to admit that it was partly due to a certain mental laziness and self-indulgence. For example, you have a free day in front of you. Now is the time to do some of the things you have always intended to do: start reading Hegel or Whitehead, listen to all Beethoven's quartets, brush up your calculus. But one's very freedom brings a kind of laziness. You pick up a paperback novel and read a few chapters. This lowers your intellectual temperature still more. By mid-afternoon you are idly trying to recall whether there are any jobs in the garden that need doing...

Anyone who has done even a little self-observation becomes aware of how little will we possess, how easily we allow ourselves to drift down the stream of time instead of trying to navigate. We even come to accept our laziness as a basic part of 'the human condition', and only some serious challenge or threat can wake us up to the fact that 'it would have been so easy to be a saint'.

To know this consciously is to be a large part of the way towards a solution. It means that you refuse to accept what appears to be a fixed state of consciousness. You start pushing it and kicking it. In my teens, I made the discovery that if I spent a long day trying to 'get in the mood' for ideas or for poetry, things would often improve towards evening. My thought, that had been dull and sluggish, would suddenly acquire a forward drive. As soon as it was 'off the ground', the sense of freedom would quickly develop into a semi-mystical state in which all the usual problems and obstacles seemed absurd, almost illusory. In one of these moods, I scrawled on a page of my journal: 'There is no life and no death; only beauty.'

In more recent years, my studies in phenomenology and the problem of the St Neot margin have made it easier to manoeuvre towards this state. I find long train journeys ideal for developing the necessary concentration, for they leave one no alternative to thinking.

Last time I went to America on a lecture tour is a case in point. The thought of leaving my family depressed me. I usually sleep badly on the night before a journey, so I was tired. On a cool January day, the train was overheated. I prepared myself for a boring and demoralising journey to London, a journey of six hours. A couple of hours later, when the train reached Teignmouth, I was yawning about once a minute.

Now several years ago at Teignmouth, I had an experience of almost visionary intensity. Recalling this, I went out into the corridor to look at the place where it had occurred – it was visible from the train. Suddenly, it struck me as absurd that I should allow myself to be bullied by my body in this way. If my outlook was basically pessimistic, there might seem to be some reason for surrendering to this depression. But it was not. I believed the romantics had been destroyed by laziness and inability to think clearly. The romantic vision was not an illusion, but a reality that could be achieved by mental effort.

I went back into the carriage – its only other occupant was an old lady who was dozing – and set about stirring my brain into a state of concentration. For five minutes, I stared out of the window, and concentrated as if I was clinging to the underside of an aeroplane. It took exactly five minutes. Then, at the end of that time, a curious trickle of vitality rose in me. It was like working a pump, and getting the first drops of water. A few minutes later, and the trickle had become a steady stream of mental intensity. It suddenly seemed absurd to have been depressed. Admittedly, I was leaving my family for three months; but then, not to do an uncongenial job, but to talk every day to intelligent and enthusiastic audiences about ideas that obsessed me. It could be an opportunity to prove conclusively that in the contest between mind and matter, mind *can* be the winner.

When I got off the train four hours later, my mind felt fresher than when I had got on.

Another example, that might be of some interest. I have often said, in lecturing about this, that I can, to a minor extent, induce a kind of mescalin state in myself by a certain kind of concentration.

To some extent, this is a mis-statement, since the mescalin state is so largely emotional, and the state of concentration is due to an increase of intellectual intentionality. But a recent experience produces an interesting variation of this pattern.

Again, it was on the London–Cornwall train. In this case, I had travelled to London on an overnight sleeper, spent the morning transacting business and talking to friends, and caught the afternoon train back to Cornwall. I had missed lunch, but had eaten a sandwich.

On this occasion, I felt physically tired as well as sleepy (I never manage to sleep on sleepers). As the train pulled out of Paddington, I decided that it might be more sensible to try and doze for an hour before making any effort to stir my mind. But it happened to be the hottest day of the year, and the carriage was stifling. For an hour, I sank into an increasing torpor, losing my battle against the heat, and tempted to open a bottle of vodka that I carried in my shoulder bag. But I'd left the glass behind. There was only one other person in my compartment, but I didn't like to drink from the bottle. So reluctantly, I faced the conclusion that I had to shake off my torpor. For ten minutes or so, I thought about an interesting aspect of the St Neot margin problem, and this made me feel less of a jelly. Then I settled down to the work of pure concentration. I expected it to be far more difficult than usual, because of my state of physical tiredness. In fact, about five minutes of unrelaxed effort began to roll back the clouds of laziness, and call up the first trickle of intensity. At this point, I noticed a different quality in my consciousness. It was far closer to the mescalin experience. I can clearly recall certain autumn days in childhood when a strange calm would descend on me, and the countryside would appear almost intolerably beautiful, as if seen through a prism that surrounded all its edges with bands of colour, or as if seen through a mist that gave everything a fairyland quality. This now happened again. The greenness of the countryside suddenly fascinated me, so that I had a temptation to repeat over and over again : 'Green, green, green . . .' Instead of the countryside merely passing the windows – trees, fields, rivers – each individual field and tree aroused an intense, fascinated interest, as if it were a series of paintings by a great painter. It was not entirely an agreeable sensation; I had a feeling that there was a touch of morbidity in it. This kind of glowing beauty emanating from things seemed associated with certain meanings and emotions; but I was reasonably certain that *I* was supplying the meanings and emotions. This softness had an oddly heart-rending quality. I suddenly remembered Rilke's line about beauty being 'the beginning of terror we're still just able to bear', and it seemed that beauty is the beginning of *pain* we're still just able to bear. Each twinge of beauty had that dubious quality of pleasure-pain that you had as a child when you pressed a loose tooth.

This state lasted several hours. It had vanished long before I reached home – because I allowed it to – but again I got off the train feeling fresher than when I got on.

It seems to me that this last example proves my point: that these semi-mystical states can be induced by thought and will-power alone. Apart from the single dose of mescalin I took, in 1963, I have never taken any drugs (unless one counts the occasional aspirin). I drink fairly moderately – between a half-bottle and a bottle of wine a day, seldom more; and I have never smoked. It cannot be argued that these states may be due to some physiological cause. Besides, I know better. I am aware of the steps I take to induce them, the facts that have to be fixed clearly in mind. I think there can be no doubt that, to some extent at least, I have proved my point: that the states that came to Blake and Traherne by some happy chance of temperament *can* be induced by the rigorous pursuit of a certain logic.

It must be emphasized that the investigation of these states is largely a problem of *language*. Some time ago, I lectured at a girls' school in Virginia about my 'new existentialism'. After the lecture, a group of teachers sat around discussing 'peak experiences'. A rather pleasant young man said very little, until his wife said: 'Weren't you speaking about that the other day?' He then explained diffidently that he had been able to induce mild 'peak experiences' since childhood. He had learned the trick by accident. He said that he hated being made to sit still, because he would start to itch, and as soon as he scratched the itch, it would transfer elsewhere. One day, sitting still in class, he started to think about itching, and immediately began to itch. This time he determined not to move. The itch got worse, and started up in several places at once. It now became unbearable, and he had to clench his teeth to withstand the temptation to scratch. All at once, he felt an odd sensation at the base of his spine, and was flooded with intense pleasure. He could not describe the nature of this sensation, except to say that it was 'shivery'. But ever since discovering this trick, he had been able to induce the sensation at any moment. As he said this, he suddenly smiled and said: 'There, I did it just then.'

But he found it completely impossible to explain exactly what he 'did' to induce the peak experience. And this is why I have cited the story. The mystics and then the romantics insisted that this experience was ineffable, that it could neither be expressed nor deliberately induced. This notion was largely responsible for the pessimistic character of romanticism. My own work has been an attempt to show that this is a field where the deliberate and controlled use of reason can produce precisely the same effects as when applied to the material world. This is to say that consciousness *is* within human control. And so, in that case, is our evolution into creatures with a 'third dimension'. It is all a question of using phenomenology – 'the descriptive analysis of subjective states' – to create a real psychology, and creating a language capable of pinning down these elusive mechanisms of consciousness. (I do not count the clinical psychology of Freud, Jung and Adler as a 'real psychology'. It is a clumsy structure, based upon vague generalisations drawn from experience of sub-normal human beings, and patched together with the intellectual prejudices of the psychologist.)

I learn from a book by Professor Bateson that Wordsworth came closer to some insight into 'the St Neot margin' than I had realised. De Quincey tells how he and Wordsworth were waiting for a cart from Keswick, and Wordsworth bent down and put his ear to the ground to listen for the rumble of its wheels. As he straightened up, he noticed a star on the horizon, and commented to De Quincey:

'I have remarked ... that if ... the attention is energetically braced up to an act of steady observation, ... then if this intense condition of vigilance should suddenly relax, at that moment, any beautiful ... object ... falling upon the eye, is carried to the heart with a power not known under other circumstances. Just now, my ear was placed upon the stretch, in order to catch any sound of wheels that might come down... the Keswick Road; at the very instant when I raised my head from the ground, at the very instant when the organs of attention were all at once relaxing from their tension, the bright star... fell suddenly upon my eye, and penetrated my capacity of apprehension with a pathos and a sense of the infinite, that would not have arrested me under other circumstances.' (*Wordsworth,* by F. W. Bateson, p. 25.)

In other words, the 'peak experience' is closely bound up with concentration, with not allowing the will to get flaccid and breathless. This kind of discipline is inconsistent with the self-pity in which most of the romantics indulged, which explained why the 'spirit of beauty' was so prone to fly away and leave 'this dim vast vale of tears vacant and desolate'. And if you start out with the assumption that this world *is* a dim vast vale of tears, instead of approaching the problem with a scientific briskness, you are halving your chances of achieving any result.

This outline of my 'philosophy' falsifies it in one fundamental respect: it gives the impression that it is less a 'philosophy' than a search for the peak experience. (One baffled reader of *Introduction to the New Existentialism* even wrote: 'But why do you want peak experiences?') This is to hold it upside down. The peak experience (Maslow's term) is not important in itself. What *is* important is that philosophy is an attempt to extend science to its logical limits, and that philosophy is aimed at the control of consciousness. This is true of *all* philosophy, not simply of phenomenological existentialism. It is an attempt to escape our 'worm's eye view', and to see reality as a whole. And consciousness is the instrument with which we see. The valuable part of logical positivism is its objection that imprecision of language has prevented philosophy from achieving its aim. When it declares that it is neither possible nor desirable to 'see things as a whole', it is merely invalidating itself with self-contradiction. The nature of philosophy is to grope towards this 'bird's-eye view'.

Whitehead once said that movements of thought were like cavalry charges in a battle; you are only allowed so many, so they have to be economised. I would prefer another simile. We are still creatures of the material world, and our incursions into the world of mind are necessarily brief, like a swimmer swimming under water. You have only so much air in your lungs. If you are a vague and imprecise thinker, you paddle around vaguely, and come up for air close to the spot you went down. But thought attempts to find methods by which one's breath can be economised. A good thinker knows his direction, and swims with an economy of strokes. This economy is achieved by the use of symbols. If you can make your symbols express some important concept or law – like the St Neot margin – you have achieved an even greater concentration, and can get still further. All good thinkers work by intuition, not by 'logic'; but without symbols, intuition will waste its energy in definition. Ultimately, the swimmer can achieve a velocity of thought like jet-propulsion.

Even this is not the final aim. We must learn to stay in these waters of thought for as long as we need to. We have to develop the mental equivalent of a frogman's outfit, with oxygen supply. But first, the practical business: to learn to swim fast and straight and economically. And this is done through the development of concepts and symbols; that is, of language.

The point of phenomenological existentialism is not the peak experience; it is the control of consciousness *and its extension by language*. Most of my thinking is not directly concerned with the peak experience, but with the exact definition of problems of the natural standpoint – the worm's eye view. At the moment, language is an unconscious slave of consciousness. It assumes it possesses a precision that it does not, in fact, possess, for it has tried to build its precision upon this quicksand of a variable consciousness. If it is to serve its function, it must take into account the mechanisms of varying consciousness.

Consciousness itself must be mapped and defined. For example, we must begin by recognising that consciousness appears to have two 'planes', a horizontal and a vertical plane. The plane of every-day experience is horizontal, static, and my ordinary thinking moves on this plane. On the other hand, experiences of intensity tend to penetrate vertically into consciousness, and make us aware of consciousness *as freedom* instead of as passive perception.

This enables me to state the core of my contribution to philosophy. The peculiar glory of the human mind is its ability to move in a step-wise progression: that is to say that when it confronts a problem, it treats it as a series of steps, and surmounts the problem by climbing step by step. Now I have pointed out that the problems of philosophy, as distinct from those of everyday life or mathematics, cannot be attacked on this logical principle. They look insoluble to discursive thought. You seem to exhaust them; you certainly exhaust yourself, and yet they remain untouched. They can only be attacked by varying consciousness itself. When consciousness achieves the 'peak experience', you suddenly become aware that there are new roads to the heart of the problem. This means that philosophy cannot be done in the same way as science – or at least, in the way an engineer would solve the problem of building a bridge over a ravine. It requires that *other* element, the intensity. A man without this ability is not qualified to be a philosopher (which, of course, rules out 90 per cent of all philosophers.) Without a certain glow of intensity, philosophy is like a car without petrol.

Now I have stated clearly that this 'stepwise progression principle' *can be applied to consciousness*. The peak experience, the freedom experience, the experience of escaping your subjective world of dreams and coming into contact with reality, is not a matter of accident or divine grace. It can be pursued as you would pursue the solution to any other problem. But a new psychology, based upon the variability of consciousness, is an urgent necessity.

It will be seen why I consider that this approach must revolutionise philosophy. It is not *a* philosophy; it is the mainstream of philosophy. All 'philosophies' so far have been self-contradictory if pursued to their logical extremes – and this includes current existentialism and logical positivism. My 'philosophy' (and it will now be seen why I place the words in brackets) makes the modest claim of being free of self-contradiction.

I return briefly to autobiography, although it is unimportant enough compared with ideas.

I have written twenty-two books in ten years: eight novels, seven volumes of philosophy, and various essays and studies. I have written at this speed because I felt I had too much to say, and that I would explode if I didn't get it said. I write as a dog with fleas scratches. But a point has come where I have laid the necessary foundation, and need time to think and write. This is the reason that, at the time of writing, I have accepted university posts in America for the next two years, and may accept more when the two years are up. I much prefer America to England. I love England itself, but can't stand the people. And in the artistic and intellectual sense, England is a dead and hide-bound country. Its cultural life is dominated by the universities, the BBC and Fleet Street 'intellectuals' – that is to say, by defeated would-be writers. The English intellectual is not given to thinking; it is enough for him that he is steeped in 'culture' (usually French) and is an expert in dismissive arguing. His chief glory is his ability to convince himself that his failure to think is a virtue, the final product of total sophistication. Basically he is second rate. In due course, his type will vanish by the ordinary process of survival of the fittest. For he is anything but fit; he is mentally flabby and short winded.

England is closed and static, and in this sense, America is certainly open and kinetic. It also has its small-minded academics – plenty of them – and its little cultural conspiracies; but there is none of that sense of stale air that you get in England. On my last trip there, I went to a cinema in Pittsburgh to see Braine's *Life at the Top*. It brought back keenly all the things I hate most about England: the mass-produced BBC types churned out by the universities, and the dreary provincial anti-snobs like Lampton, who have nothing else in their heads but a sterile hatred for the sterile 'upper classes'. It seemed to me that the film could have been called *Much Ado About Nothing*, since everyone in it is useless and dispensable. I came out of the cinema steeped in an uncomfortable dislike for everything English that was as nasty as heartburn. Then I got into a taxi, and the driver said: 'Where to, bud?', and the heartburn vanished, and I suddenly felt happy again. For in a fundamental sense, all men *are* equal, and the human race *is* a family. I may find most of my brothers and sisters intolerable, but there can be no doubt about the relationship. I conclude that I am a born communist: not an ideological one, but an instinctive one. No man deserves respect for his 'position' (which in England often amounts to his accent) but for what he is; and then, only so long as he is not conceited about what he is. America has its faults – thousands of them – but at least this is taken for granted. All this came to me in a rush with the driver's 'Where to, bud?', and I suddenly felt an immense affection for America. It is a country where I can feel comfortable and do my best work.

At thirty-five, I am suddenly aware of the absurdity of the shortness of human life, and can find deeper meanings in *Back to Methuselah*. Time accelerates steadily. It is not really twenty years since I was fifteen; it is about five. Sometimes, when I speak to younger people, I can see that they are congratulating themselves on being young; and I smile ironically. It is impossible for a sixteen-year-old to realise that in five years' time he will not be twenty-one, but thirty... And a year after that, thirty-five. And six months later, forty ... Time accelerates so as to swindle us.

But Shaw is right. This absurdity has got to stop. Man must be able to calculate on living at least a hundred and fifty years. At least, the creative men must. The average person stops developing at twenty anyway, so another hundred and thirty years of life would be of no use to him. But how can any really valuable advances take place if a new generation comes along and starts back at the beginning? The confusion of philosophy – the fact that it has never developed into a science, although it has had twenty-five hundred years to do it in – is due to this brevity of human life. Once something has been achieved on the 'horizontal plane' of consciousness – some new advance in building or living or practical thinking – it can be passed on intact to the next generation. But the really big problems – the problems that challenge religious or philosophical thinking – require a kind of grasp and maturity that can only be acquired by seventy years or so of hard and continuous thinking. If this body and brain of mine could be driven on for another hundred years or so, I could probably solve all the problems of philosophy single handed. As it is, I have been thinking pretty consistently and continuously since the age of twelve, and it will take me another twenty years to create a basic terminology, to complete the foundations of a real philosophy.

When I decided to be a writer at the age of fourteen or so – instead of a scientist – I felt guilty at choosing what I supposed to be the path of least resistance. I should have known that once a scientist, always a scientist. But twenty years of work have not taken me far. (This is not modesty. I know I have come further than any of my contemporaries; I would be a fool if I didn't know it, and a coward if I was afraid to say so.) But at least the years seem to have taken me to a point from which I can make a beginning.

1962–1967

INDEX

Abbott, E. A., 31
Abraham, Jonathan, 89, 94, 111
Actionalism, 78
Act of Creation (A. Koestler), 155
Adeane, Louis, 135, 136, 153
Adler, Alfred, 41, 172
Adrift in Soho (C. Wilson), 125, 158, 160
'Adventure of the Blue Carbuncle' (A. Conan Doyle), 37
Adventures of Tom Sawyer (M. Twain), 36, 37
Affluent Society (J. K. Galbraith), 152, 155
Age of Defeat (C. Wilson), x, 9, 152, 153, 154, 155, 156, 158
Agrippa, Henricus Cornelius, 6
Akademia Duncan, 78, 79
Alexander the Great, 163
All for Love (J. Dryden), 150
Allsop, Kenneth, 146
Amazing Stories, 25
Amis, Kingsley, 123
Anarchists, *see* London Anarchist Group
Andy, *see* Baines, A.
Angry Decade (K. Allsop), 146
Angry Young Men, 93, 123
Aran Islands (J. M. Synge), 68
Arlen, Michael, 5
Armstrong, Ethel (the author's aunt), 76
Artzibashef, Michael, 4, 5
Atlantis, 18, 19
Auden, W. H., 126
Axel, 162
Ayer, A. J., 116, 128

Back to Methuselah (G. B. Shaw), 127, 177
Baines, Andrew, 32, 33

Banker and Baron (*Bankár és Báró*, Hugo), 156
Barbusse, Henri, 115
Bardot, Brigit, 131
Barnum, P. T., 135
Bartók, Béla, 134
Bateson, F. W., 172, 173
Baudelaire, Charles, 134
Bax, Clifford, 67
Baxter, George, 34, 60
Beatles, 131
Beaverbrook, W. M. A., 1st Baron, 139
Becket, Samuel, 150
Beethoven, Ludwig van, 133, 168
Beiderbecke, Bix, 89
Berdyaev, N. A., xi, 127
Bergson, Henri, xi, 116
Berkeley, George, Bishop, 39, 47
Berlin, Irving, 54
Bernanos, Georges, 116
Bertrand, Aia, 78, 79
Betjeman, John, 131
Betty, *see* Hexstall, B.
Beyond the Outsider (C. Wilson), 148
Bhagavad Gita, 57, 58, 66, 67, 69, 71, 94
Bible, 44, 72
Bible of the World, 72
Birth of Tragedy (F. Nietzsche), 132
Bizet, Georges, 54
Bjornson, B. M., 142
Blake, William, 70, 84, 85, 127, 144, 159, 171
Blondel, Maurice, xi
Blue Carbuncle (A. Conan Doyle), 37
Bohème (G. Puccini), 103, 133
Book of the Dead, 82, 105
Books and Art, 139
Books and Bookmen, 141, 146

INDEX

Brahms, Johannes, 133, 142
Braine, John, 176
Brecht, Bertolt, 157
Bredin, Mark, 159
'Bridge' group, 102, 114
British Museum, 84, 111, 112, 114, 115, 116, 117
Brooke, Rupert, 52, 69
Brothers Karamazov (F. M. Dostoevsky), 81, 127
Brown, Curtis, 151
Browne, Sir Thomas, 87
Bruckner, J. A., 133, 134
Brush, Katherine, 5
Buckle, Richard, 149
Buddha, 94
Burns, Robert, x
Burroughs, William, 150
Butler, Samuel, 84
Byng, Cranmer, 94
Byron, George Gordon Noel, 6th Baron, 62, 65, 146

Café Tournon, Paris, 101
Campbell, J., 53
Campton, David, 52
Camus, Albert, x-xi, 132, 152, 153
Capote, Truman, 131
Carlyle, Connie (the author's aunt), 24
— Frank (the author's uncle), 24
— Thomas, 126
Carmen (G. Bizet), 54
Casanova, Giacomo, 158, 163
Chaucer, Geoffrey, 94
Chesterton, G. K., xii 17, 39, 52, 151
Childe Harold (Lord Byron), 146
Children's Encyclopedia (A. Mee), 18
Christie, J. R. H., 95
Christ in Concrete (P. de Donati), 151
Clements, Sir John, 104
Cloud of Unknowing, 104
Coates, Eric, 54
Coleman, Kenneth, 49
Coleridge, S.T., 41
College of Art & Technology, Leicester, 32, 33, 36, 39
Concept of Mind (G. Ryle), 162

Concerto, a film, 54
Confucius, 94
Connell, John, 122, 123
Connie, Aunt, *see* Carlyle, C.
Connolly, Cyril, 122, 131, 155
Corot, J. B. C., 54
Coward, Noel, 150
Crabbe, John, 103, 105
Cranston, Maurice, 147
Crime and Punishment (F. M. Dostoevsky), 82

Daily Express, 123, 129
Daily Mail, 124
Daily Mirror, 126
Dalmas chemical works, Leicester, 81
Dangerous Moonlight, 54
Dante Alighieri, 82
Darwin, Charles, 167
David Copperfield (C. Dickens), 21
Davis, Gladys, 32, 33, 34
Dean, James, 23
Death of God (C. Wilson), 138, 141
Death on the White Horse (T. Storm), 40
Delius, Frederick, 42
Del-Rivo, Laura, 89, 90, 92, 99, 120
De Quincey, Thomas, 172
Desmond, *see* Norman, D.
Devine, George, 138
Diaghilev, Sergei Pavlovich, 149
Diary of Vaslav Nijinsky (ed. R. Nijinsky), 51
Dickens, Charles, 21, 46, 53, 126, 149, 150, 151
di Donati, Pietro, 151
Diogenes, 23
Divine and the Decay (B. Hopkins), 93, 124, 133, 141, 147
Doktor Faustus (T. Mann), 53
Dora, Aunt, *see* Tarrat, D.
Dostoevsky, Fëdor Mikhailovich, 68, 81, 88,127
Doyle, Sir Arthur Conan, 18, 152
Dryden, John, 50
Duncan, Isadora, 79
— Raymond, 78, 79
— Ronald, 138, 139, 141
Dürrenmatt, Friedrich, 152
Duxbury, May, 32

INDEX

Ecclesiastes, 44
Eckermann, Johann Peter, 9
Eddington, Sir Arthur Stanley, 36
Einstein, Albert, 31, 39, 167
Elder Statesman (T. S. Eliot), 131
Eliot, T. S., 5, 45, 47, 51, 67, 68, 69, 82, 84, 91, 112, 116, 124, 126, 131, 134, 137, 141, 150, 151, 157
Ellis, Henry Havelock, 14, 64
Emergence from Chaos (S. Holroyd), 125, 146, 147
Emperor's Clothes (K. Nott), 116
Encounter, 107, 123, 128, 147
Encyclopaedia Britannica, 149
English, Lil (the author's aunt), 15
Entertainer (J. Osborne), 27
Essays on the Life Aim (C. Wilson), 40-41
Ethel, Aunt, *see* Armstrong, E.
Eton College, 124, 127
Evening News, 122
Existentialism, x, xi, 142, 143, 144, 145, 147, 152, 160, 161, 162, 164, 167, 175; *see also* New existentialism

Faber & Faber, 141
Falla, Manuel de, 81
Fantasia (W. Disney), 54
Fantasy Magazine, 25
Farson, Daniel, 124, 133, 135, 139, 141,
— Negley, 135, 139, 152
Fathers and Sons (C. Wilson), 45
Faulkner, William, 150, 151
Faust (J. H. von Goethe), 53, 57, 163, 165, 167
Feu (H. Barbusse), 115
Finnegan's Wake (J. Joyce), 53, 57, 60
Firbank, Ronald, 42
Firebird (I. F. Stravinsky), 81, 133
First Gentleman (N. Ginsbury), 62
Fitzgerald, F. Scott, 50, 115, 132, 150
FitzGibbon, Constantine, 123, 124
Flagstad, Kirsten Malfrid, 81
Flatland: A Romance of Many Dimensions (E. A. Abbott), 31
Fleming, Ian, 49
Flight and Pursuit (S. Holroyd), 147

Flynn, Cyril, 39
Forster, E. M., 46
Four Quartets (T. S. Eliot), 69
Fox, George, 17
Foyle, W. & G., 97
France, Anatole, 151
Franck, César, 81, 133
Franco, Francisco, 157
Frankenstein, 24
Frazer & Glass, 82, 85
French Revolution (T. Carlyle), 126
Freud, Sigmund, 172
From Here to Eternity (J. Jones), 146
Future Indefinite: Autobiography (N. Coward), 150

Gabriele, 117
Galbraith, J. K., 152, 155
Galli-Curci, Amelita, 103
Gateway Secondary Technical School, Leicester, 30, 31, 32, 33, 36, 45, 46, 60, 62
Gautier, Théophile, 71
Gem, The, 36
Genêt, Jean, 17, 150
'Gerald', 50, 51, 52, 54, 60, 68, 74, 76, 103
Gibson, Tony, 86
Gide, André, 42, 91
Gill, Eric, ix, xii
Ginsbury, Norman, 62
Giorgione, 54
Gladstone, William Ewart, 17
Gladys, *see* Davis, G.
Glass Cage (C. Wilson), 158, 160, 161
Glass Mountain, 54
Glinto, Darcy, 16
God, 29, 115, 127; *see also* Jesus Christ
Goethe, J. H. von, 9, 10, 53, 165
Gollancz, Victor, 116, 117, 118, 119, 121, 122, 123, 125, 128, 129, 133, 134, 140, 141, 146, 147, 151, 152, 153, 154
Goncharov, Ivan Aleksandrovich, 60
Gorran Haven, xii, 113, 153
Gospel of Sri Ramakrishna, 113
Great Gatsby (F. S. Fitzgerald), 115

181

INDEX

Greene, Graham, 93, 116, 137, 150, 157
Guardian, 147
Guide to Philosophy (C. E. M. Joad), 39, 154
Guillaume, Claude, 78, 98, 101
— Marie, 98
— Mme, 98
Gurdjieff, George Ivanovitch, 68, 115

Haggard, Sir Henry Rider, 126
Halliday, 'Flax', 102, 103, 104, 105, 106
Hamann, Johann Georg, 160
Hamlet, 22, 115
Hamilton, Gerald, 134, 135
Hardy, Thomas, x
Harris, Frank, 93, 158
Hastings, Michael, 123
Hegel, Georg Wilhelm Friedrich, 168
Heidegger, Martin, x, xi, 142, 143, 152, 162
Hemingway, Ernest, 1, 23, 91, 92, 137, 150, 152
Hemlock and After (A. Wilson), 112
Henry, 49
Henry James, the Major Phase (F. O. Matthiessen), 76
Hesse, Hermann, 69, 111
Hexstall, Betty (also called Ginger), 32
Highways and Byways in Devon and Cornwall (A. H. Norway), 113
Hipwell, Barry, 104
Hitler, Adolf, 19, 22, 23, 83, 103
Hoffmann, Ernest Theodor Amadeus, 92
Holroyd, Stuart, 114, 115, 124, 125, 146, 147, 152, 153, 157
Holst, Gustav Theodore, 54
Hopkins, Bill, ix, 90, 91, 92, 93, 94, 98, 99, 100, 101, 106, 112, 114, 120, 122, 124, 132, 133, 138, 139, 141, 145, 146, 147, 149, 152, 153, 157
— Ted, 138
Horn, Alfred Aloysius, 35
Hotspur, The, 36
Houghton Mifflin Co., 125

Hugo, Charles, 156
—— Victor, 91, 124, 156
Hulme, T. E., 68, 91, 115, 116
Hungarian Literature (E. Reich), 156
Hungarian revolution, 145
Hurok, Sol, 130
Huson, Eric, 60
Huxley, Aldous, 49, 150
— Sir Julian, 163, 164
Hydrogen bomb tests, 145
Hylton, Walter, 104

Ibsen, Henrik Johan, 142
Immaturity (G. B. Shaw), 115
Inquire Within for Everything, 16
Intelligent Woman's Guide to Socialism (G. B. Shaw), 155
Introduction aux existentialismes (E. Mounier), x
Introduction to the New Existentialism (C. Wilson), 161, 162, 173
Isherwood, Christopher, 134

Jack-the-Ripper, 84, 87, 88, 135, 151
James, Henry, 5, 76, 151
— William, 40, 81, 127, 161
Janson, Hank, 49
Jaspers, Karl, xi, 162
Jeans, Sir James, 31, 36
Jehovah's Witnesses, 28, 57
Jerusalem (W. Blake), 70
Jesus Christ, 18, 19, 127; *see also* God
Jim the Penman, 17
Joad, C. E. M., 39, 154
John, Cousin, *see* Tarrat, J.
John Bull's Other Island (G. B. Shaw), 132
Johnson, Dr Samuel, 13
Joiner, H. D., 49
Jones, Anetta and Ernest Henry (the author's grandmother and grandfather), 9, 10, 13, 18, 26, 34, 35, 118
— Maude (the author's aunt), 9
— Roy (the author's cousin), 11
Jonson, Ben, 41

INDEX

Joyce, *see* Payne, J.
Joyce, James, 5, 51, 82, 111, 124, 137, 150, 151, 152
Jung, Carl Gustav, 172

Keats, John, 66
Ken, *see* Coleman, K.
Kierkegaard, Sören Aabye, 78, 115, 116, 160
King Solomon's Mines (H. R. Haggard), 126
Koestler, Arthur, 129, 155
Kropotkin, Petr Alekseevich, Prince, 87

Ladder of Perfection (W. Hylton), 104
Lambert, J. W., 156
Lao-tse, 94
Last of the Mohicans (J. F. Cooper), 35
Late Days (M. Willows), 105
Latham, A. G., 53
Lawrence, D. H., x, 50, 62, 119, 150
——T. E., 23, 30, 167
Leicester, 2, 3, 9, 16, 20, 25, 26, 27, 33, 36, 38, 46, 50, 51, 52, 55, 60, 64, 65, 71, 73, 74, 79, 80, 83, 85, 86, 88, 95, 96, 102, 103, 104, 105, 118, 120, 127
L'Enfer (H. Barbusse), 115
Lermontov, Mikhail Yurevich, 103
Lessing, G. E., 156
Lewis's Ltd, Leicester, 102, 104, 105
Life at the Top (J. Braine), 176
Lil, Aunt, *see* English, L.
Lodge, Sir Oliver, 18
Logical positivism, 127, 128, 144, 162, 167, 173, 175
Logue, Christopher, 100, 101, 157
London Anarchist Group, 86, 87, 88, 89
London Transport, 86
Lonely Crowd (D. Riesman), 152
Look Back in Anger (J. Osborne), 49, 123
Loom of Youth (A. Waugh), 140
Lord of the Flies (W. Golding), 147
Lovecraft, H. P., 42, 46-47
Lowell, Percival, 24
Lyons, J., 86, 113, 114

Macaulay, Thomas, Baron, 41
Macdonald, Dwight, 130
Machiavelli, Niccolò, 124
MacNeice, Louis, 126
Mademoiselle de Maupin (T. Gautier), 71
Magic Mountain (T. Mann), 81, 88
Magnet, The, 36
Mahler, Gustav, 133
Malatesta, Errico, 87
Mallarmé, Stéphane, 134
Man and Superman (G. B. Shaw), 42, 44, 45, 66, 81, 104, 105
Manual of General Science (C. Wilson), 34, 35, 36
Man Without a Shadow (C. Wilson), 135
Mankowitz, Wolf, 126, 129
Mann, Thomas, 53, 81, 88, 137
Marcel, Gabriel, xi, 116
Mars, 24
Marvels and Mysteries of Science, 24
Mary, 72, 73, 74, 75, 80, 95
Maschler, Tom, 135
Maslow, Professor A. H., 173
Matthiessen, F. O., 76
Maude, Aunt, *see* Jones, M.
Maugham, W. Somerset, 5, 54
May, *see* Duxbury, M.
'Maze of Maya' (C. Wilson), 57
Metal Flower Blossom (C. Wilson), 90, 94, 104, 105
Mee, Arthur, 18
Mein Kampf (A. Hitler), 103
Meistersinger (R. Wagner), 103
Merlin, 100, 101
Michelangelo, 167
Miller, Arthur, 129
Millicent, 49, 51, 60
Millionaire, The (M. Artzibashef), 4
Milton, John, 124
Mind at the End of its Tether (H. G. Wells), 115
Mind Parasites (C. Wilson), 160
Mohini Chatterjee (W. B. Yeats), 58
Monroe, Marilyn, 23
Moon and Sixpence (W. S. Maugham), 54
Morris, William, 78
Mortimer, Raymond, 140
Mounier, E., x

INDEX

Mr Norris Changes Trains (C. Isherwood), 134
Murger, Henri, 92
Music, xii, 29, 54, 81, 89, 103, 133, 134, 143, 158
Musset, Alfred de, 91
Mysterious Universe (J. Jeans), 31

Naked Lunch (W. Burroughs), 150
Napoleon I, Emperor, 22, 32
Necessary Doubt (C. Wilson), 152, 160
Nero, Emperor, 87
New existentialism, (phenomenological existentialism), x, xi, 152, 157, 161-167, 171, 173, 174
New Lindsay Theatre, London, 123
New-Paris-York, 78
News Chronicle, 138
New Statesman, 123, 147, 157
Newstead Abbey, 62, 64
Newton, Sir Isaac, 87, 167
New Yorker, 130
New York Times, 120, 122
Nichols, Anne, 120, 121
— Beverley, ix
Nielsen, Carl August, 142
Nietzsche, Friedrich, xi, 31, 68, 72, 115, 126, 127, 132
Nijinsky, Vaslav, 51, 114, 119, 127
Norman, Desmond, 49
North London Syndicalist Group, 87
Norway, A. H., 113
Notes from Underground (F. M. Dostoevsky), 88
Nott, Kathleen, 116

Oblomov (I. A. Goncharov), 42, 60, 115
Observer, 122, 129, 140
Odyssey (Homer), 82
Of Time and the River (T. Wolfe), 50
Organisation Man (W. H. Whyte), 152
Original sin, 7, 29, 68, 83
Osborne, John, 27, 123, 131
Outline of History (H. G. Wells), 27

Outsider (C. Wilson), ix, x, 30, 68, 107, 114, 115, 116, 117, 118, 119, 121, 122-25, 126, 127, 128, 129, 130, 131, 132, 133, 137, 138, 140, 146, 147, 149, 151, 154, 155, 156, 157

Paganini, Niccolò, 81
Pain Threshold, see *Outsider*
Palgrave, Francis Turner, 44
Paris Review, 98, 100, 101
Pastoral symphony (Beethoven), 133
Pat, 104
Patti, Adelina, 103
Payne, Joyce, 48
Peace, Charles, 17
Pearson, Edith, 48
Penman, Mr, 84, 85
Peter Pan (J. M. Barrie), 30
Phenomenological existentialism, *see* New existentialism
Pickwick Papers (C. Dickens), 46, 126
Planets (G. Holst), 54
Plato, 59, 69, 167
Platonic idealism, 167
Plimpton, George, 98, 99, 100
Pocket World Bible, 72
Poe, Edgar Allan, 91
Portrait of the Artist as a Young Man (J. Joyce), 111
Pound, Ezra, 67, 141
Practical Knowledge for All, 34, 41
Praz, Mario, 130
Present Indicative: Autobiography (N. Coward), 150
Priestley, J. B., 123
Proust, Marcel, 51
Puccini, Giacomo, 133
Pushkin, Aleksandr, 103

'Queer Feet' (G. K. Chesterton), 37

Rachmaninov, Sergei Vasilievich, 54, 81
Raymond, Ernest, 140
Read, Sir Herbert, 87, 89
Rebel, The (A. Camus), quoted x-xi
Reich, Emil, 156

INDEX

Relativity: the Special and the General Theory: a Popular Exposition (A. Einstein), 31
Religion, 18, 19, 41, 59, 70, 71, 73, 82, 83, 115, 116, 131, 144, 145, 152
Religion and Science (B. Russell), 27
Religion and the Rebel (C. Wilson), x, 42, 128, 131, 132, 133, 137, 139, 140, 141, 143, 146, 147, 149, 154, 155, 156
Reynolds, Alfred, 101
Richter, Johann Paul Friedrich, 53, 92
Riesman, David, 152
Rilke, Rainer Maria, 171
Rite of Spring (I. F. Stravinsky), 81
Ritual in the Dark (C. Wilson), 40, 78, 82, 83, 84, 91, 93, 101, 104, 105, 106, 111, 114, 119, 120, 121, 134, 141, 149, 151, 152, 153, 154, 156, 157, 158, 159
Robinson, H. M., 53
Roman Catholic Church, 28, 59, 70, 71, 73, 82, 83, 132
Romantic Agony (M. Praz), 130
Rousseau, Jean-Jacques, 78, 88
Rover, The, 23
Roy, Cousin, *see* Jones, R.
Royal Court Theatre, London, 123, 129, 138, 157
Russell, Bertrand, Earl, 27, 116
Ryle, Gilbert, 162

Sade, Marquis de, 151
St Etheldreda's, Ely Place, 81
Saint-Exupéry, Antoine de, 23
St Neot margin, 7, 29, 42, 167, 168, 170, 172, 174
Salazar, Antonio de Oliveira, 157
Salinger, J. D., 131
Sanine (M. Artzibashef), 4
Sarto, Ben, 16, 17
Sartre, J.-P., x, xi, 68, 115, 122, 128, 137, 138, 142, 143, 144, 152, 153, 161, 162, 164
Saturday Critic, 90, 93, 94, 99, 101
Schonfield, Hugh, 115
Schopenhauer, Arthur, 42
Schumann, Robert Alexander, 167

Secker & Warburg, 118
Seddon, Richard, 7
Sellars, Peter, 131
Seven Pillars of Wisdom (T. E. Lawrence), 104
Shakespeare, William, 134, 161
Shaw, G. B., 6, 24, 26, 38, 41, 42, 43, 44, 45, 46, 49, 54, 58, 59, 66, 67, 68, 81, 84, 89, 91, 99, 104, 115, 116, 124, 126, 127, 132, 137, 143, 151, 155, 161, 167, 177
Shelley, P. B., 59, 87, 91
Shostakovich, Dmitry Dmitriyevich, 133
Siddartha (H. Hesse), 111
Sidford, J. W., v, 48, 49, 53
Simpson, 5
Sitwell, Dame Edith, 156, 157
Skeleton Key to 'Finnegan's Wake' (J. Campbell & H. M. Robinson), 53
Smith, Godfrey, 123
— Hugh Heckstall, 132
Socrates (C. Bax), 67
Spain, Nancy, 140
Spender, Stephen, 74, 107, 126
Spengler, Oswald, 22
Spenser, Edmund, 41
Spillane, Mickey, 16
'Standing Outside a Lunatic Asylum', 21
Stekel, Wilhelm, 64
Stevenson, Robert Louis, 74
Stewart, Joy, *see* Wilson, Joy
Stonehenge, 70, 71
Stories of Detection, 37
Storm, Theodore, 40
Stravinsky, Igor Fedorovich, 81, 133
Strindberg, August, 147
Students' Association, 122
Suetonius Tranquillus, Gaius, 87
Summers, Montague, 59
Sunday Times, 122, 123, 128, 140, 156
Swedenborg, Emanuel, 18
Symposium (Plato), 59
Syndicalists, *see* North London Syndicalist Group
Synge, J. M., 68

Tao Te Ching, 72, 76

INDEX

Tarrat, Dora (the author's aunt), 16
— John (the author's cousin), 15, 19
Tell England (E. Raymond), 140
Tenth Chance (S. Holroyd), 157
Thais (A. France), 151
Thomas, Dylan, 91, 123, 124, 150
Thrilling Wonder Stories, 25
Thurber, James, 36
Tiberius, Emperor, 87
Time Magazine, 125, 140
Time of Totality (B. Hopkins), 93, 100, 145
Times, 123, 155
Tolstoy, Leo, Count, 68, 103
Tomkins, Warrant-Officer, 61
Tono Bungay (H. G. Wells), 37
Toynbee, Arnold Joseph, 22
——Philip, 122, 131, 140
Trader Horn (A. A. Horn), 35
Traherne, Thomas, 171
Tricorne suite (M. de Falla), 81
Tristan und Isolde (R. Wagner), 81
Twenty-five (B. Nichols), ix
Twenty Thousand Leagues Under the Sea (J. Verne), 18
Tynan, Kenneth, 129, 138

Ulysses (J. Joyce), 46, 51, 82, 104, 105, 111, 112, 121, 150

van Gogh, Vincent, 51, 70, 119, 127
Vastation experience, 40, 47, 96, 122, 126-127, 152
Verne, Jules, 18
Varieties of Religious Experience (W. James), 81
Vaughan College, 49, 52, 53, 60, 95
Veen, Philip, 100
Victoria Wine Co., 109, 110
Vision of Asia (C. Byng), 94

Wagner, Richard, 54, 103
Wain, John, 123
Wainwright, David, 122, 123
Warburg, Fred, 118, 119, 121
Walmesley, Margot, 123, 124
Warsaw Concerto (R. Addinsell), 54
Washington, George, 17
Waste Land (T. S. Eliot), 71, 82, 104
Waugh, Alec, 140

Weil, Simone, 116
Wells, H. G., 27, 34, 37, 68, 84, 103, 115, 124, 126, 163
Wesker, Arnold, 138
Western Fever Hospital, Fulham, 88, 103
Wheels of Chance (H. G. Wells), 34
Whitehead, Alfred North, 160, 161, 168, 174
Whiting, John, 129
Whitman, Walt, 72, 78, 79
Whyte, William Hollingsworth, 152
Wilde, Oscar, 6, 50, 51
Williamson, Henry, ix
Willows, Freda, 106
— Maurice, 74, 103, 105, 106, 107, 117
Williams, Tennessee, 131
Wilson, Angus, 106, 112, 114, 118, 120, 121
— Annetta (the author's mother; *née* Jones), 2, 3, 9, 10, 11, 12, 13, 35, 64, 71, 72, 118, 120
— Arthur (the author's father), 2, 3, 11, 12, 13, 14, 15, 18, 19, 20, 57, 68, 69, 72, 120
— Barry (the author's younger brother), 9, 11, 14, 20, 21
— Betty (the author's first wife), 80, 81, 82, 83, 84, 85, 86, 88, 95, 96, 97, 102, 104, 105, 108, 110, 111, 112
— Colin
  on the narrowness of human consciousness, 1-8
  the story of the old woman in the vinegar bottle symbolic of human nature, 1-2, 66
  rents a cottage in Cornwall, 2
  on the way in which people affect one another's personalities and self-assessments, 6
  definition of his private term, the St Neot margin, 7
  much spoiled as a child, 9
  his fundamental 'anxiety' about the universe, 9
  possesses a need for withdrawal, 10
  an abnormally affectionate child but dislikes being mollycoddled, 11

early life bound up with his mother, 11
becomes the confidant of his mother's disappointments, 12
takes his mother's side in family quarrels, 12
inherits his father's sentimentality, 13
mania for collecting, 13, 25
disposed to thieving, 13, 15, 16, 17, 19, 25, 26, 41, 48, 86
regarded as a 'scrapper', 13, 15
little interested in sex, 13, 14, 20
likes dressing in his mother's clothes, 14, 64
shows distinct tendencies to sadism, 14, 20
lack of sympathy for his father's enthusiasms, 15
the essential quality of his childhood, 17
his contempt for adults, 17, 31
early religious convictions, 18, 19
problem of distinguishing between fact and opinion, 19
escapes possible murder or sexual assault, 21
learns the danger of over confidence, 22
given to lying extensively and gratuitously, 24
becomes interested in astronomy, 24
works as a newspaper boy, 25, 32
develops interest in chemistry, particularly explosives, 25, 26
makes money selling explosives, 26
Shaw's 'moral passion' is born in him, 26
he discovers the world of science, 26-28
reads Bertrand Russell's *Religion and Science*, 27
and H. G. Wells, 27
profound revulsion from triviality, 27
discovery of the *impersonal*, 28
and of states of 'higher consciousness', 29
on man's lack of free will, 29
defines the term 'outsider', 30

becomes a 'teacher's pet' at school, 30
reads Einstein, Abbott and Jeans, 31
imagines himself to be a prodigy, 31
moves from scientific relativity to moral relativity, 31, 39
his first girl friends, 32
acquires a reputation for womanizing, 32-33
becomes aware of the power of sex, 33
undergoes a period of bad language, 33
rejected by his girl friend, 34
conceives the idea of writing a book, 34, 35
discovers ability to ride a bicycle, 34
his first films and subsequent debt to the cinema, 35
determines to reject an 'ordinary' future, 36, 95
realizes he has talent for neither art nor technology, 36
enjoys speaking at school debates, writing for school magazine and organizing theatricals, 36
learns disproportionately little from his eleven years' schooling, 36
reads, and is greatly impressed by, *Tom Sawyer*, 36-37
on education, 37
on the educational value of comics and boys' papers, 37
is always attached to one girl and sometimes as many as ten, 37, 38
his feeling of ultimate immunity vanishes, 40
revolts against the universal self-delusion of superiority, 40
his *Essays on the Life Aim*, 40-41
disagrees with Adler's theory of neuroses, 41
has moments of detestation of other people, 41
starts a passion for poetry, 41

INDEX

Wilson, Colin—ctd.
retreats into literature and avoids contact with people, 41
discovery of Shaw deepens his pessimism, 42
takes his School Certificate and fails to matriculate, 42
applies for a job at the labour exchange, 43
obtains employment in a wool factory, 43
begins to think of himself as a writer, whose task is to investigate the meaning of human existence, 43
his state of unhealthy intensity alarms some friendly adults, 44
life becomes a desert, 44
determines to write a sequel to *Man and Superman*, 44-45
greatly influenced by Eliot, 45
becomes a laboratory assistant, 45
writes quantities of plays and short stories, 46
experiences a profound feeling of lack of identity, 47
contemplates suicide, 47
contemplates murder, 48
loses his job, 48
is employed by the Collector of Taxes, 48
forms a relationship with a young married woman, 49
and a friendship with a homosexual, 50
his friendship with David Campton, 52
becomes an established civil servant and is posted to Rugby, 52
is introduced to and admires Rupert Brooke's poetry, 52
begins to write a comic novel, 52
and a version of Faust in free verse, 53
loses his job and lodgings, 54
studies painting and sculpture, 54
his love of music, 54; *see also* Music
receives a small windfall and takes the first holiday of his life, 55
is called up and enters the RAF, 56
resolves to 'face life', 57
attends meeting of Jehovah's Witnesses to gather material for a story, 57
begins his training in RAF, 57
is brought before his superior officer and narrowly escapes becoming a defaulter, 59
is shocked by the abuse of power in the RAF, 59
is placed on a charge and receives a fortnight's confinement to camp, 61
declines invitation to chastise a masochistic warrant officer, 61
is placed on another charge and awarded extra duties, 63
represents himself to the MO as a homosexual in order to obtain his release, 64
is interviewed by the RAF police, 64-65
and sent to a psychiatrist, 65
certified as 'nervously unstable' is discharged from the service, 65
begins to plan an immense work on outsiders, 68
resolves to abjure 'safe jobs', 68
determines to become a 'wanderer', 69
tries in vain to become an actor, 69
takes a job on a building site, 70
considers becoming a Catholic, 70, 73
on man's need for symbols of the unseen, 70
on the right attitude towards reality, 70
his preference for the Catholic Church, 71
works as a fairground barker, 72
begins to read the Bible with interest, 72
meets Mary, 72
loses his job and becomes a building worker, 73
his thoughts turn to the possibility of entering a monastery, 73

INDEX

begins taking instruction to become a Catholic, 73
becomes a farm labourer, 74
terminates his relationship with Mary, 75
sets out for Dover with half-a-crown in his pocket, 75
on travel, 76
first impressions of France, 76-77
becomes involved with another girl, 77
suffers a severe defeat, 77
recognition that truth is objectivity, 78
befriended by Raymond Duncan, 78
hitch-hikes to Strasbourg, 79
returns to Leicester, 79
takes an office job, 80
meets a nurse who is subsequently to become his wife, 80
on work, 80
becomes a navvy, 80
persuades his employers to allow him to work part time, 80
on the British workman, 80
his employers withdraw concession and he leaves the job, 81
goes to work in a chemical factory, 81
revives his interest in music, 81
is married, 81
migration to London, 81
takes another labouring job, 81
followed by another in a plastic factory, 82
attends mass, 82, 83
discovers the *Book of the Dead*, 82
on his novel, 82
on the Catholic Church, 83
his wife becomes pregnant, 83
on landladies, 83
changes his job, 85
is given notice, 85
the worst ordeal of his married life, 85
his wife returns to Leicester, 86
becomes involved with anarchists, 86

summonsed for defrauding London Transport, 86
speaks in Hyde Park, 86
on anarchism, 87
on the disease of our civilization, 87
is banned from the anarchists' platform, 87
joins the Syndicalists, 87
becomes a hospital porter, 88
some questions concerning death, 89
writes a revue, 89
on Laura Del-Rivo, 89-90
his first experience of drunkenness, 90
his revue is 'performed', 90
begins writing a play, 90
on Bill Hopkins, 90-94
is disappointed in Soho, 92
moves to Paris, 94
resolves never to accept boredom and unfulfilment, xii, 95
disagreement with his wife, 96
determines to leave London, 96
attacks of 'vastation', 96
realises that man is wholly 'mechanical', 97
leaves his wife, 97-98
sets out for France, 98
settles in Paris, 98
reflections on American rudeness and charm, 99
is repatriated by the Foreign Office, 101
goes to Leicester, 102
recollections of Maurice Willows, 105-107
returns to London, 108
is employed in a laundry, 108
and later a garage, 109
and a wine merchants', 109
becomes the confidant of his landlady's daughter, 110
her spare-time occupation, 110
and her unattractive practice in bed, 110
finds brief employment in a plastics factory, 110
on leisure, a problem of modern civilisation, 111

INDEX

Wilson, Colin—ctd.
  sleeps rough at night on Whetstone golf course and later Hampstead Heath, 111
  works by day at British Museum, 111-112
  finds temporary job in a dairy, 113
  takes a holiday, 113
  a job at Lyons Corner House, 113
  completes first version of *Ritual in the Dark*, 114, 120, 121
  his hardest and most unpleasant job, 114
  works as a washer-up, 114
  plans and begins writing *The Outsider*, 114-115
  a major criticism of *The Outsider*, 116
  finds a publisher, 117
  works as a telephonist, 117
  his mother becomes critically ill, 118
  The Outsider accepted for publication, 118
  another publisher becomes enthusiastic, 118
  completes *The Outsider*, 119
  becomes a house decorator, 120
  again experiences the 'vastation' feeling, 122
  publication and acclaim of *The Outsider*, 122
  expresses himself on Dylan Thomas, 123-124
  becomes an immediate popular success, 123-125
  the problem and meaning of human existance, 126
  some results and problems of his sudden success, 126-135
  begins writing *Religion and the Rebel*, 128
  a general reaction develops against *The Outsider*, xi, 128
  and unprovoked attacks, 128
  on the persecution complex of most successful writers, 131
  his reaction to the attacks, 132
  determines to leave London, 132
  buys a gramophone and begins collecting long-playing records, 133
  his preference for music to poetry, 133-134
  a sudden irruption of publicity wrecks all remnants of serious reputation he has left, 134-136
  leaves London, 136
  no longer has any reason for optimism, 137
  his great interest in Sartre, 137-138
  writes an open letter to George Devine, 138
  publication and hostile reception of *Religion and the Rebel*, 139-140
  lectures in Oslo, 141-145
  a summary of the philosophy of Sartre and Heidegger, 142-143
  the centre of his own philosophy, 143
  existentialism the only philosophy that attempts to place things in perspective, 144
  a month in Hamburg, 145-148
  two victims of his publicity, 146-147
  a resurgence of optimism, 149
  begins a new version of *Ritual*, 149
  attitude of the modern writer to his world, 149-151
  writes *The Age of Defeat*, 152
  his publisher offers an unexpectedly generous advance, 153
  buys a house, 153-154
  finishes *Ritual* and his publisher accepts it, with certain cuts, 154
  polite and dismissive reception of *The Age of Defeat*, 155
  Ritual appears and is better received than anything since *The Outsider*, 156
  hopes of promising film sale of *Ritual* fail to materialise, 157-158
  the difficulty of living by writing, 158

INDEX

his enjoyment of writing, 158
about *Ritual in the Dark,* 158-159
futility of sex as a vocation, 158
on man's sense of continuity, 159
his preference for writing novels to philosophy, 160
his reason for writing novels, 160
goes on lecture tour of U.S., 161
a bad traveller, 161
suddenly becomes able to see his ideas as a whole, 161
his *Introduction to the New Existentialism* largely ignored by British press, 162
on the two negative attitudes of western philosophy and an outline of the author's alternative, 162-173
effect on him of mescalin, 166, 169-170, 171
an experience of almost visionary intensity at Teignmouth, 169
another semi-mystical experience, 170-171
on inducing peak experiences, 171-173
maintains that consciousness is within human control, 172-173
on phenomenological existentialism, 174
on the two 'planes' of consciousness, 174-175
on the core of his contribution to philosophy, 175
the author's philosophy alone free from self-contradiction, 175
his reasons for accepting university posts in U.S., 176
his preference for America to England, 176-177
on the English intellectual, 176
on the brevity of human life, 177
— Joy (the author's wife), 104, 105, 108, 110, 111, 112, 113, 115, 117, 118, 122, 133, 134, 135, 145, 153, 161; her family, 134, 135
— Roderick Gerard (the author's son), 83, 86, 96, 111
— Rodney (the author's youngest brother), 13, 113
— Sally (the author's daughter), 161
— Sandy, 138
— Susan (the author's sister), 2
Wittgenstein, Ludwig, 128, 161
Wolfe, Thomas, 50, 137, 138
Woolworth, F. W., 15, 16, 19, 72
Wordsworth, William, 167, 172, 173
Wordsworth (F. W. Bateson), 173
World of Violence (C. Wilson), 152, 160

Year of Grace (V. Gollancz), 117
Yeats, W. B., 5, 22, 55, 58, 91, 105, 108

Zarathustra (F. Nietzsche), 72
Zola, Emile, 41